colin rose edge to edge

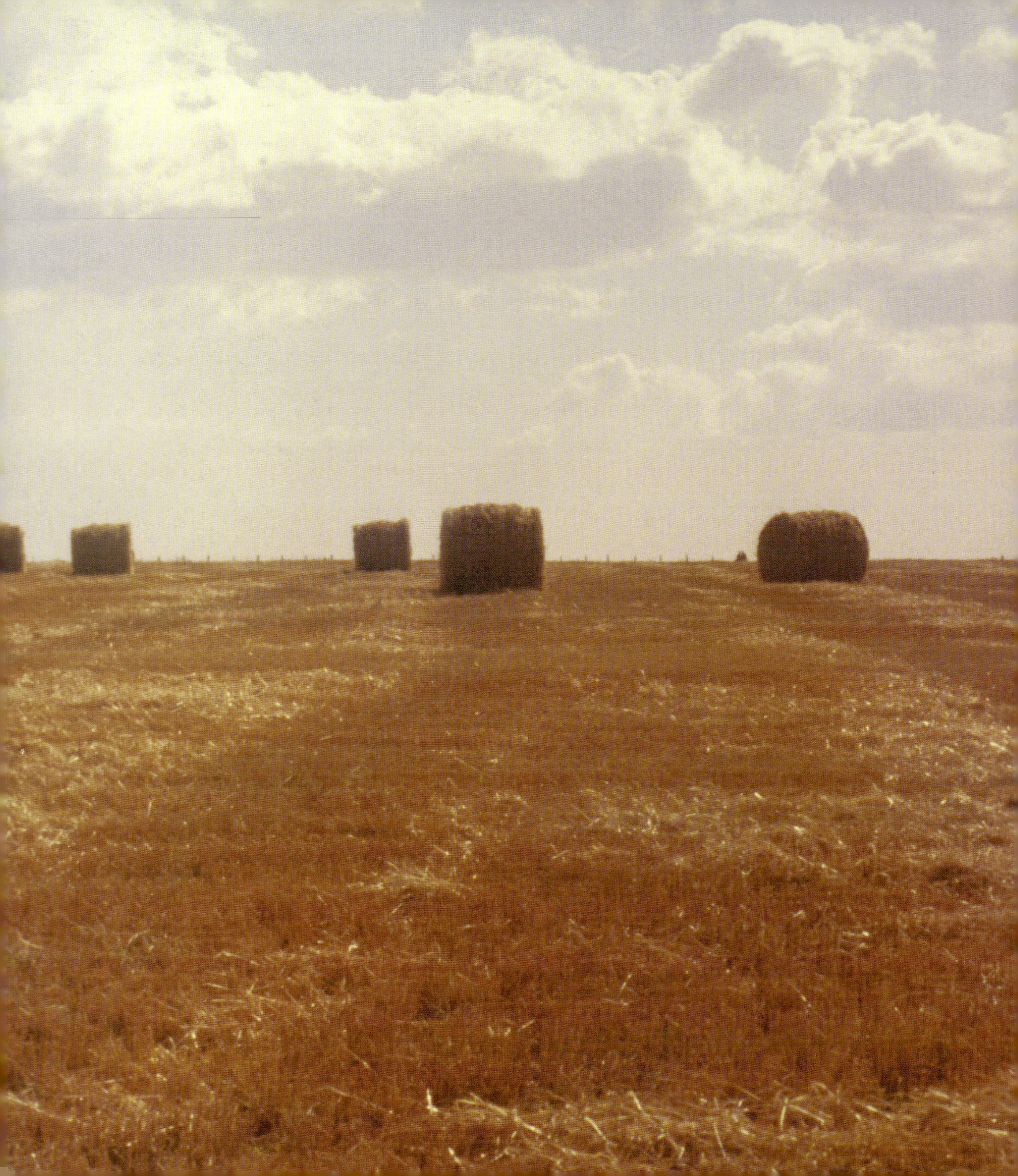

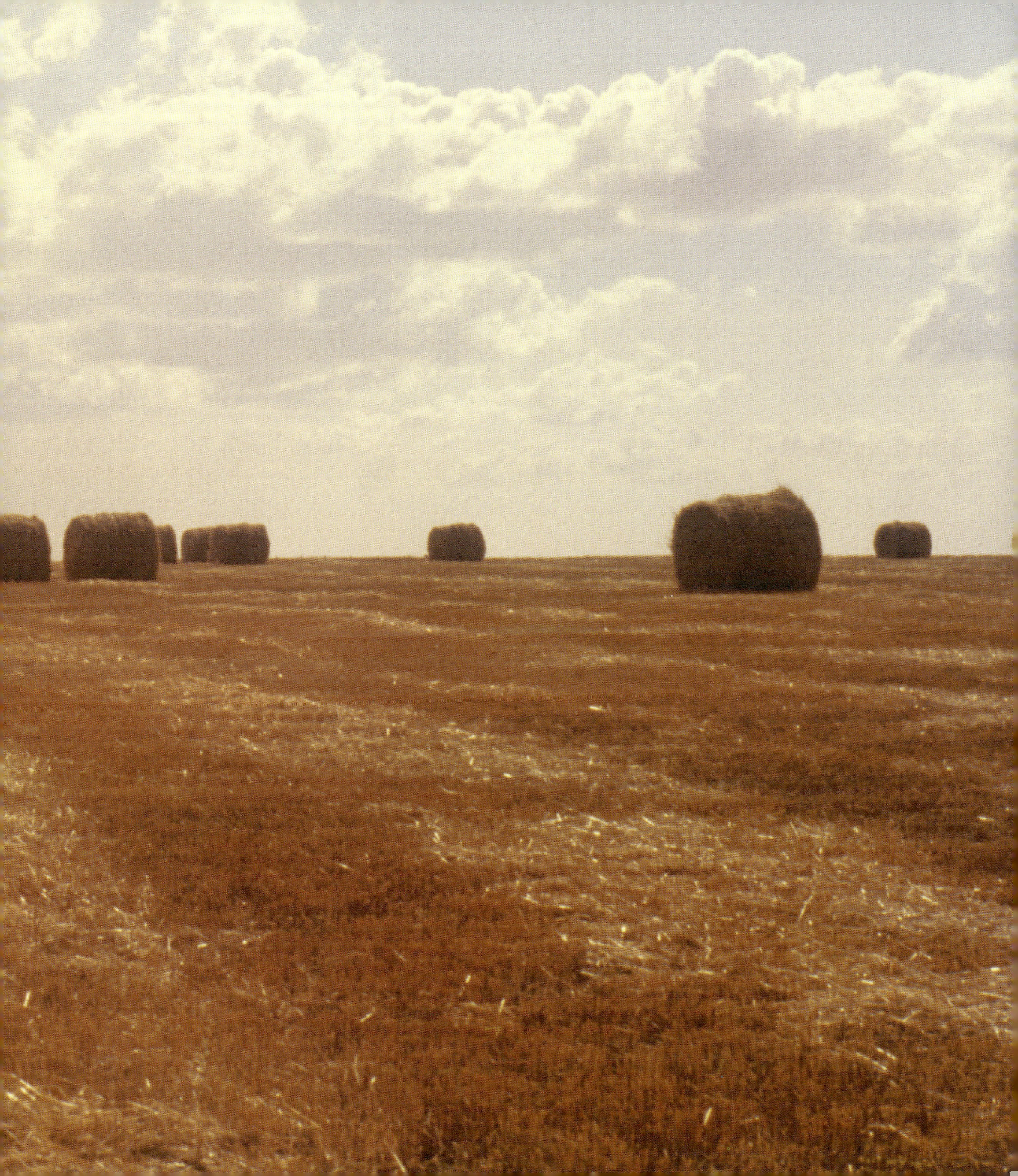

colin rose edge to edge

Ian Thompson & Marina Vaizey

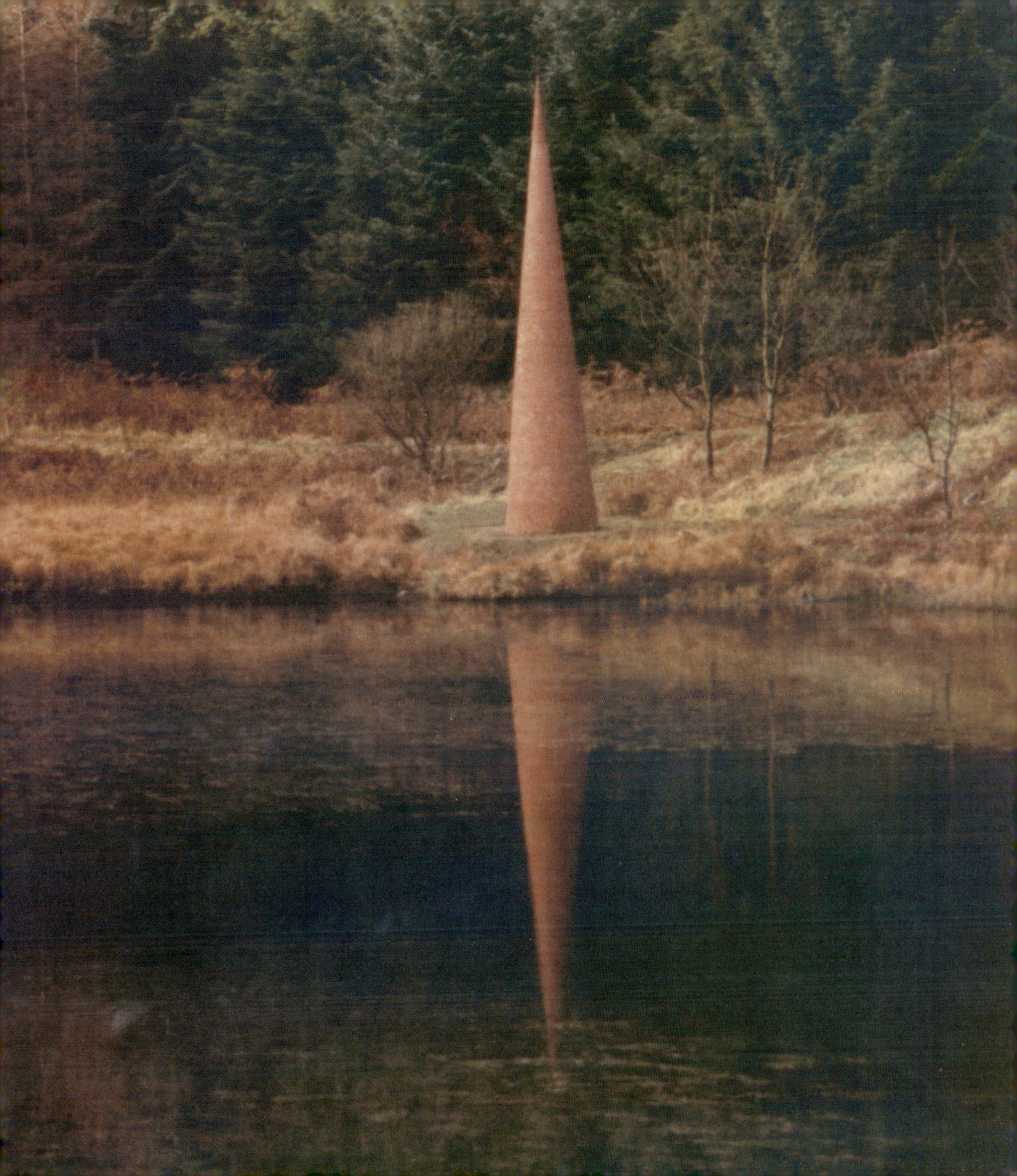

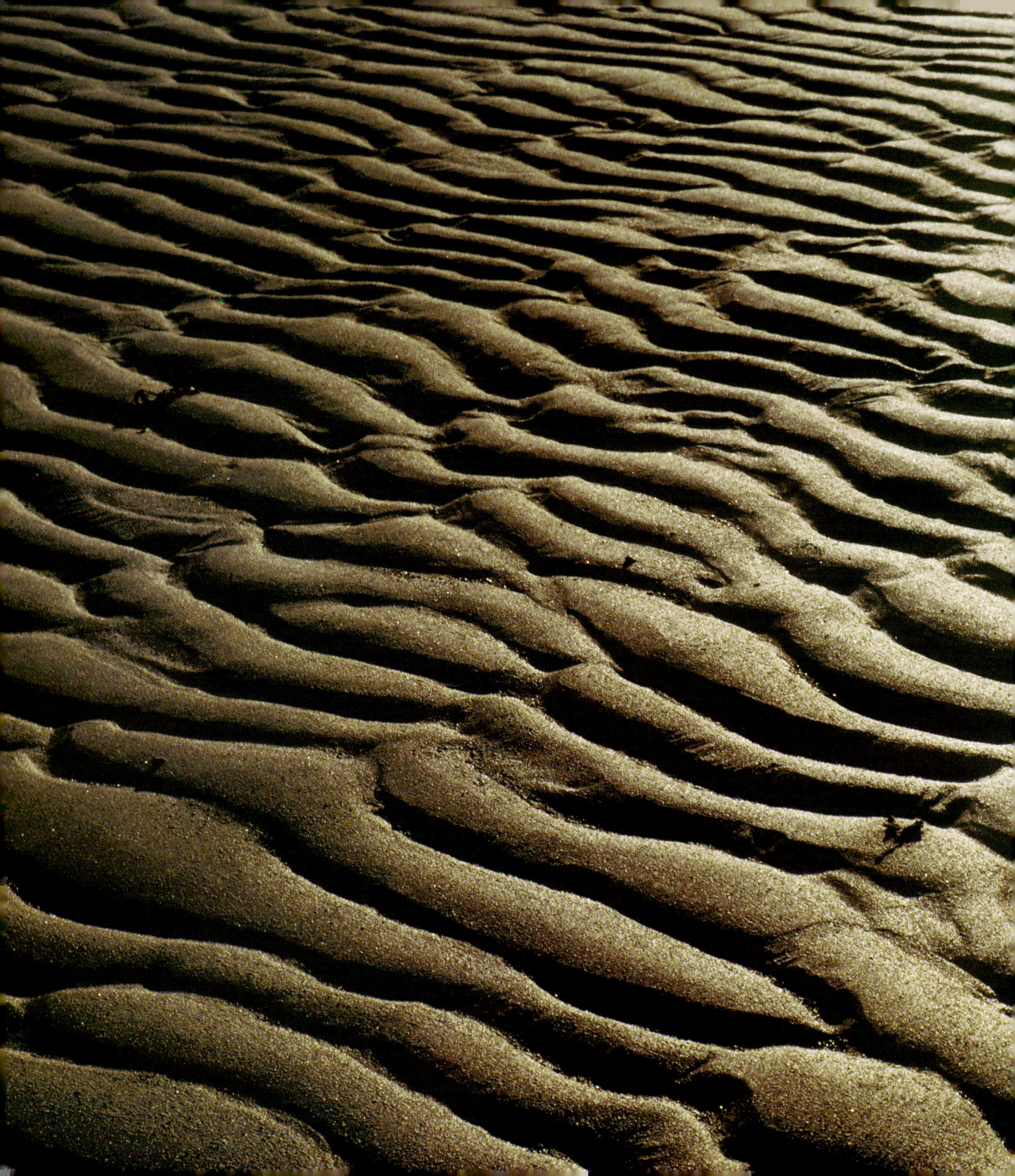

Contents

Introduction

Peter Murray
Director of Yorkshire Sculpture Park

I remember the first time I met Colin Rose. It was in the late spring of 1984. He arrived at the Yorkshire Sculpture Park (YSP) in a van crammed full of linear semi-circular pieces made from metal, which, joined together, would form a huge circle. This seemed relatively straightforward until we discovered that this circle, with a diameter of 13 metres, had to be mounted on a tree, with the top threaded through the high branches and the bottom edge of the circumference gently caressing the lush green grass of the parkland.

Unfazed by the complexity of this request Colin Rose, in his reassuringly straightforward manner, persuaded some of the YSP staff to abseil up and down the tree as the piece was assembled in mid air. Once assembled a method of stabilising the sculpture had to be devised to ensure that the majestic beech tree, which was to become a welcome home for the sculpture, was not damaged.

The result was a beautiful pristine circle aptly named *Ting*. This simple, minimalistic statement became part of the tree, existing in harmony with the organic cycle of change: glazed by the spread of beech leaves in the summer, silhouetted by the stark muscular intensity of the tree in the winter. *Ting* seemed so at home at Yorkshire Sculpture Park, so much part of the landscape, and yet, upon moving to Grizedale in 1985 it adapted to another tree, and taking on a more horizontal feel, has settled well into the Cumbrian landscape which is now its permanent home.

Reflecting on this experience in 1993 Colin Rose said that it was at Yorkshire Sculpture Park that he first developed the idea of a tree being a 'place' in the landscape, offering a harmony with the elements, which in turn relate the work to the landscape.

In 1988 Colin Rose was selected to participate in a practical sculpture symposium at Krefeld in Germany. Supported by the skilled workforce from Kleinewefers he had an opportunity to work in a fabrication plant and was provided with a generous supply of metal. Working with designers, fabricators and welders he constructed a large freestanding sculpture. This robust work consisted of two rectangles fabricated from heavy metal. One was firmly rooted into the ground supporting the other which, tilted at an acute angle, appeared to catch the large circle before it crashed to the ground. A coat of dense blue paint unified the sculpture (*Cloud*, 1988) which became a marker, activating an immense area of space.

This industrial experience rekindled the artist's engineering skills acquired as an apprentice engineer prior to going to art college. It also provided him with an insight into the importance of team work which is a vital part of manufacturing large scale sculptures for public places.

In 1992 Colin Rose was awarded a Henry Moore Foundation bursary to work at Yorkshire Sculpture Park, providing valuable support for research and reflection. He started by exploring the landscape and studying the ancient trees. He observed the changing seasons, discovered a geometry and order which unified the diversity of natural abundance and helped create wonderful spaces and vistas. He also observed how the public interacted with nature, in a playful and relaxed manner.

Following this period of research he created a distinctive exhibition where the sculpture lived in the trees. Developing further his interest in the linear quality of the circle he made a series of works constructed from lightweight aluminium, some coated with light reflecting tape. A good example is *Night and Day*, 1992. From the ground this work has the appearance of a silvery drawn circle set against the sky. It is, in fact, a vast circle constructed from aluminium and held in place, 12 metres above ground, by the support of a jagged line of aluminium. During the production of this work he said: "a large proportion of my sculpture is derived from the elements – sun, rain, wind, clouds, waves and the natural rhythms and cycles underlying them". Placed high in trees along the main drive and adjacent to the car park these sculptures took on a different life when caught by the beams of car headlights.

Colin Rose once told me that he liked rubbing shoulders with trees which possess an enormous strength and yet, with the slightest breeze can demonstrate gentleness and delicacy of movement. Exploring this notion further he placed a beautifully constructed sculpture called *Pine Ball*, 1989, on the dusty green branches of a cedar tree. Snuggly cradled in the arms of the tree it seemed to rock the sculpture gently, providing a form of protection from the elements. Another sculpture re-emphasising his interest in volume was *Whirling Beans*, 1990. Several large roped coil spheres were delicately placed high up in a Cedar of Lebanon. The large limbs of the tree seemed to protect and nourish these spheres attracting great wonderment from the viewers, as the tree became, 'a place', for the sculptures.

The trees chosen for these works had at some point lost branches creating what the artist felt was an imbalance, so much so that it became hard for him to imagine the trees without the sculptures. This beautiful and haunting exhibition emphasised Colin Rose's ability to create simple elegant statements which, although both physically and conceptually complex, appeared to be effortless in their execution and placement.

These early years and his strong involvement with nature enabled Colin Rose to move on to bigger and more complex works, particularly for the urban environment. The simple minimalist approach of the artist belies the complexity of his thought and the technical aspects which support the creations of his powerful works. His brush with nature also ensures that he and his work do not lose contact with the environment and, although he often drools over the technology essential for some of his sculptures, he still likes to enjoy the tactile qualities of natural materials enabling him to construct remarkable works such as the *Stone Cone* and the *Earth Cone* series. Marina Vaisey presents a perceptive insight into Colin Rose, the artist and thinker. Ian Thompson writing in some detail about Colin Rose's public sculptures, refers to the artist's view that the test for art in public places is whether people would notice if it was taken away. At YSP we certainly missed *Ting* when it went to Grizedale in 1985, but the memory of his tree pieces linger on and often when I look at the trees near to the Camellia House I still seem to catch glimpses of *Pine Ball* and others.

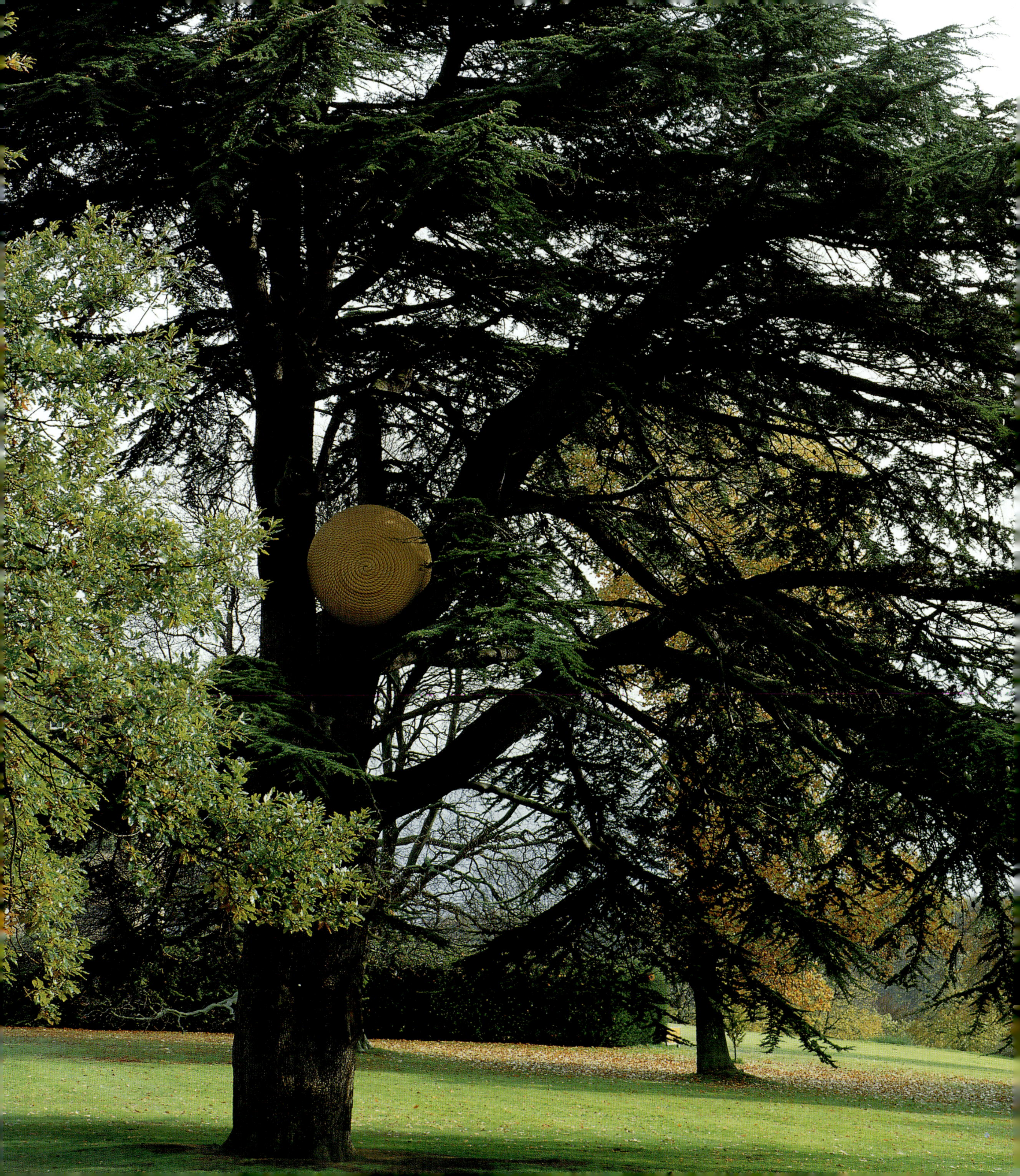

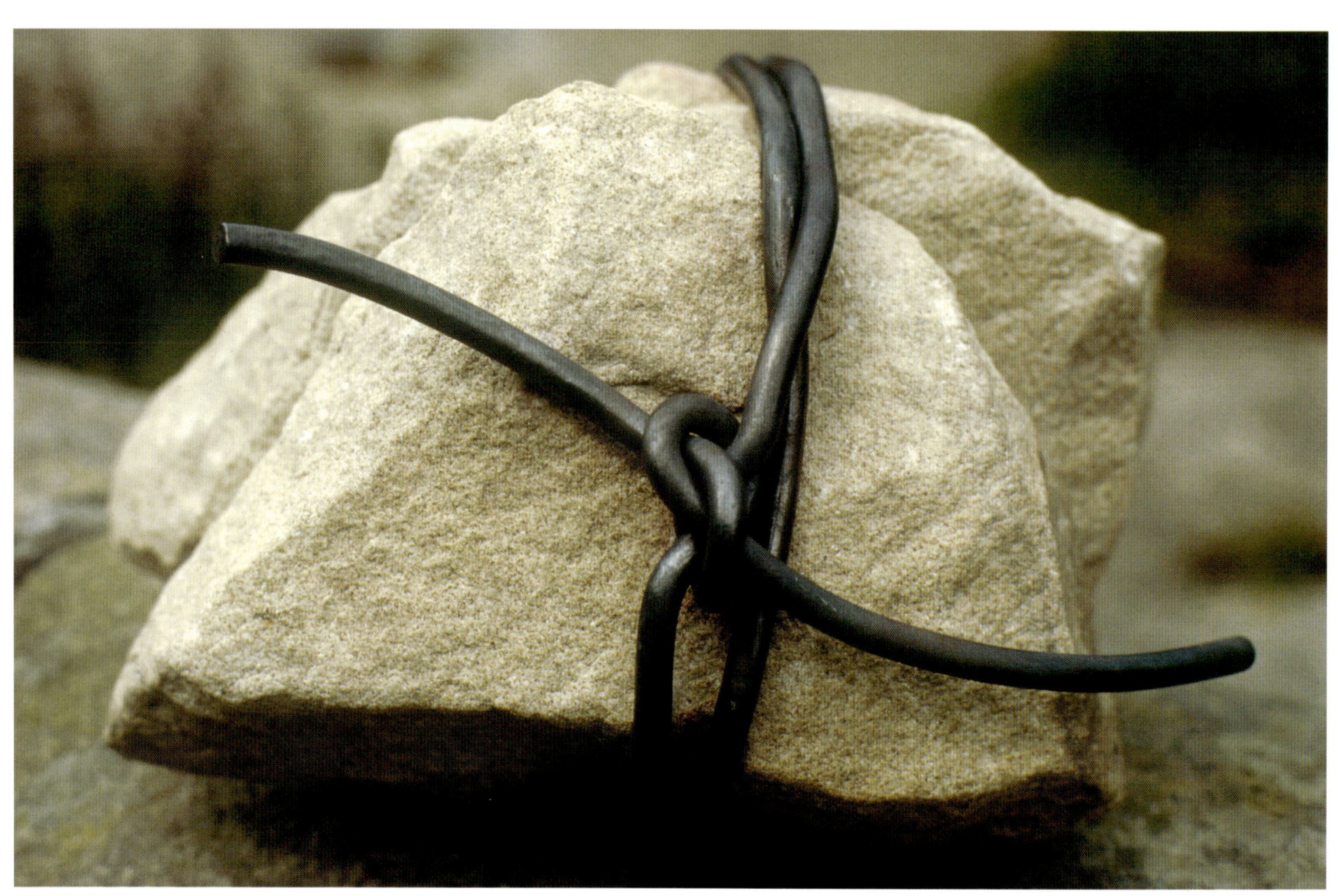

Colin Rose

Marina Vaizey

The past century has seen a remarkable redefinition of sculpture and its meaning within the Western tradition. Yet the classic dictionary definition remains: the art of forming representations of objects in the round or in relief by chiselling stone, carving wood, modelling clay, casting metal or similar processes. During the technologically minded twentieth century the processes and materials expanded to include found objects, industrial components and plastics. The process now, as with an artist such as Richard Long, may mean moving found objects – stones, flints – into various permutations. Many proponents of Minimalism, an ism now nearly 50 years old, also took sculpture as a kind of rearrangement of existing materials, or prefabricated units, playing on both the notion of the found object and an art that was back to basics, as one critic put it, "an A B C art". Dan Flavin took as his unit fluorescent light tubes; Carl Andre, industrial components such as bricks or metal squares formed into rectangles or squares. Carving and modelling became minority interests.

Equally, land artists took their work to remote places, and ambitions soared; the American James Turrell has spent decades altering the crater of an extinct volcano in the American south west. The scale of the metal sculptures of Richard Serra can be breathtaking: huge curved or straight Corten steel walls, manufactured by industrial methods. Performance and gesture may now also be inescapably a part of modern and contemporary sculpture, as well as existing as a method in its own right. There are artists who imaginatively defy category, and exploit individual working methods of their own, such as the working couple Gilbert and George, who use more directly than most their own life and attitudes as the crucial core of their subject matter. They burst upon the public imagination by defining themselves as 'Living Sculptures', challenging their audience's notions of what sculpture could be.

From these examples it is clear that sculptural vocabulary has been radically expanded. Thus the defining characteristics of the past century, in areas other than, as well as, the visual arts, may be summed up in one word: more.

There is more of everything: more people, more countries, more things. Above all we have more information and more access to that information. There is more knowledge of all kinds, including a continual bombardment of visual imagery through a variety of media, particularly electronic media, not to mention print and photography. These images may be drawn not only from the present, as well as visual speculation about the future, but also from past millennia, constructed from souvenirs, and remnants: evidence, scientific and imaginative. Art, it seems, cannot even shock anymore, and perhaps now that is art's most shocking characteristic. Anything is available on the Internet. We are deluged with visual imagery, from advertising to tourism, from photography to television, from magazines to books. The whole of the past in the visual arts, however mutilated, is available to us if we look: from the rock art of the Sahara to Buddhist caves in western China.

Against all the newness, there are still remarkable public sculptures which have well defined if distressing but communally understood public purposes. Maya Lin's Vietnam memorial in Washington, DC, and the war memorials of Michael Sandle in Britain and Malta, commemorate, in elegiac fashion, specific events. There are still extraordinary contemporary public sculptures which are understood to commemorate something, even if what the sense of shared euphoria and delight – or, conversely, outrage – is actually about is less certain. From groups such as Barbara Hepworth's *The Family of Man*, to Antony Gormley's *Angel of the North*, there has been a sense of ritual, of memorialising some human concern in a secular society.

There are sculptures, too, which occupy communal public space whilst expressing private emotion that also capture the imagination – the air of controlled menace, for example, in Louise Bourgeois' outsize spider, *Maman*, now installed by the river Nervion outside the Guggenheim Bilbao, or the sheer euphoric improbability of Jeff Koons huge *Puppy Dog*, covered with flowers, standing outside the main entrance to the museum. As the hierarchies of society have become blurred or questioned, so has the sense of heritage or history. Moving away from the commemorative, the memorial, the triumphant, the piece of public sculpture that was understood to an extent by the community in which it was placed, to sculpture that was expressionist, impressionist, highly personal and individual, has been a complicated procedure.

It seems to me that Colin Rose, against the odds for contemporary sculpture to play a role in fulfiling artist, backers and public, has produced an individual voice, syntax, grammar and language. His work that plays with the unexpected, is satisfying and strong, and at its best both strange and beautiful; its placidity and calm underlined by a curious otherness. His sculpture hides effort, disguises the arduous nature of its making. Whilst the product of sophisticated visual thinking, it appears simply to be, to happen, to exist without artifice, without pretension or awkward self-consciousness. We do not expect trees to bear such geometric fruit, such bursts and clusters of geometric forms, visible by day or night, or rocks to float in ponds, or spires to appear in wooded glades. But Colin Rose imagines such things, and makes them tangible.

Right: **Floating Rocks** 1996 (detail)
Approx. 200 x 200 x 300cm
Watergate, Whickham, Tyne & Wear

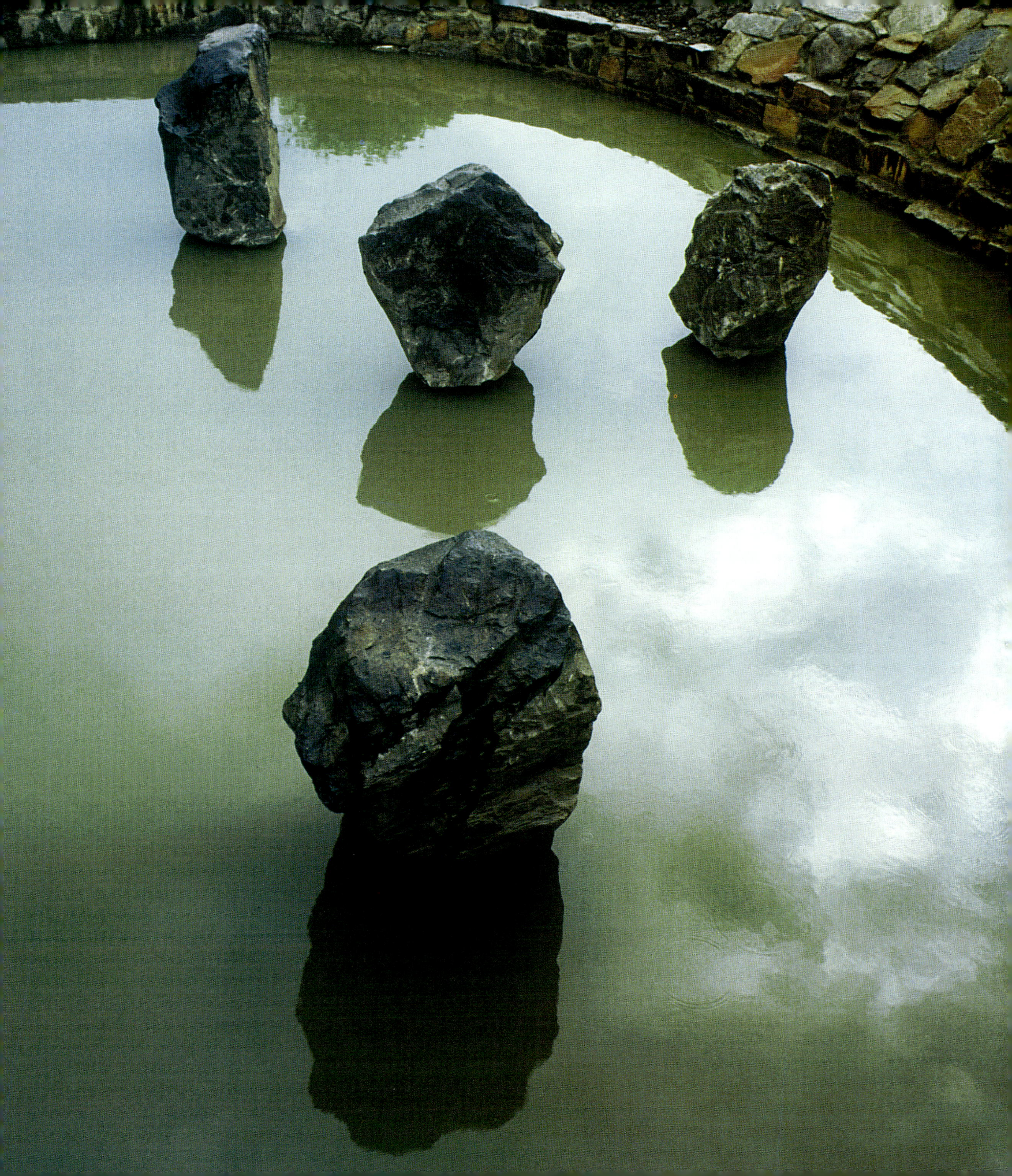

A series of playfully serious sculptures based on geometric structures – a metal circle, wooden spheres – were over several years placed in trees near and by roads. They were visible by day, accentuating the natural forms and structures they inhabited – inhabited without colonising and without aggression. *Ting*, made of steel, threw up an interesting debate, situated as it was at Grizedale. Grizedale, a mixed deciduous and coniferous woodland owned and managed by the Forestry Commission, has had an on-going programme of artists at work in the forest, making sculpture out of natural materials: slate, stone, wood, and so on.

Ting, Colin Rose's great airy circle, an enormous shiny silvery ring, glinting in sunlight, rain and in the headlights of passing cars, was of course metal, the only metal sculpture then allowed. That in itself was a gentle act of subversion, questioning as it did the perceived authenticity at Grizedale of organic materials for the making of art. This assumption in itself of course was contradictory: Grizedale embraced the natural decay of sculptures by Andy Goldsworthy and David Nash, for example, yet as a forestry operation, was reliant on the use of sophisticated machinery for tree husbandry. *Ting* neither decayed in the way that organic materials may, nor did it disguise itself and insinuate itself in the way that much sculpture did within the context of the forest. The visitor was surprised by *Ting*, simple and euphoric in its effect. But its material and geometric shape subtly echoes machinery, the matching of the man-made and the natural. And what could be more man-made and man dominated than a husbanded forest, for all that the forest appears to the uninitiated so natural, so uninterfered with?

Ting was the first in a number of sculptures that related to the landscape: *Ripple*, *Wriggle* and *Swirl* are all pieces which use reflective tape to work in different ways – the geometric against the organic – by both day and night. Colin Rose has taken the tradition of the non-objective world, the geometries of the imagination as the subject matter of his sculpture. His sculptures become objects which are literally set against the natural in the real world, that world which filtered through the Western imagination has in the past provided the subject matter for the artist.

Ting 1984 (detail)
Painted steel
Grizedale Forest

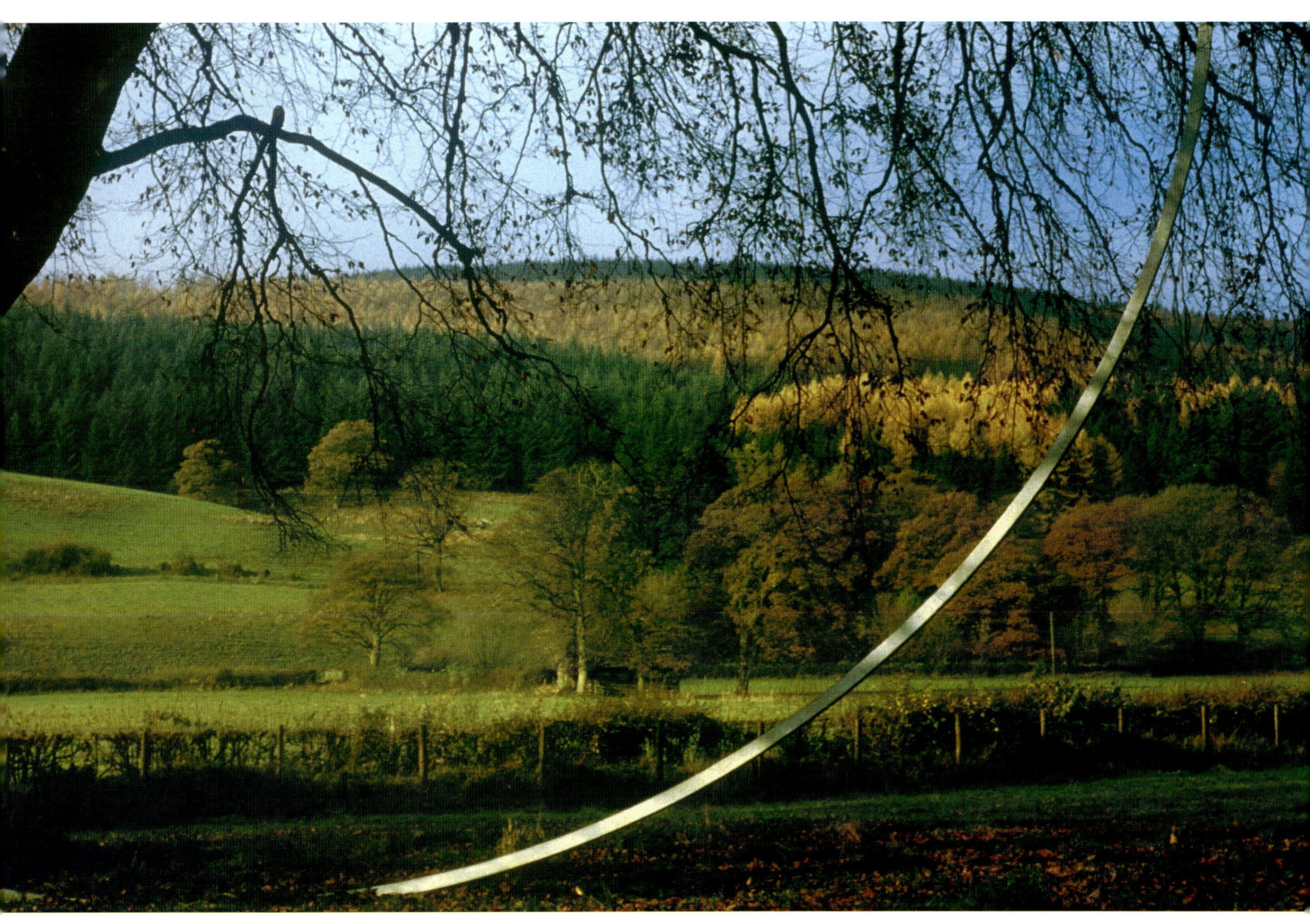

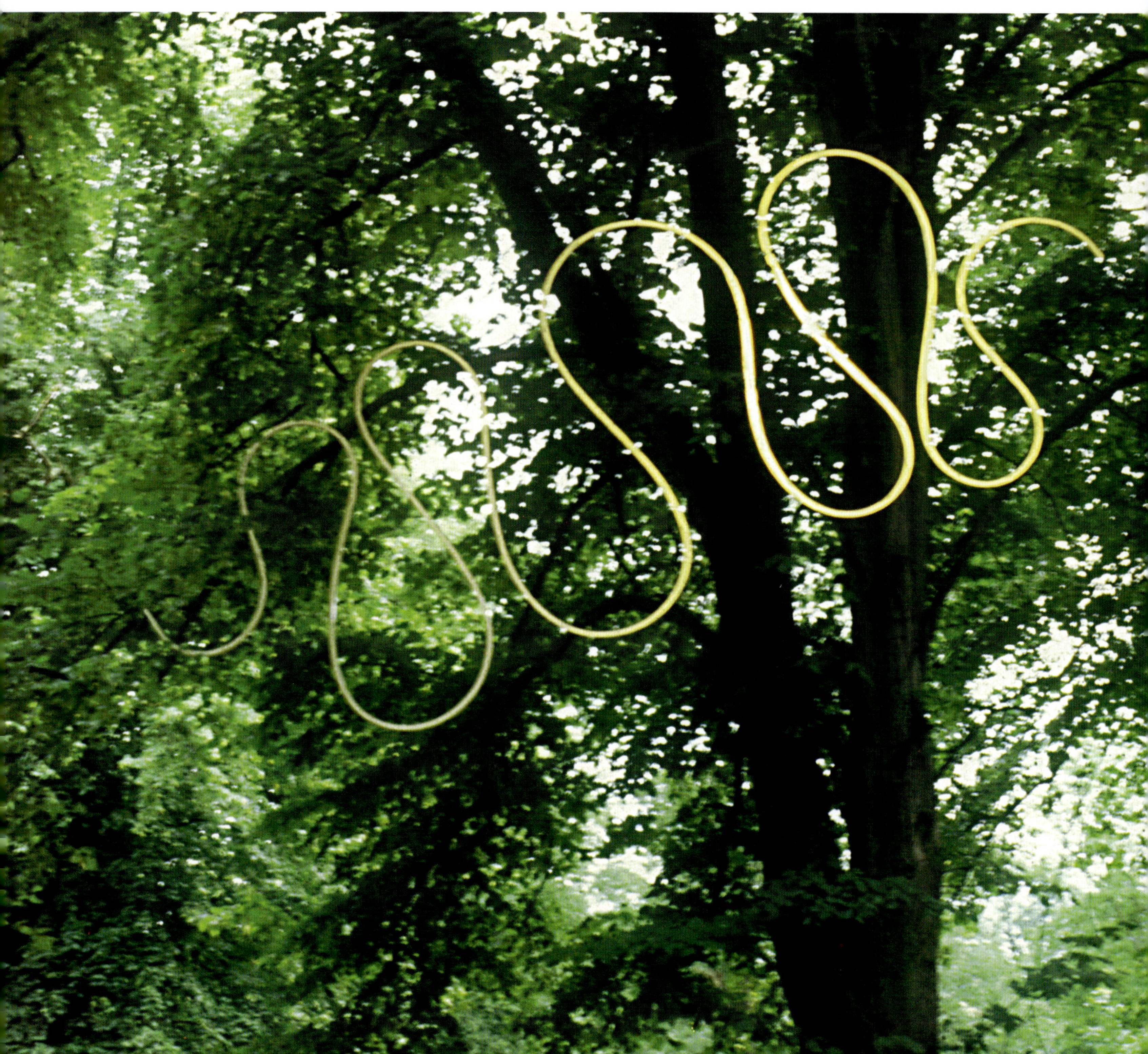

Wriggle 1992
Aluminium and reflective coating
300 x 600cm
Yorkshire Sculpture Park

Ripple 1992
Aluminium and reflective tape
300 x 400cm
Yorkshire Sculpture Park

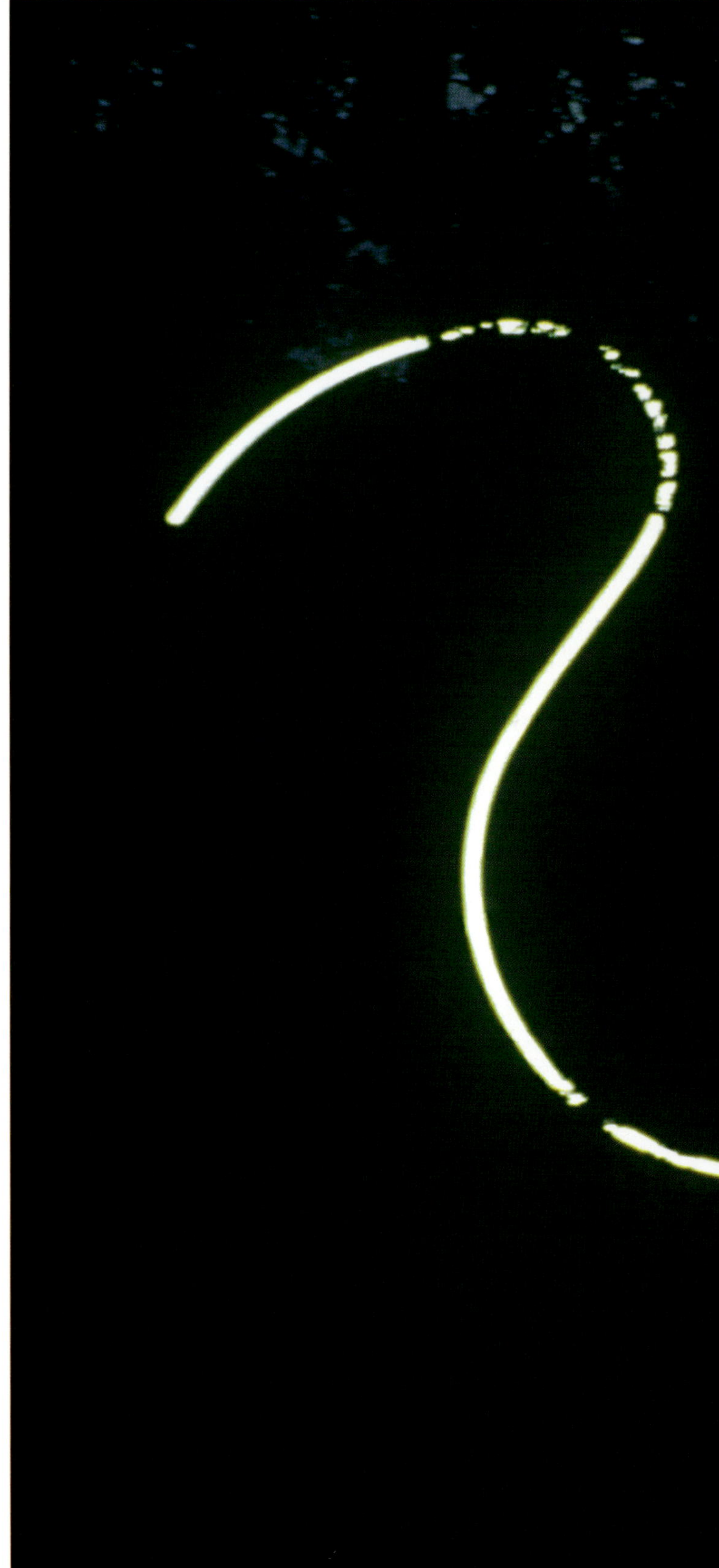

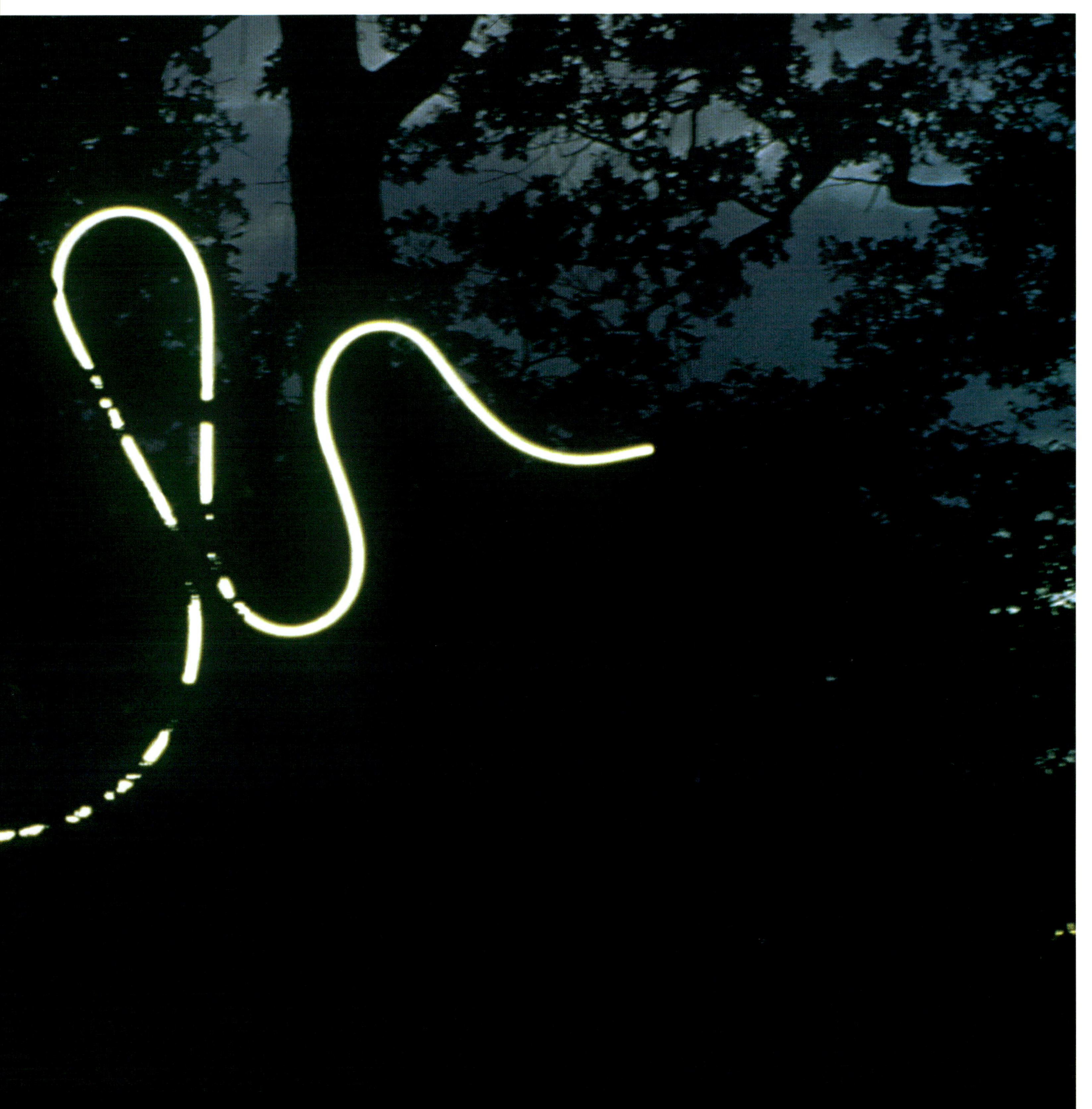

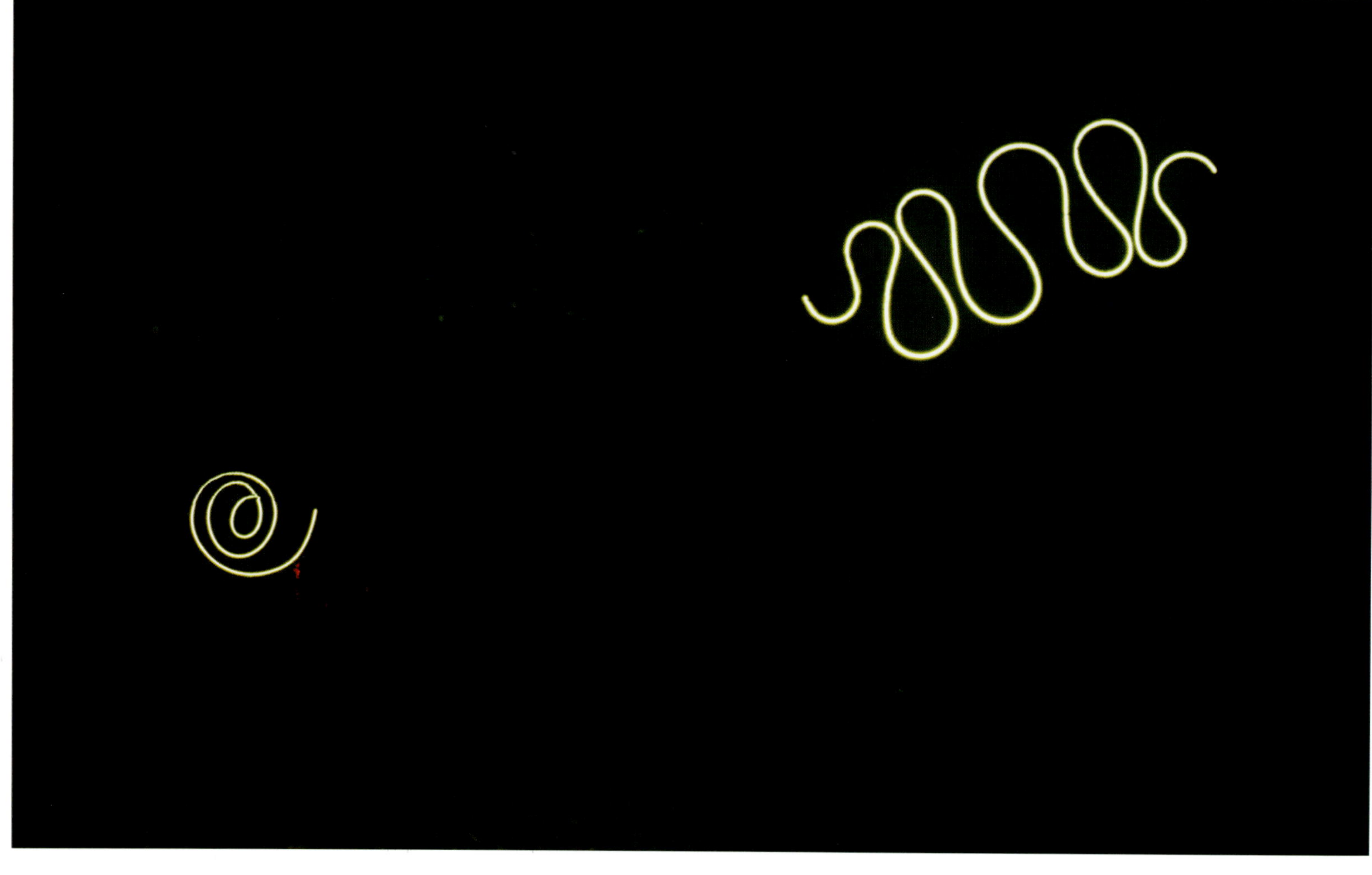

Left:
Swirl & Wriggle 1992
Yorkshire Sculpture Park

Below:
Swirl & Wriggle 1992 (night car lights)
Yorkshire Sculpture Park

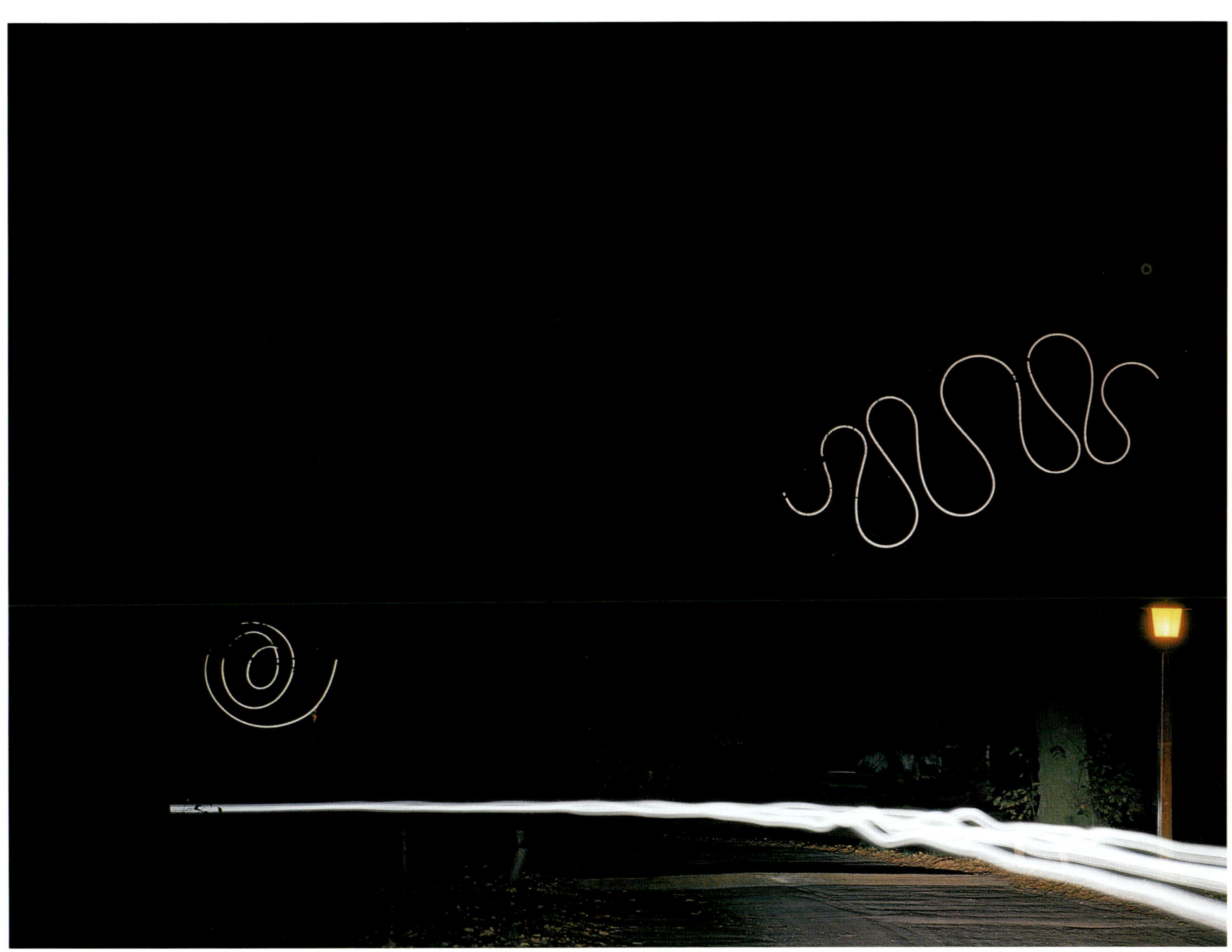

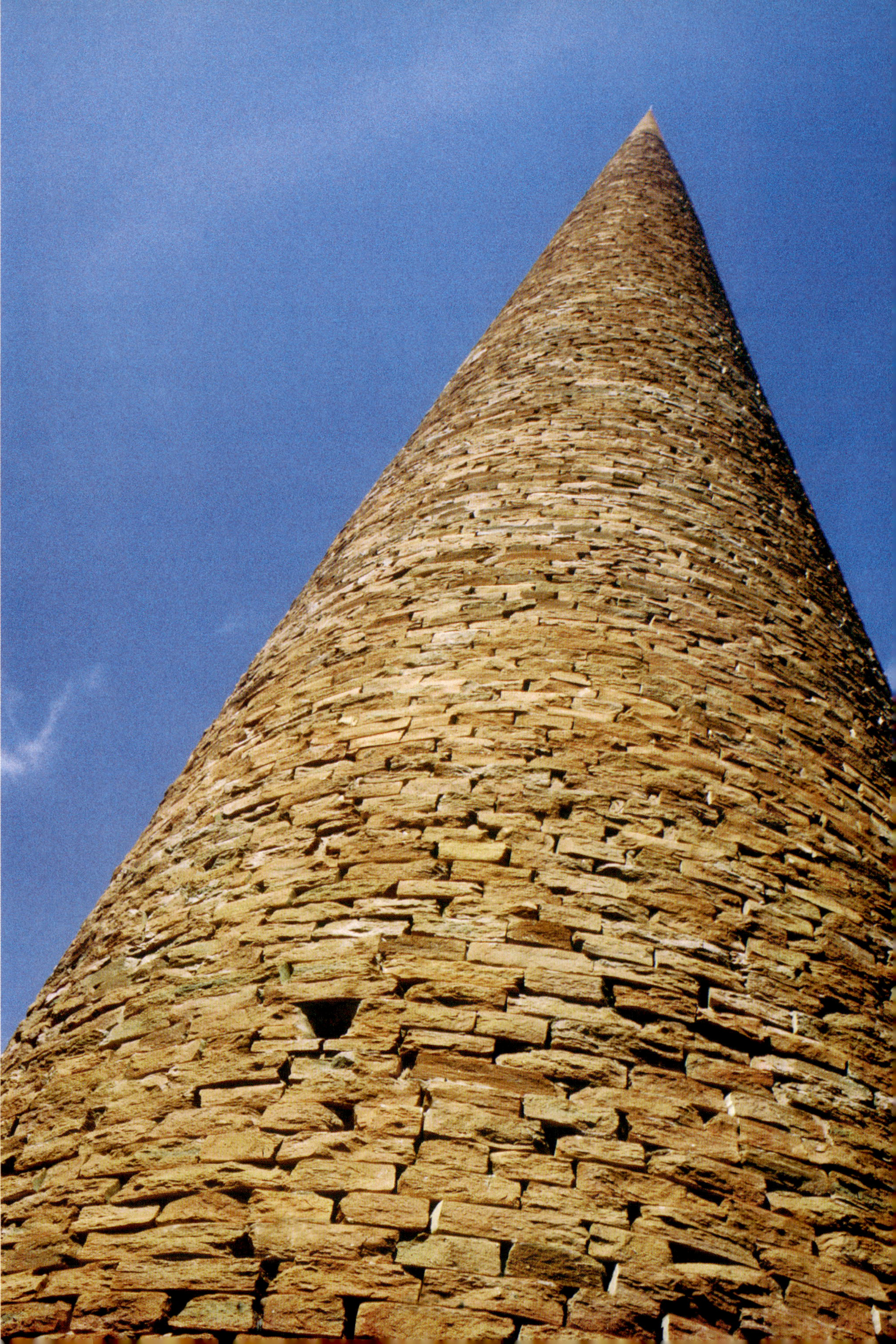

Left:
Eye 1999 (detail)
Split quarry tiles
10 x 3m Ø
The Black Loch, Dumfries and Galloway

Below:
Voices in Stone 1997
Sandstone
150 x 150cm
Runcorn Priory, Cheshire

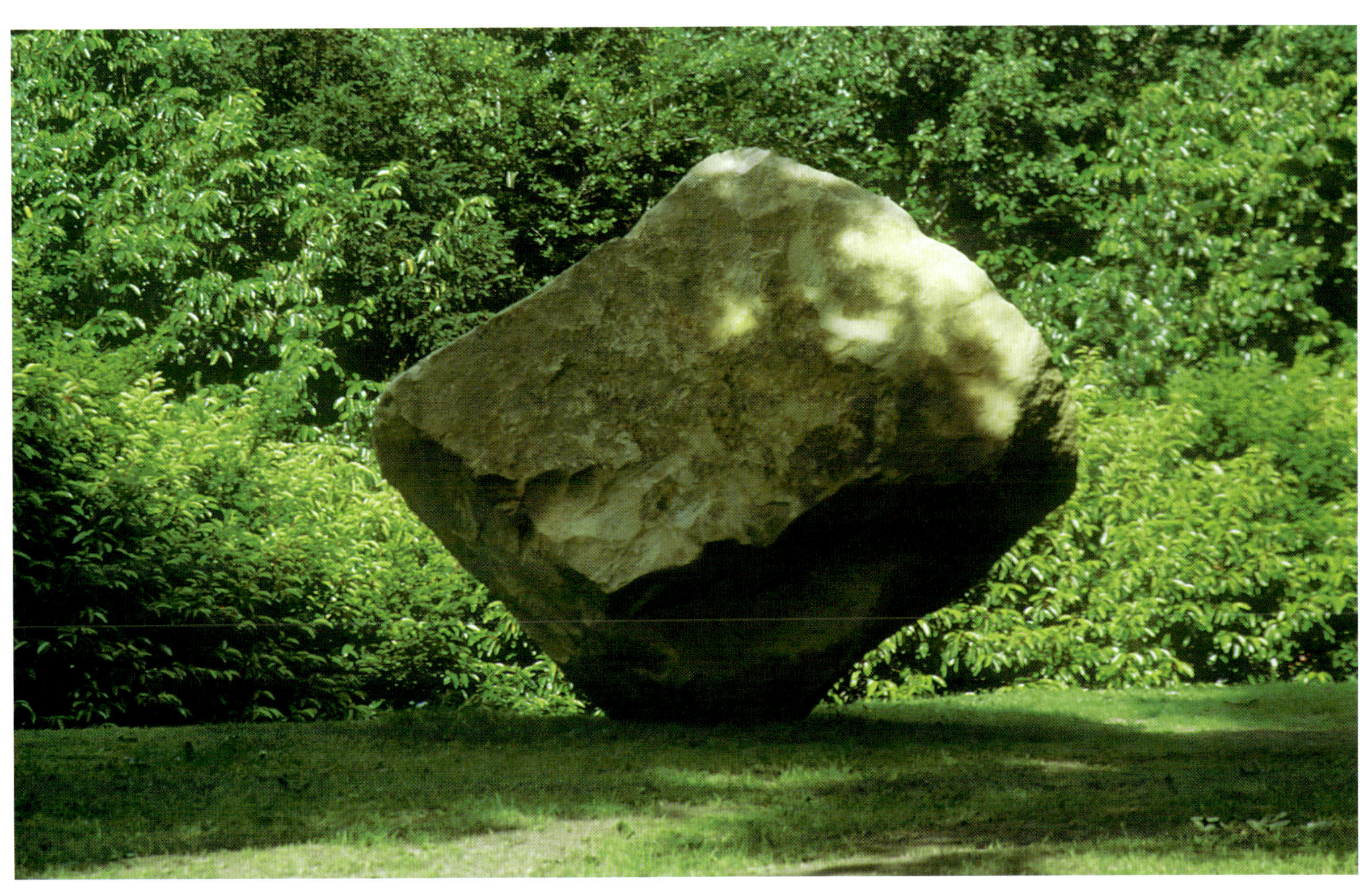

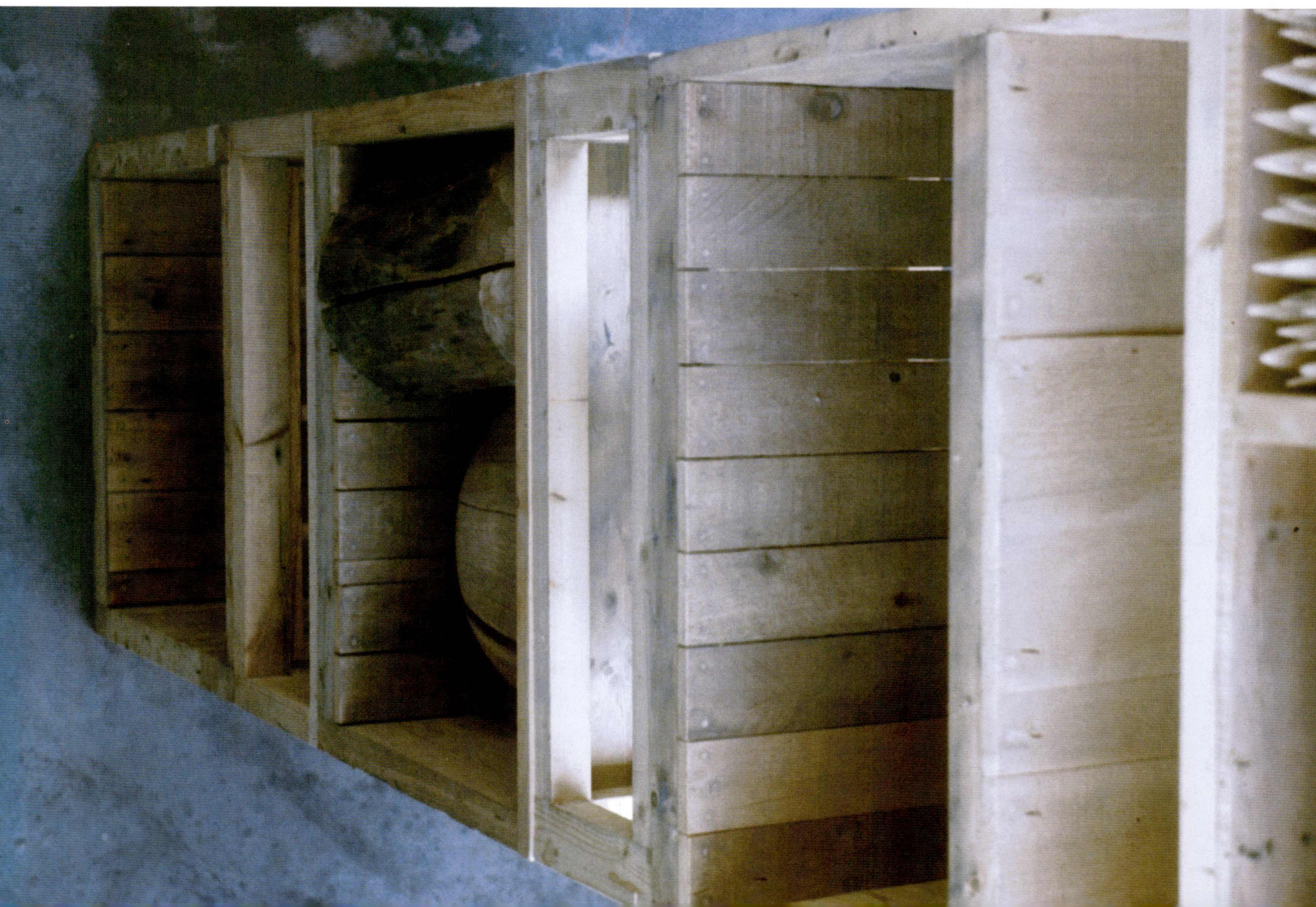

Tower 1976 (detail)
Wood
600 x 120 x 100cm

An intuitive geometry informs Colin Rose's visual imagination. All art, good, bad and indifferent, embodies literally, as well as metaphorically, an idea, an intention, a concept – but not necessarily a theory. Nevertheless there are two distinct aspects to Rose's art, which began on a domestic level, a playful, private level. Working within the constraints of the objects around him, Rose first investigated domestic furniture and negative space, the air inside the drawer of a bureau or a table, the space beneath, long before turning things inside out became the prerogative of a sculptor like Rachel Whiteread. The form, the notion, is dredged from within, but placed outside, in an environment which frames it and makes sense.

Thus from his early work on, the sculpture – serious, attentive – deliberately takes as much from its special place and framing as from its own form. Rose's sculptures are inhabitants. They have a life. They alert us to much that goes on around them, as well as to themselves.

His art is not revolutionary. He uses a formal vocabulary, with forms that have been combined and recombined by many artists over the past 100 years: sculptors such as Alexander Calder, David Smith, Anthony Caro. Although he eschews the reportage of the directly representational, does not play with the figurative, there are inevitable and beguiling references to landscape and to architecture, the placing of the man-made in three dimensional space. We recognise the spheres, the cones, the pyramids, the peaks and waves and rivers, the combinations of curves and straight lines, as part of that thoughtful geometry, a kind of lyrical mathematics so characteristic of the burgeoning into abstraction of the past century: the geometric shapes floating in space, as in Malevich, the lines anchored by colour as in Mondrian, the geometric particles of dreams and imagination as in Kandinsky, the lines going for a walk as in Paul Klee.

Below:
Untitled 1991
Formica
30 x 30cm

Opposite:
Two Rivers 1990
Painted wood
120 x 240cm

Following pages:
Eye

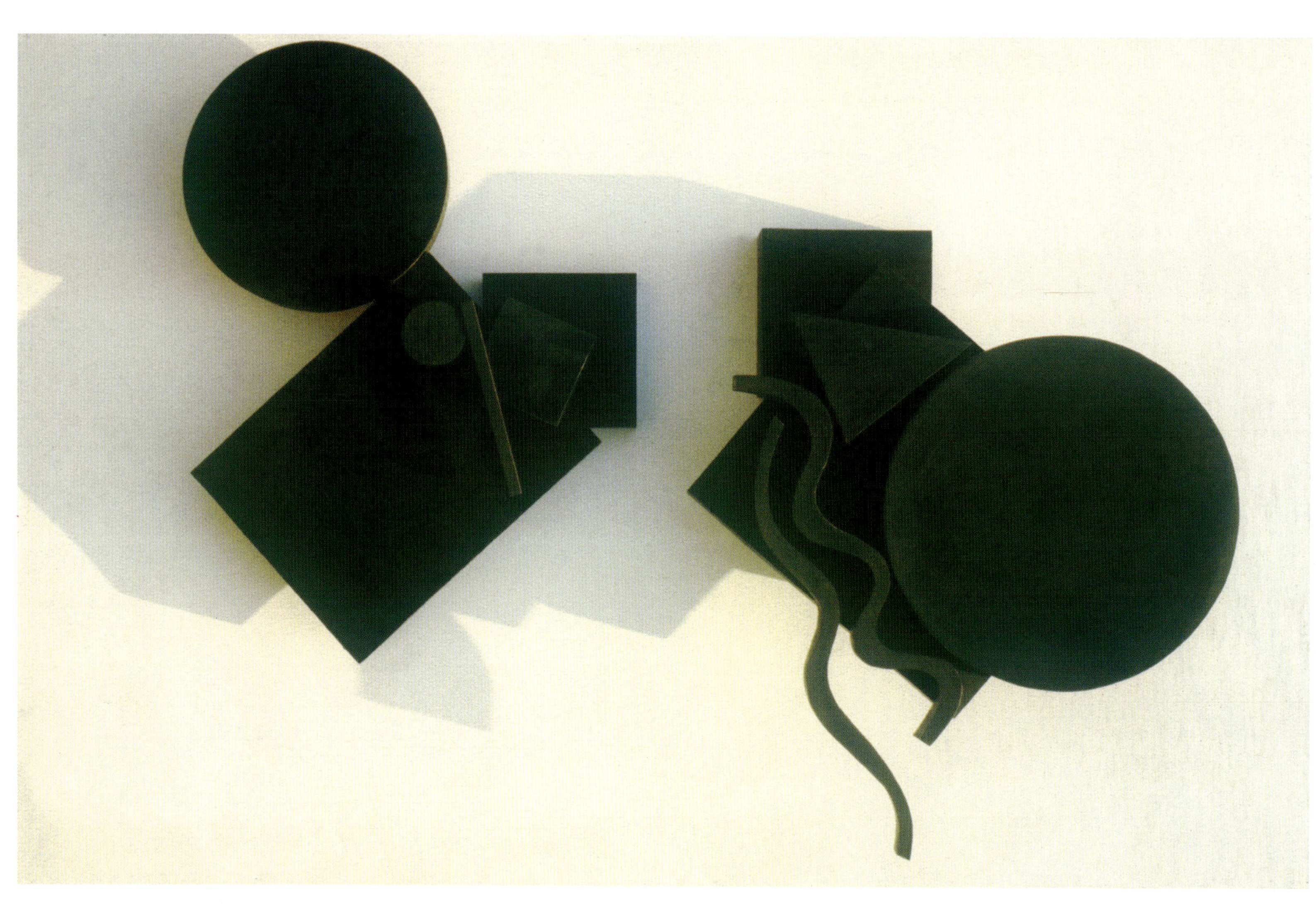

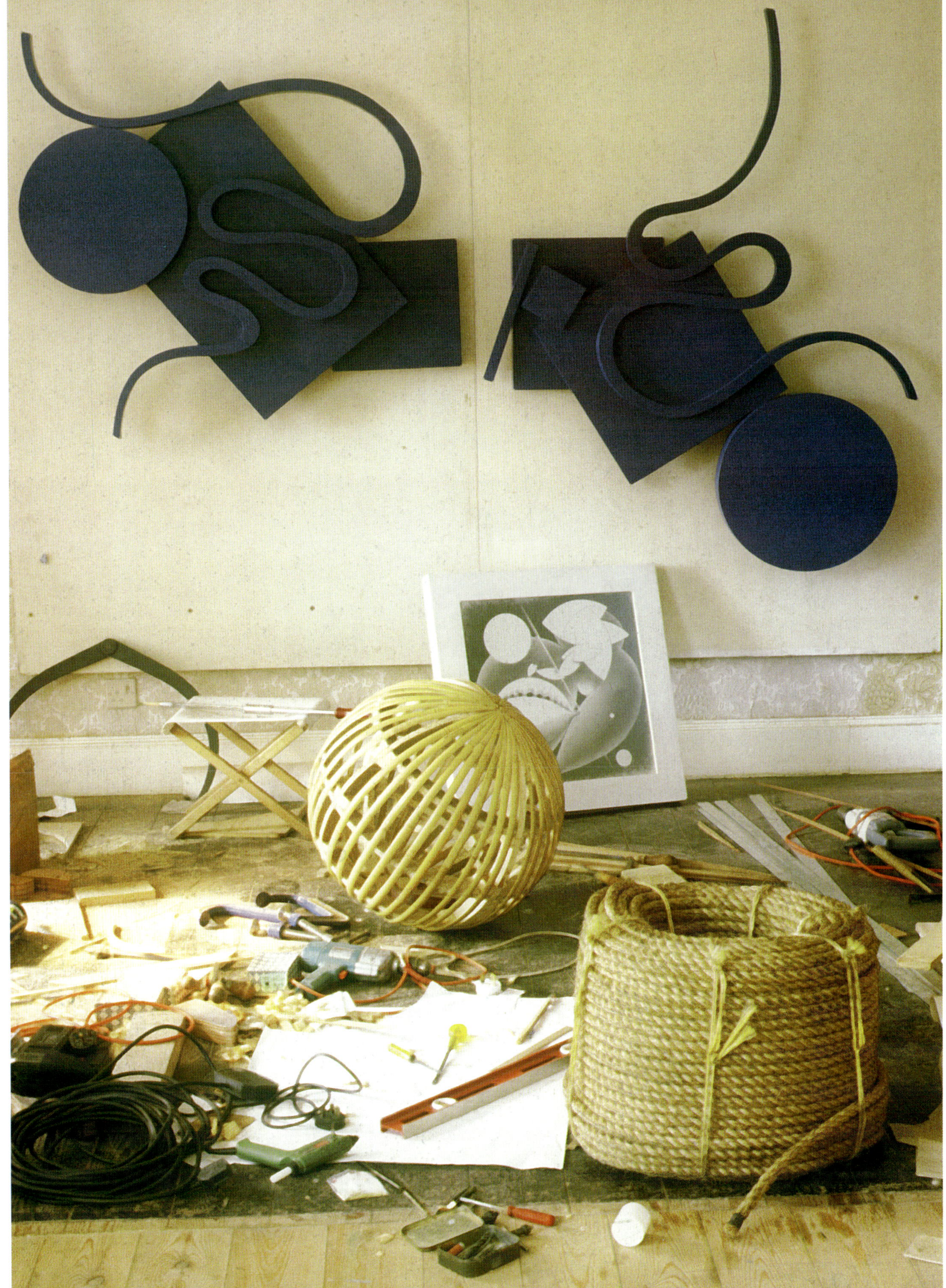

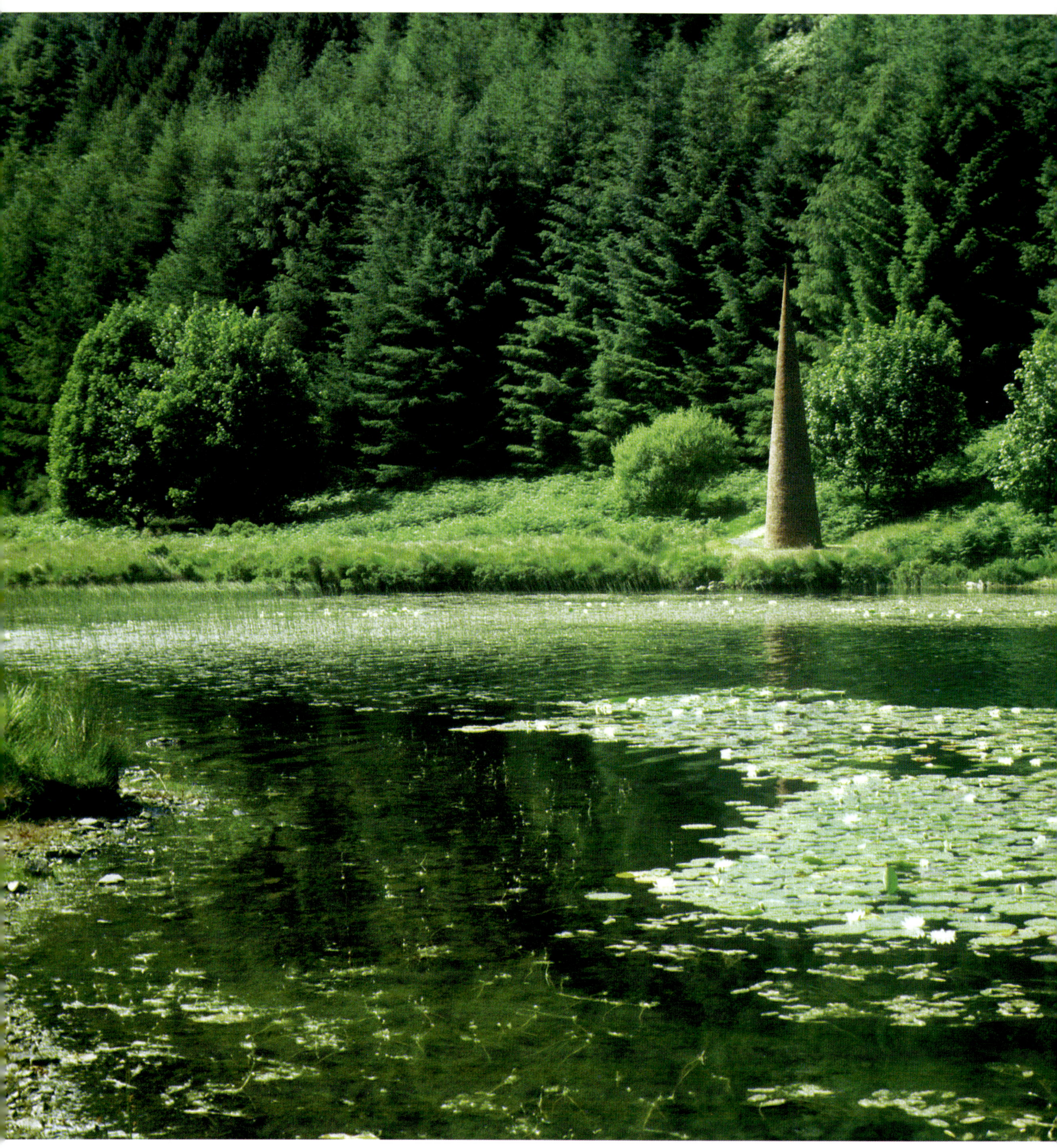

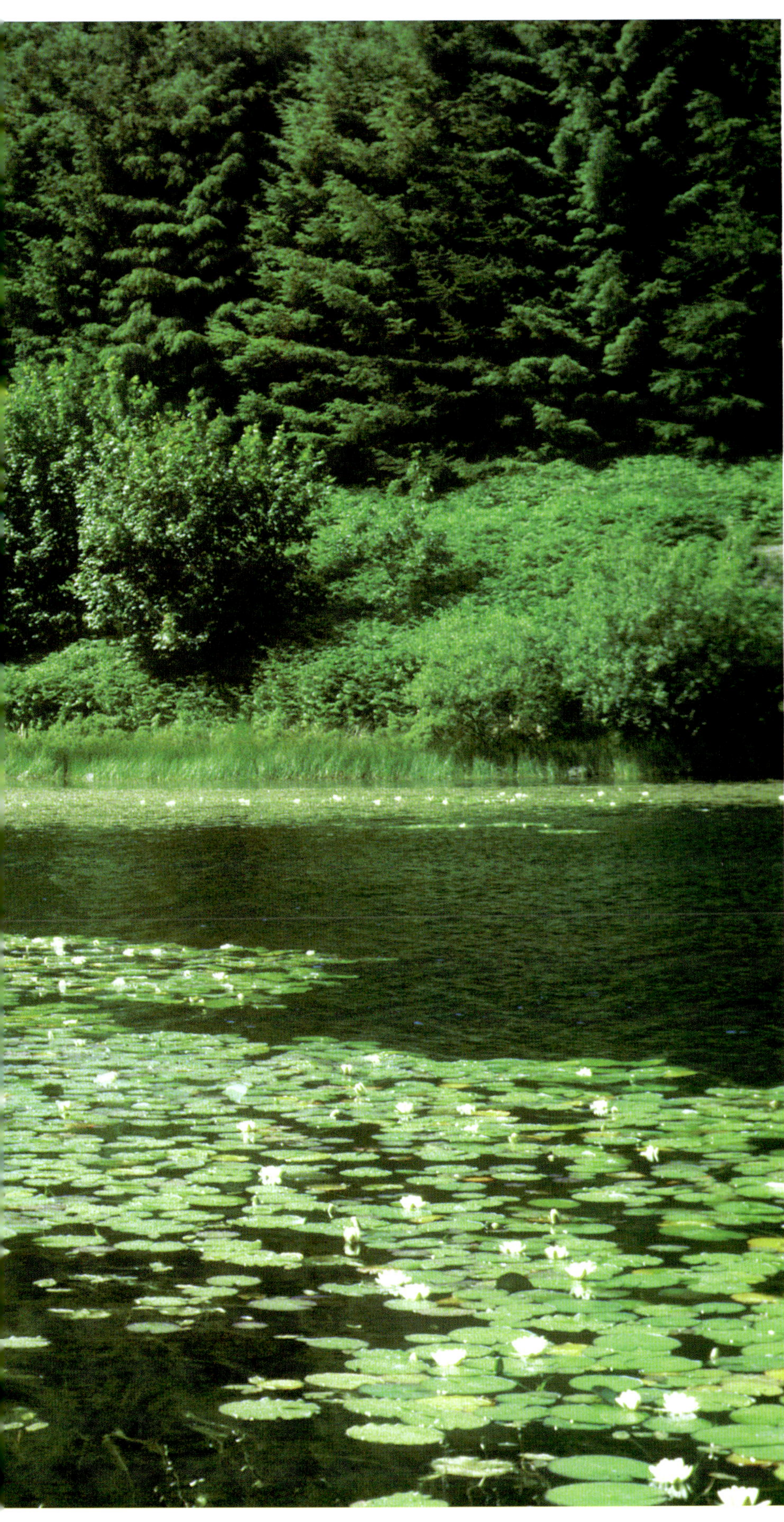

Swirl 1992
Approx. 500cm Ø
Yorkshire Sculpture Park

Colin Rose uses idioms and materials that have become part of the expanded visual language since Western art transcended a need to signify specific aspects of the observed world. Three dimensional objects based on intuitive geometry and the language of machines, construction, industry, fragments of the built environment, have migrated to a public space outside the gallery and the museum – outside the white cube. But there is a pervasive and persuasive aspect to his art that makes his structures particularly distinctive and recognisable. They are not exaggerated or overgrown, rather they are alluring, beguiling, inevitable. However artificial the metal circle nesting in the tree, or the forms emerging from the water may appear to be, they look like visitors who have arrived to stay. As the natural forms that surround them, the sculptures bear no message except in so far as we react to their presence; they are. Rose's works enter into a debate with the natural: his artifice is clear, and of course the deliberate placing of a sculpture is an indivisible part of the work. Rose insinuates his art into a natural framework.

Sculpture in landscape, sculpture at home, sculpture on the wall. The art of Colin Rose takes place perhaps initially in the studio and then moves out, and moves of course too from the study to the engineered result magnified in size. The concept of site-specificity has become increasingly important, with urban spaces and country fields being hosts, often permanent, to sculptures conceived with the spaces they will inhabit firmly in the mind of the artists. Much sculpture has indeed been startlingly direct, actually manipulating the landscape, rather than creating a discrete piece which comes to inhabit its surroundings. Such classics, often ephemeral, include Robert Smithson's *Spiral Jetty*, Christo and Jeanne-Claude's *Running Fence*

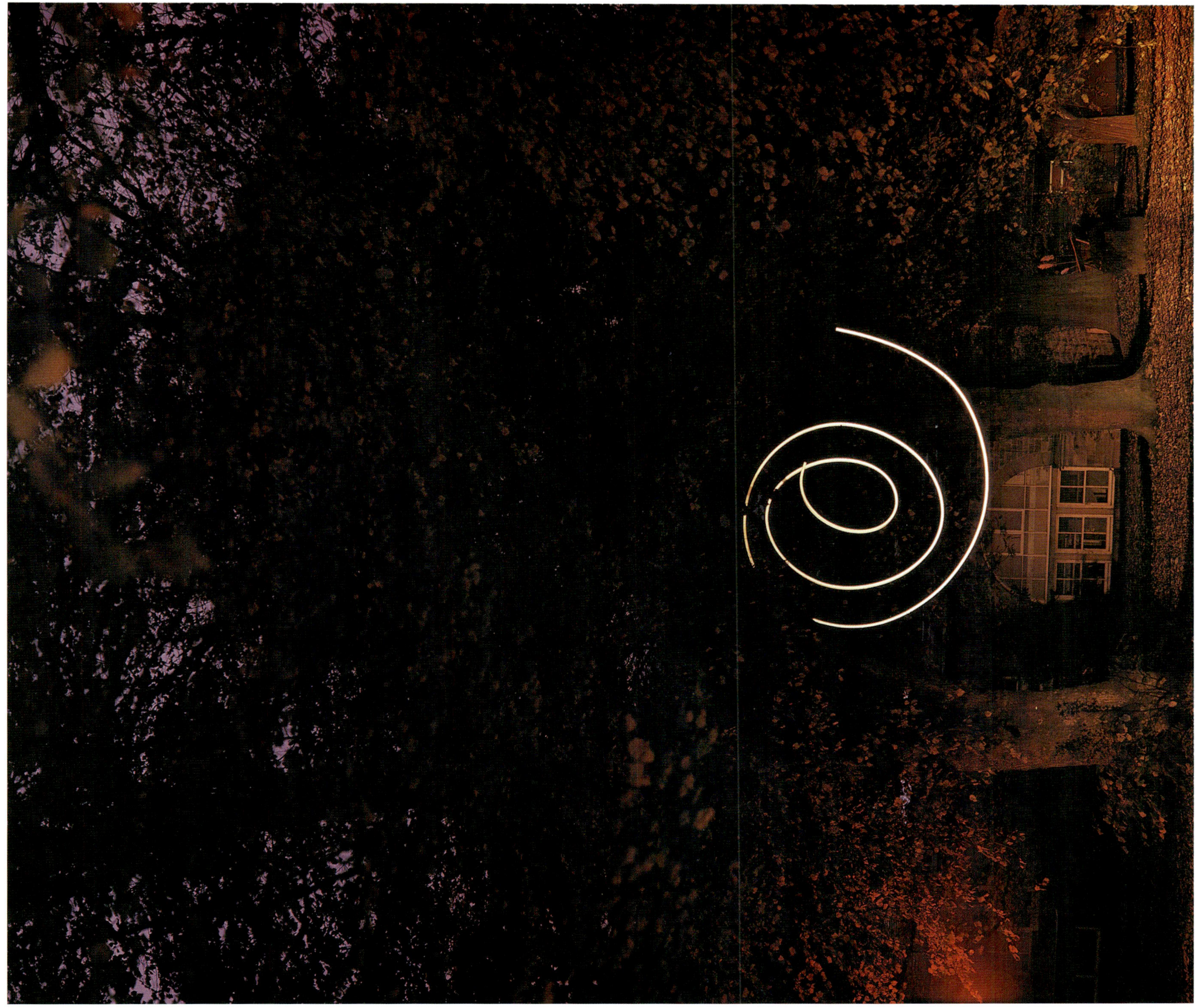

in northern California, James Turrell's *Roden Crater* and Walter de Maria's *Lightning Field*. These are works which have room to breathe, and whilst imposed on their environment, are not imposed on the public who make a journey, almost like a pilgrimage, to visit them. (And the controversy of the public placing some years ago of Richard Serra's *Tilted Arc* in New York City, which eventually was moved elsewhere, can indicate the delicacy of the situation when art meets the public in a way that some might resent.) Successful pieces are works which become embedded in the visual imagination as are the photographs of ephemeral structures taken by those artists who strike out into the landscape, from Richard Long to Andy Goldsworthy. At times only an activity is commemorated: a walk by Richard Long or Hamish Fulton appears in the making of a map, a captioned photograph, a diagram.

Although the process of the making may be evident with Colin Rose's sculptures, and is also occasionally documented – such as aspects of a work's transport or fabrication – he is always determined on the actual and the concrete. Perhaps this is why Colin Rose began from the domestic, with gentle, beguiling parodies of daily life. Neatly encapsulating a particularly British brand of surrealism, one of his earliest works is a hand, neatly tied up in brown paper and string, complete with its label: a posting label, an identifying label, a label you might have at a sale, an auction, or a storeroom. The label bears the ghostly image of the hand, unpacked. Rose has continued to explore his fascination not only with the domestic object, but with transport systems (including the postal system) and communication, with the processing of different kinds of parcels being an on-going game.

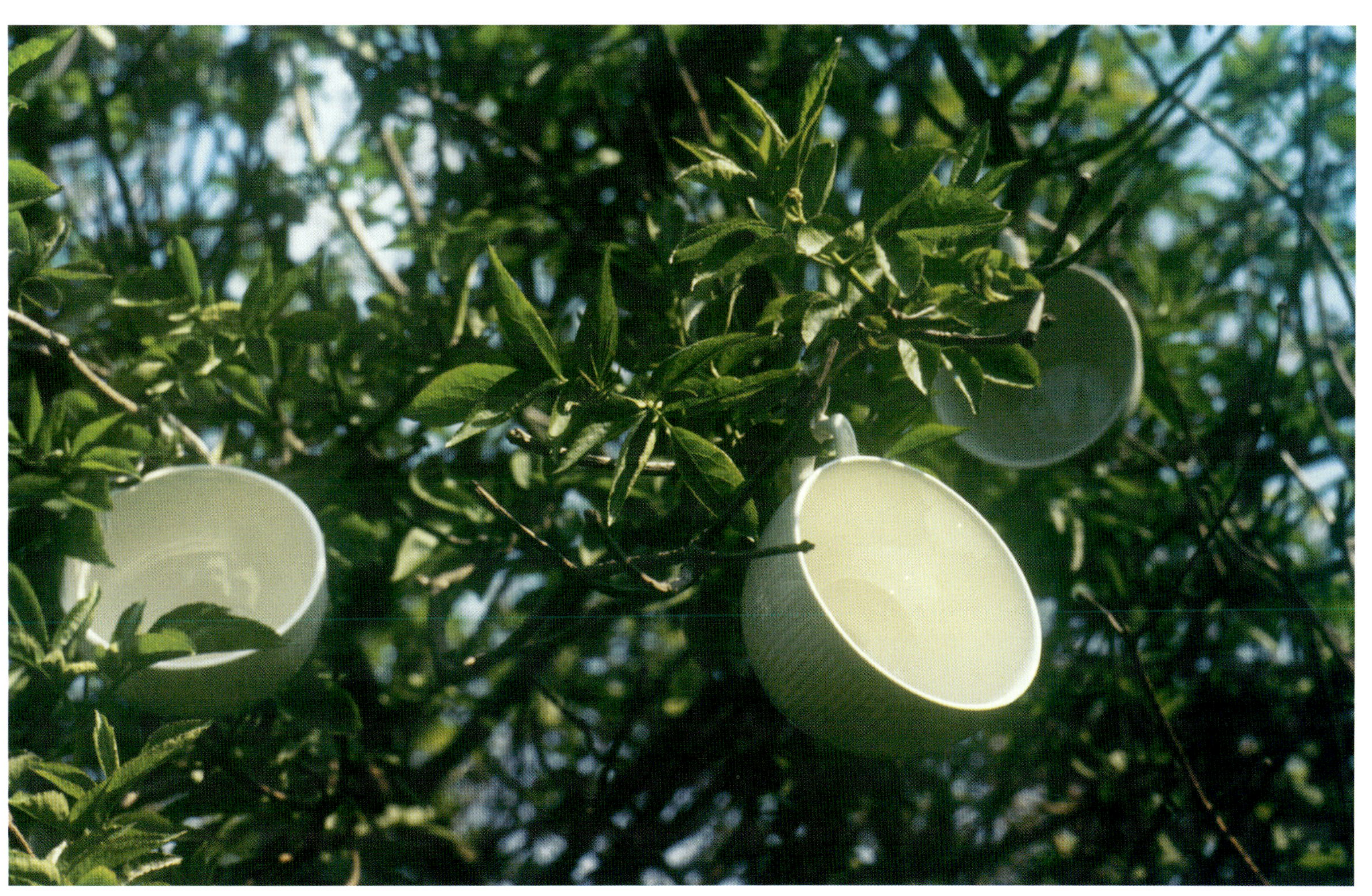

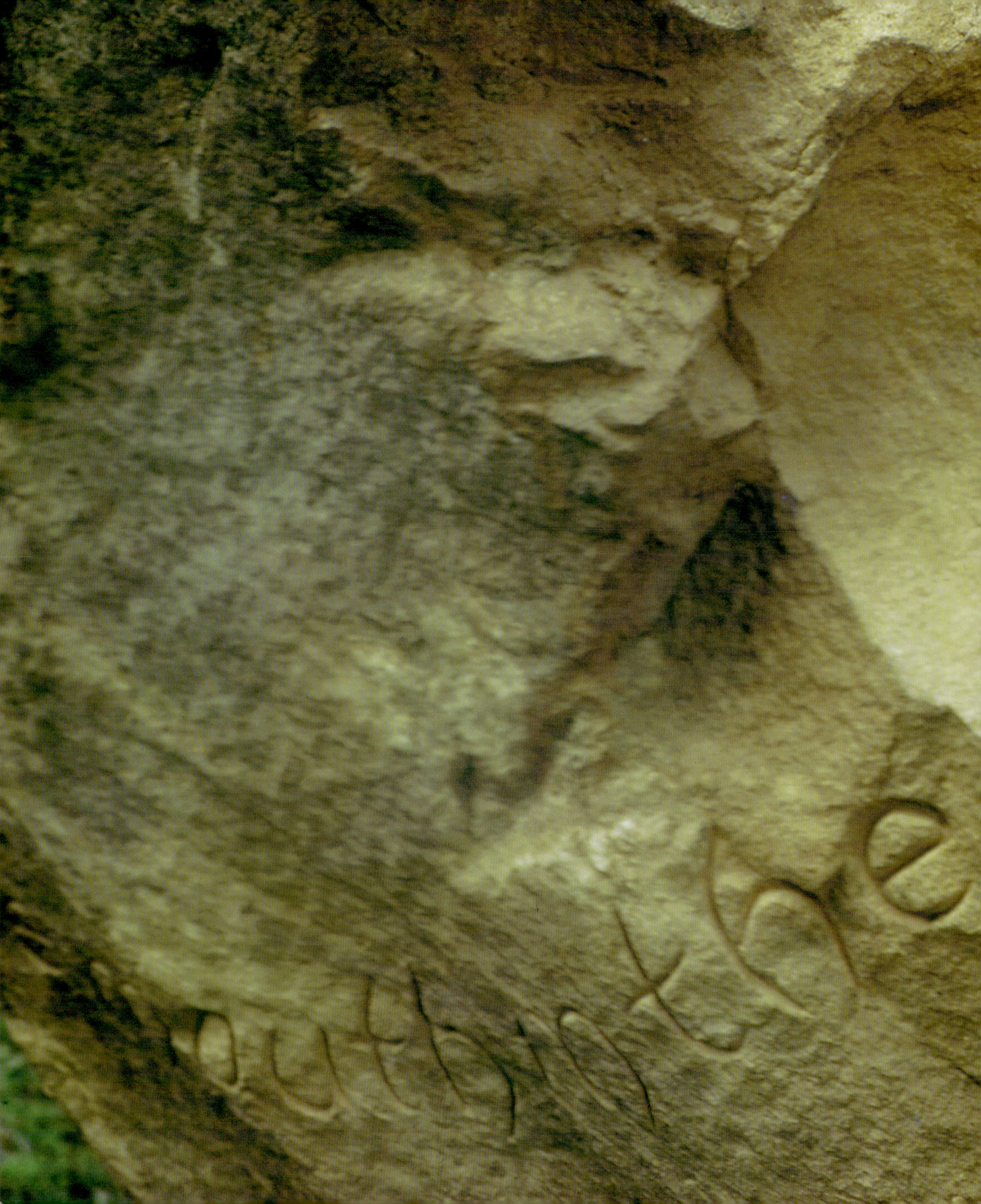
outh in the

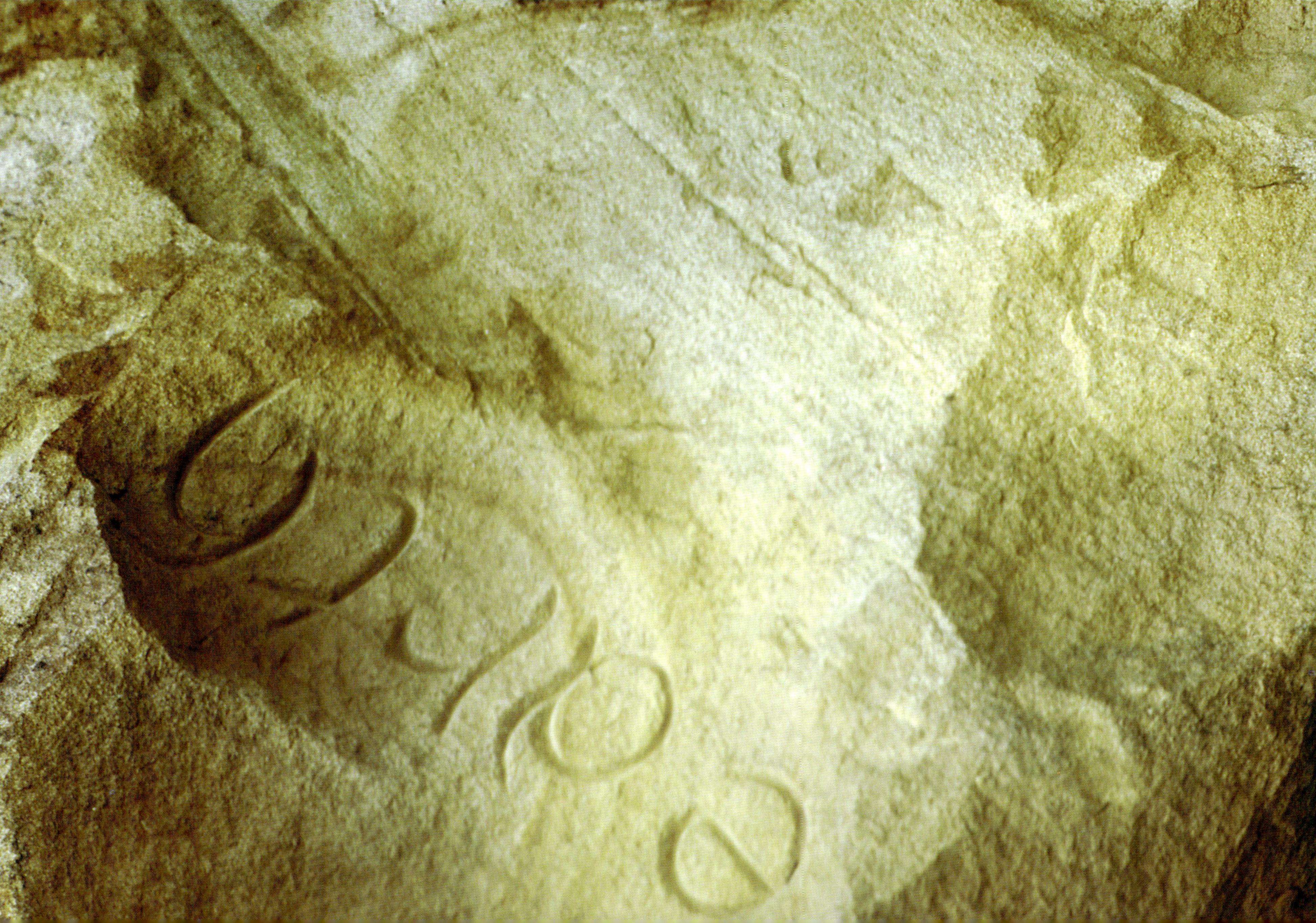

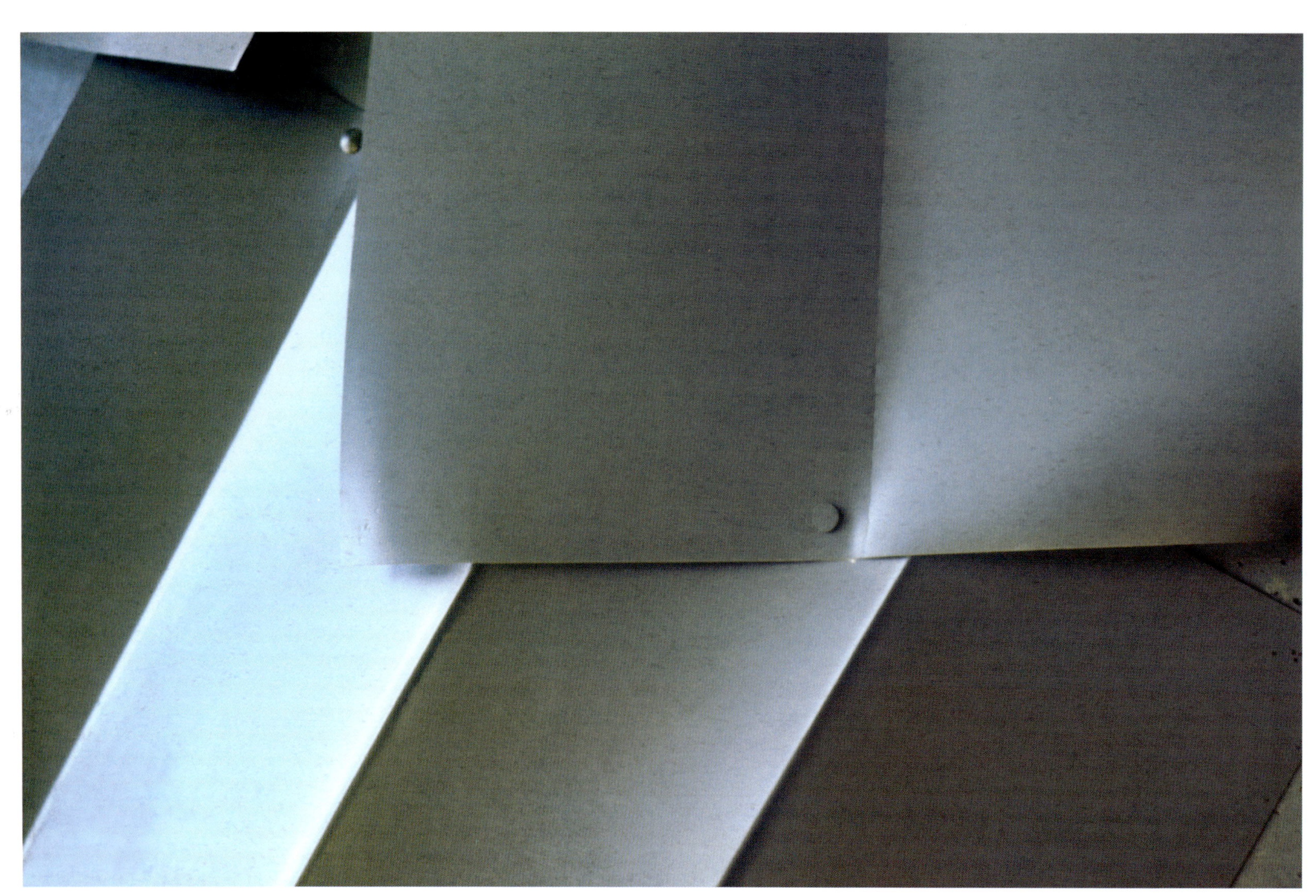

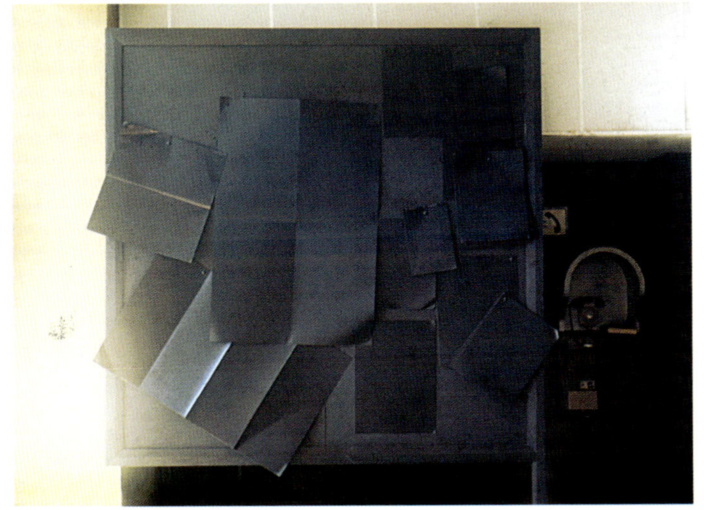

Notice 1976
Painted steel and wood
240 x 240cm

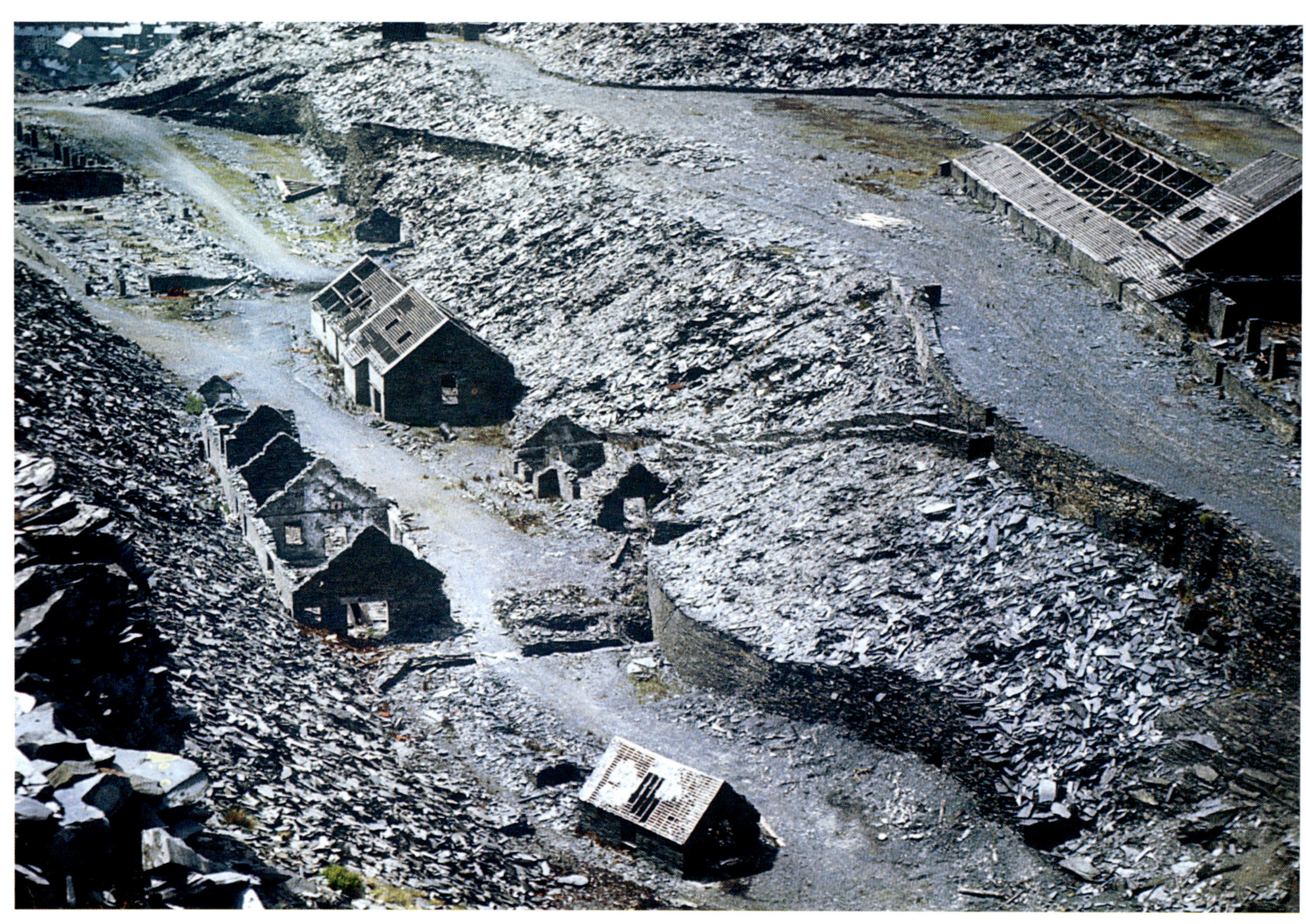

Slate Mine
Bleanau Ffestiniog

Early paintings hint at the life of things, like Ravel's *L'enfant
and le sortilege*, or *The Nutcracker*, with its toys come to life.
Cup Dreaming shows a teapot arching its spout skywards –
is it a yearning teapot, a 'dreaming teapot'? A saucer
leaning nonchalantly against the pot, and bearing upon
itself the linear depiction of the cup, into which we are
looking – an empty cup, made whimsical and lively by the
stem of the spoon, the handle of teapot, the spoutish
protuberance, animating the composition. The style is
diagrammatic. Is the artist dreaming of a cup of tea,
supposedly the leading passion of the English? No cup is
visible, but only the appurtenances, without which the cup
has neither content nor context: the teapot, the saucer.
Rose is planning a controlled viewing, with objects having
their own coloured shadows, fixed and immutable, unlike
shadows which change with changing light. *Tea*, of 1977,
shows teacups – at last – but they are inaccessible, hanging
as they are, in a tree. It is one supposes literally a tea tree.

There are other uses of found objects, of humble things.
Tyre is a photograph of an old truck tyre nestling in its own
shallow grave in a green lawn: it existed 'naturally', recorded
as source material for future work. Coming upon something
disregarded, Rose regarded it, and used it, a piece of
driftwood, of flotsam and jetsam washed up inland. For and
in Wales there are evocations of slate quarries, with pieces
called *Map*. One *Map* is a framed wall piece, with shards and
squares and tiles and chunks of slate both contained within
the frame and spilling out of it. From the same early period
comes *Map 2*, mine-destroyed houses and structures of
slate. These were Rose's first ever site specific works, in
the disused slate quarry at Bleanau Ffestiniog.

There are other domestic pieces: hanging shelves bearing
seemingly domestic objects made of spliced wood, like
crowded three dimensional Morandis. They are fossilised,
immovable, fixed. There are teasing domestic objects,
redolent of a gentle menace which might – or might not –
gather momentum. A table has a tiny surface, its elaborate
turned legs are scrunched together in impossible proximity
and are complete with ball bearings so this souvenir of a
table could be sent skittering any which way.

Dark Light 1976
10 x 6cm

Dark Light is a black bulb which could give no light. It is another contradiction, an ambiguity, a tease: can something be a dark light? Is darkness not the antithesis of light? Yet in English lightness is hardly ever a straightforward antithesis of darkness but something else altogether to do with weight and substance as well as gradations of light and dark. Rose suggests an interest in how we understand both the world we see and the world we inhabit (much of it invisible to our naked eye).

Rose's playing with objects not being quite what they were expected to be is part of a process which slowly moved beyond the domestic into the use of a vocabulary which was to combine natural forms – the organic – with the geometric. These preoccupations are to do with the artist's concern with the underlying processes that we cannot see, but which shape what is visible. An example would be the wind, which we cannot see, but all around us its effects are strikingly visible, or the skeleton clothed in flesh which obscures it, but which nevertheless shapes the body. The domestic moves into the abstract, making visible that which is hidden.

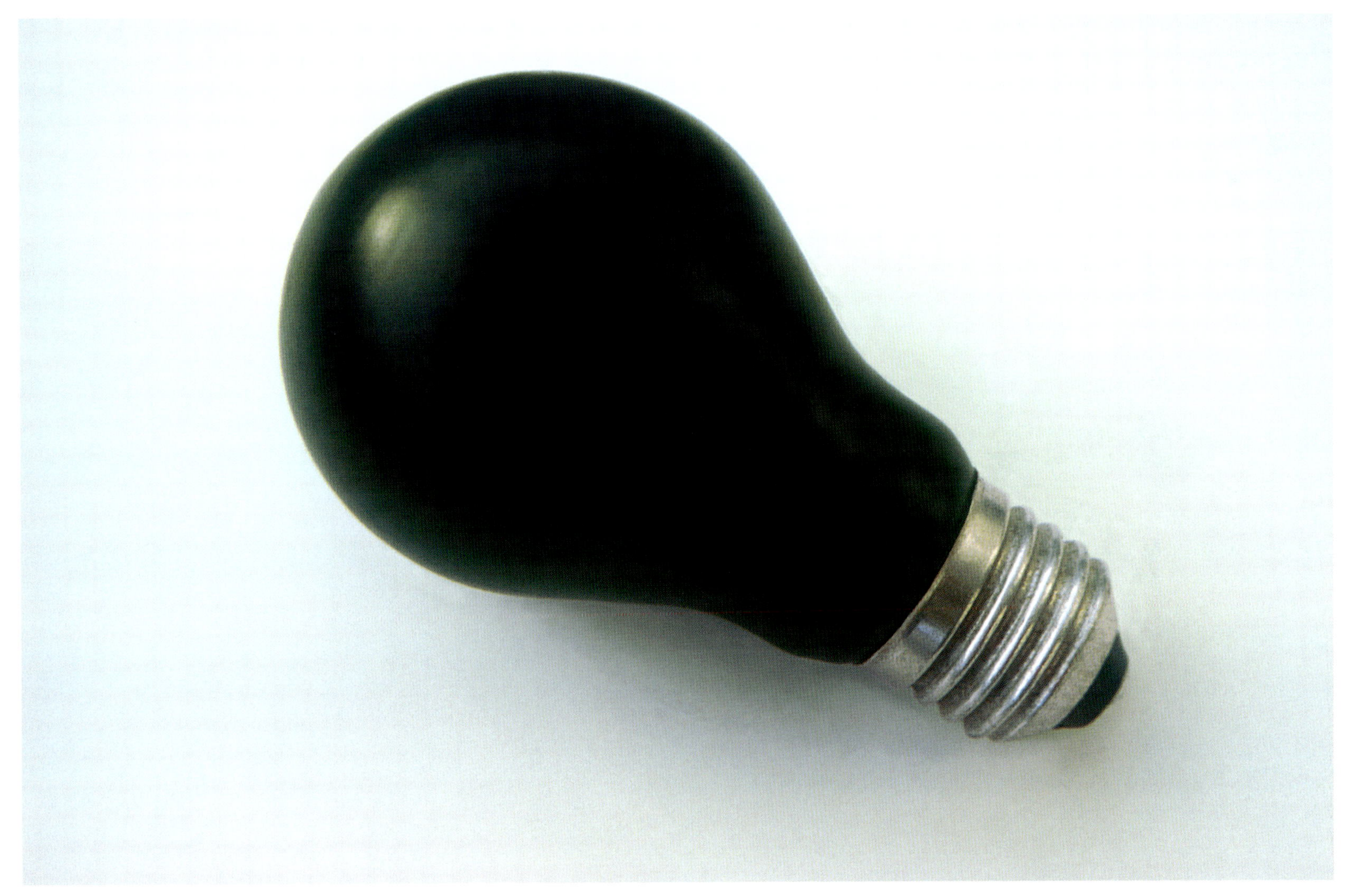

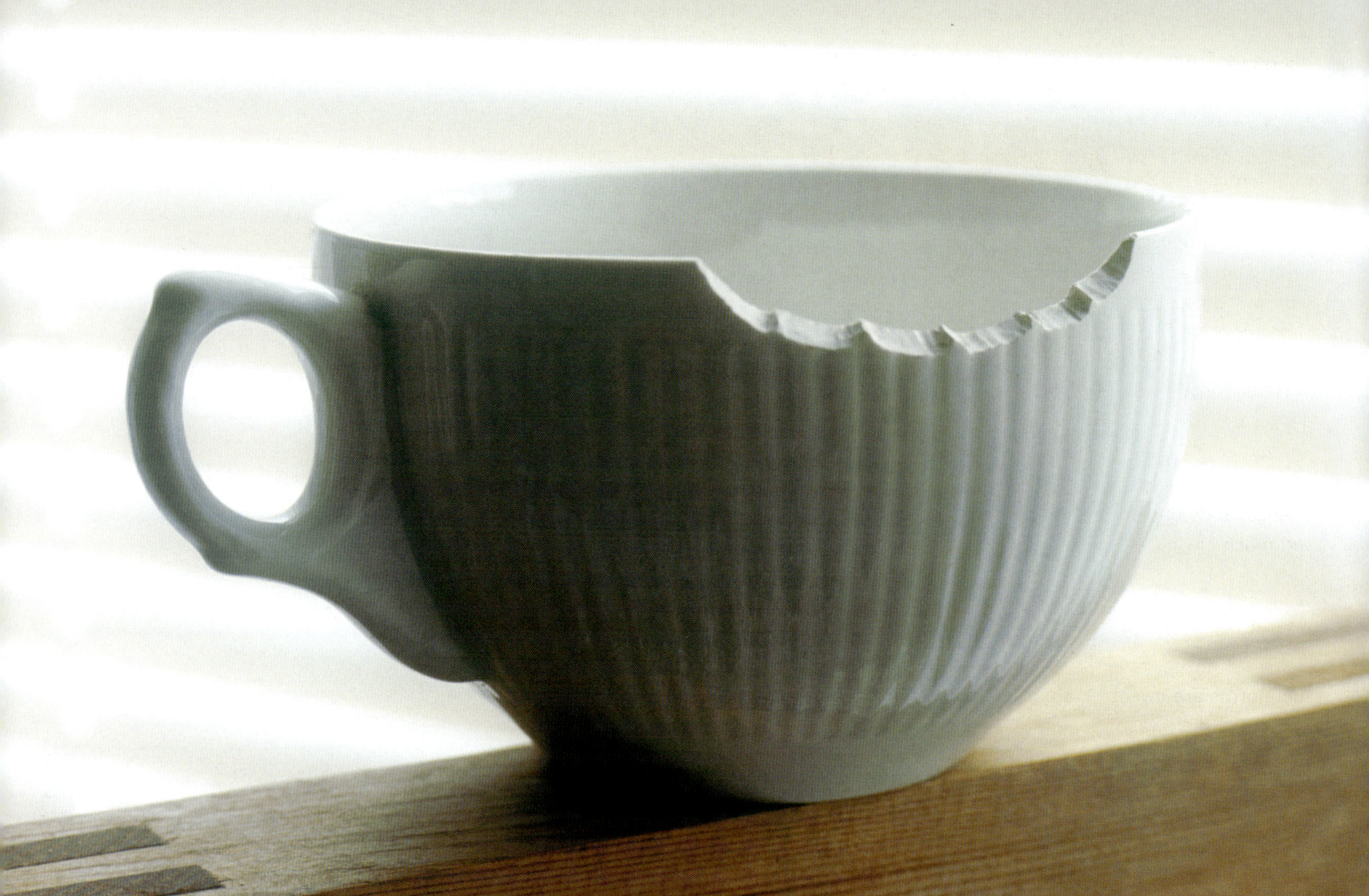

Above:
Cup 1978

Opposite:
Starball 1995
Charcoal on paper
150 x 150cm

Starball 1995 (maquette)
Card
30cm Ø

The process really began with a transformation of the
domestic. A teacup had bites taken out of it: shades of
the Marx brothers when they crunched sugar crisp crockery
to the astonishment of their audience. Years ago, in a
small publication from the Natural History Museum called
Taken from Life, the scientific investigators from the museum
presented simply as aesthetic delights and fascinating
descriptive insights, photographs of natural forms taken
with the new techniques available by using an electron
microscope. In unscripted echoes, unconsciously
complementary, artists have been developing and inventing
with their own intuition shapes which were curiously
related to scientific investigations. C H Waddington's
seminal study, *Behind Appearances*, explored the
relationships in the modern period between painting and
science, and concluded that they were complex, subtle
and much closer than those between literature and science.
As for painting so in many ways for sculpture: imagery,
preoccupation, technique, materials. A three dimensional
form, for example, the double helix, is at the metaphoric
heart of the science of genetics. In Colin Rose's aesthetic,
such forms are invented: a prime example is a form like
Starcone, which was first worked out in drawings, but
emerges eventually as a three dimensional work; so too
with *Starball*. These formations have a lyrical fascination,
a curious combination of solidity and delicacy. Tension
is provided by a constant interplay between an intuitive
geometry and natural form: geometric figures are often set
in context because they are framed in landscape or actually
inserted into trees. Clusters of artistic decisions and the
determination on a specific site are the joint determinants
of the appearance of a particular work.

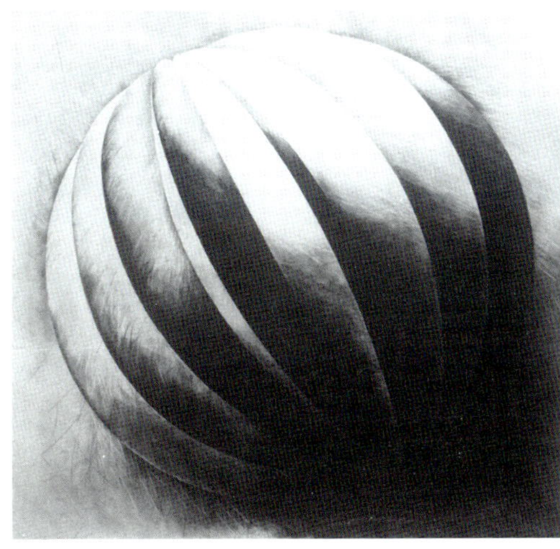

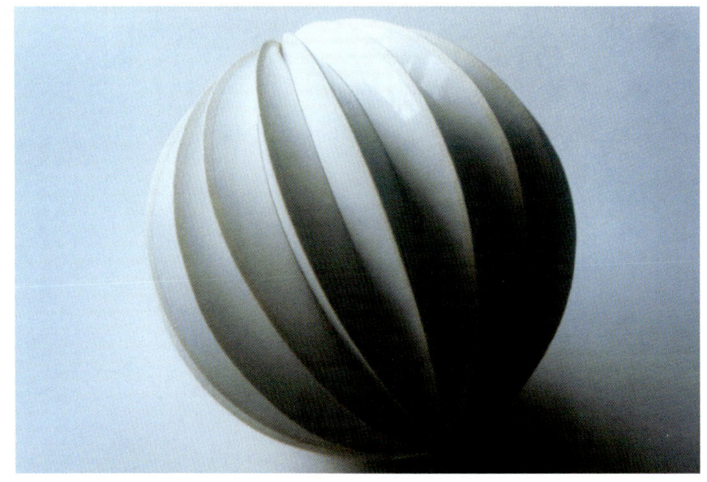

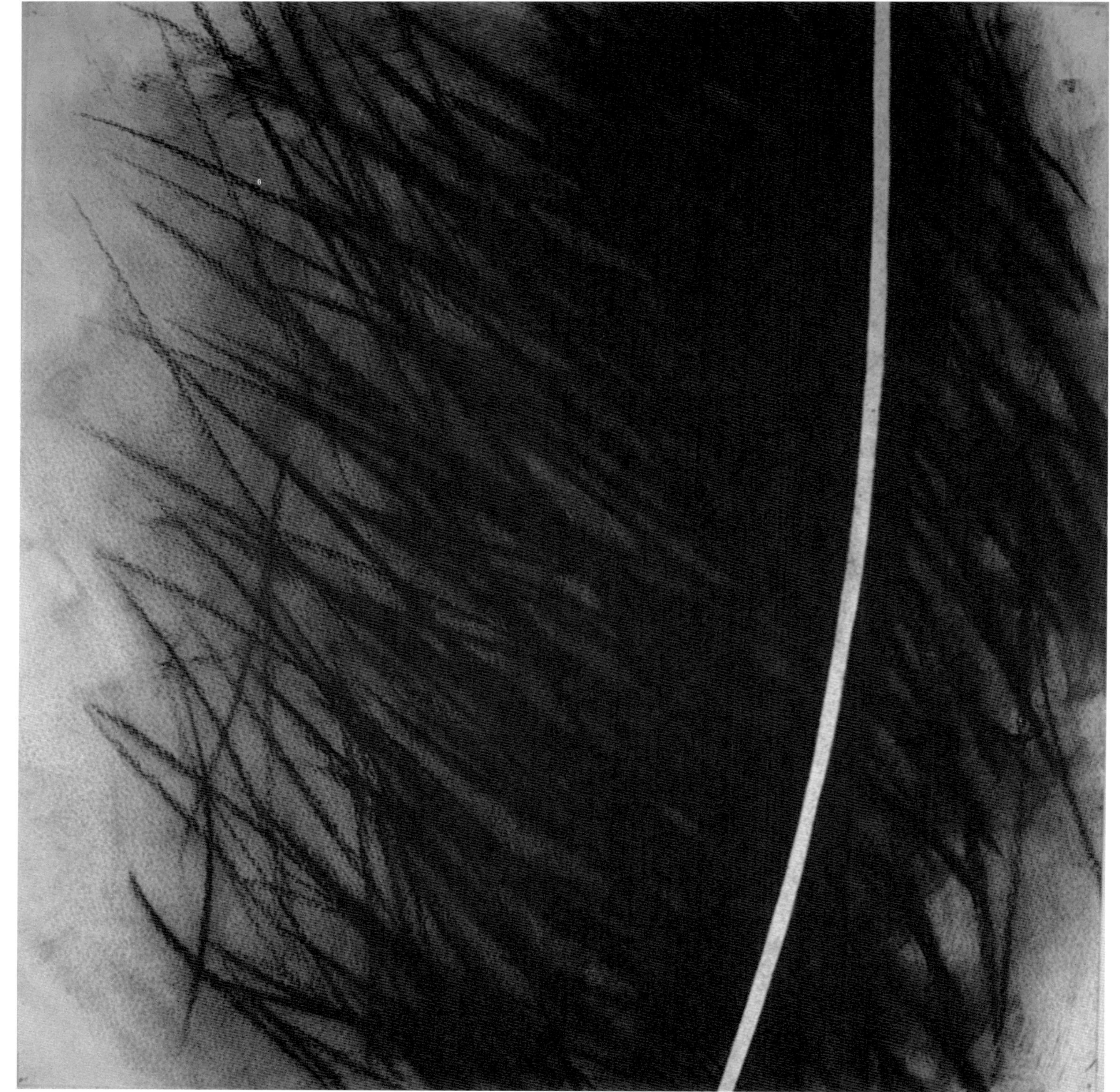

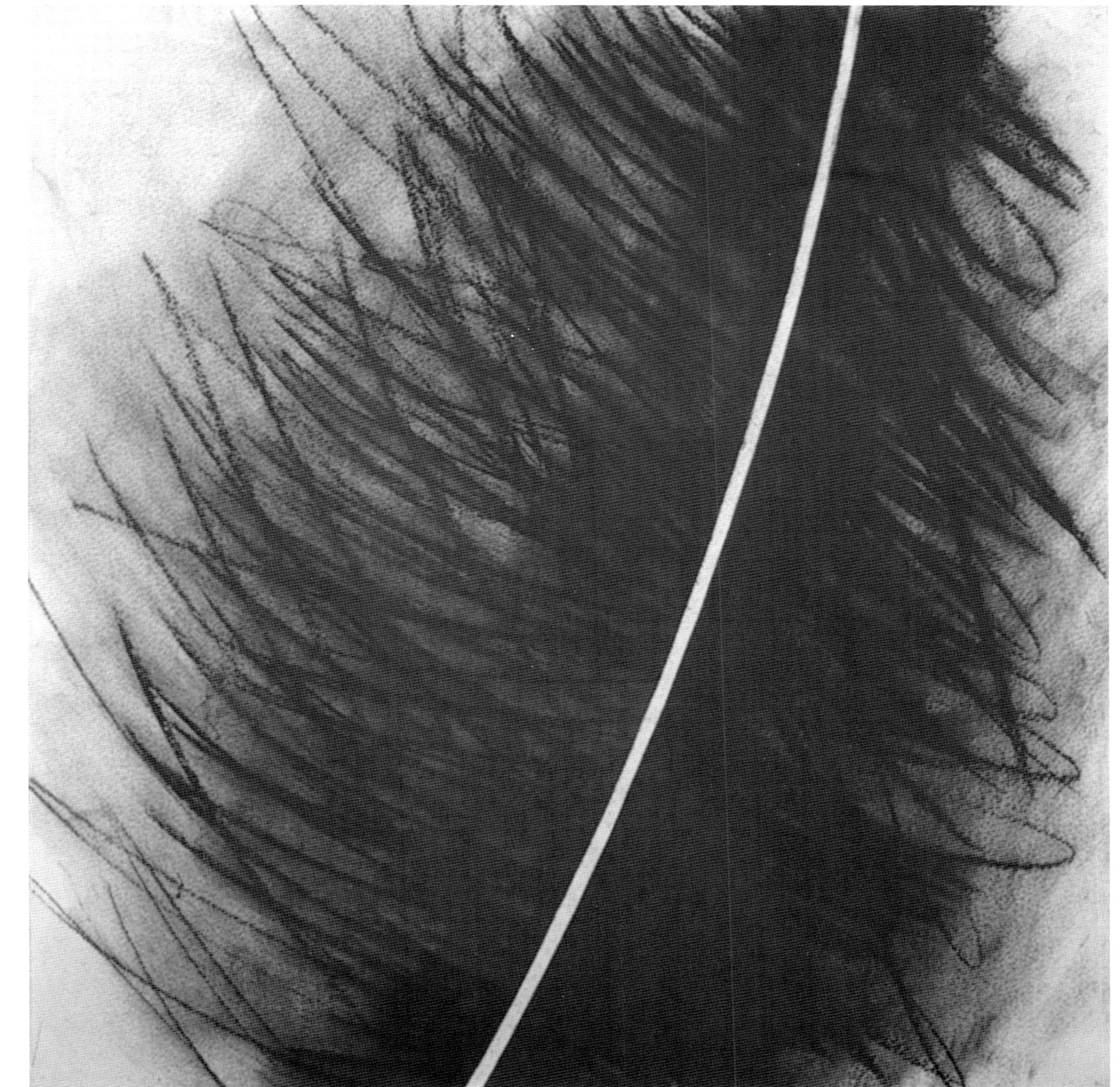

Previous pages and below:
Broken Wave 1996
Charcoal on paper
50 x 50 x 1900cm

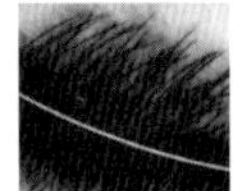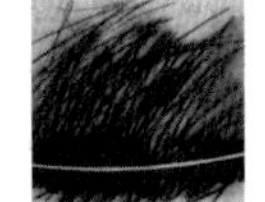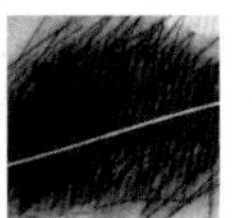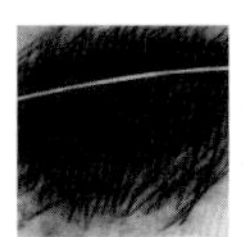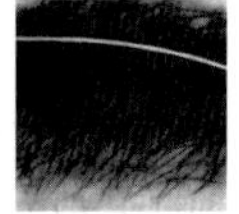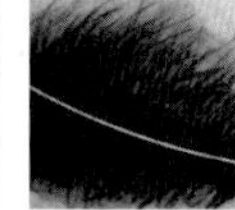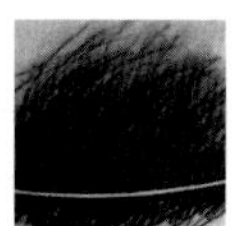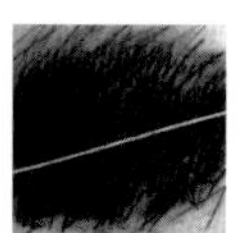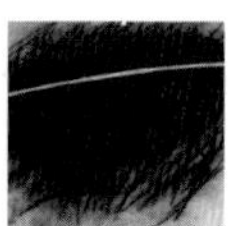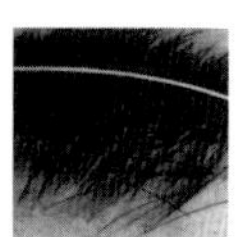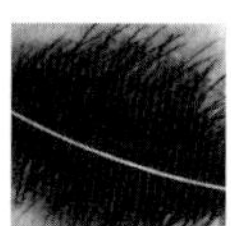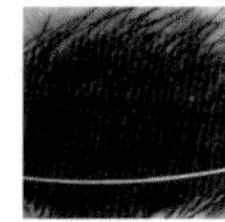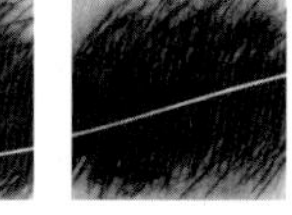

Titles suggest Rose's formal preoccupations with symbolic
or quintessential form: *Broken Wave*, *Rolling Moon*, *Dancing
Drum*, *Floating Rocks*. In certain ways, Colin Rose's art is
part of a much wider but little explored post war, and
perhaps even postmodern, aesthetic, in which there is
specifically a yearning for a kind of simplified ritual. A long
wall drawing, accomplished on successive paper squares,
23 in all, *Broken Wave*, shows a graceful curve cascading
against a crowded brushing of charcoal lines. The *Broken
Wave* is actually a continuous line, punctuated although
not distorted by the spaces between the paper squares.
It is an expansive, euphoric gesture, evidenced in a natural,
captivating, beguiling rhythm.

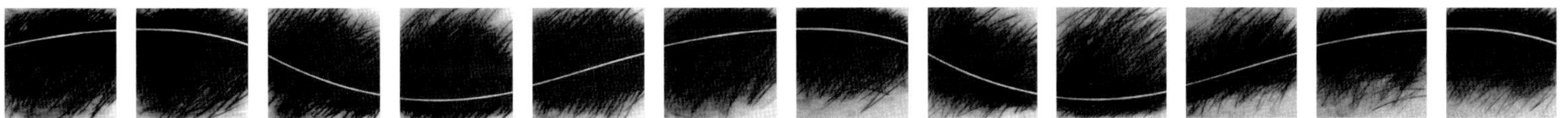

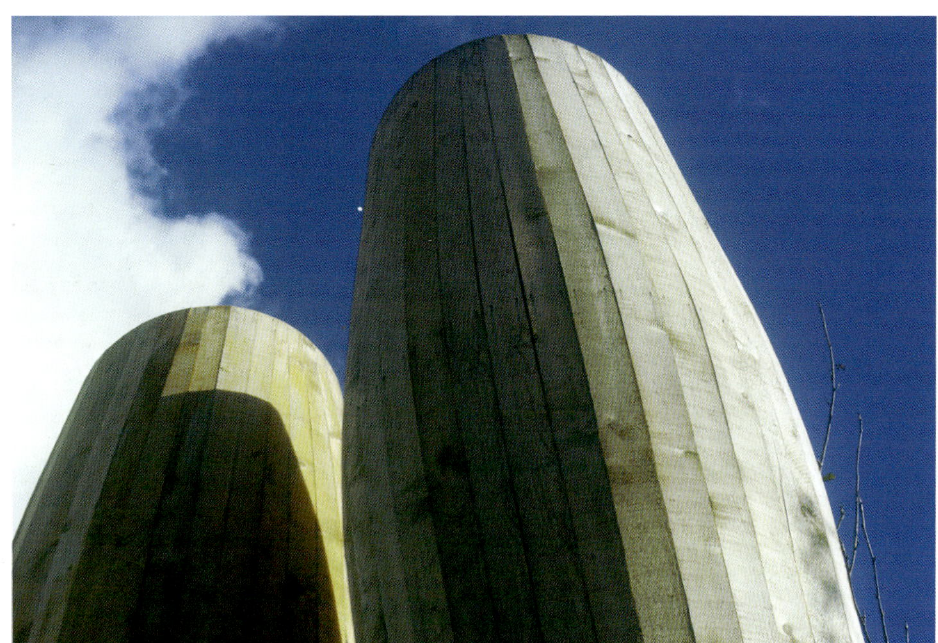

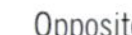

Opposite:
Dancing Drums 1989
Wood
450 x 120cm Ø
Yorkshire Sculpture Park

Left:
Dancing Drums 1990 (detail)
Wood
Gateshead NGF

Below Left:
Dancing Drums 1989 (in progress)

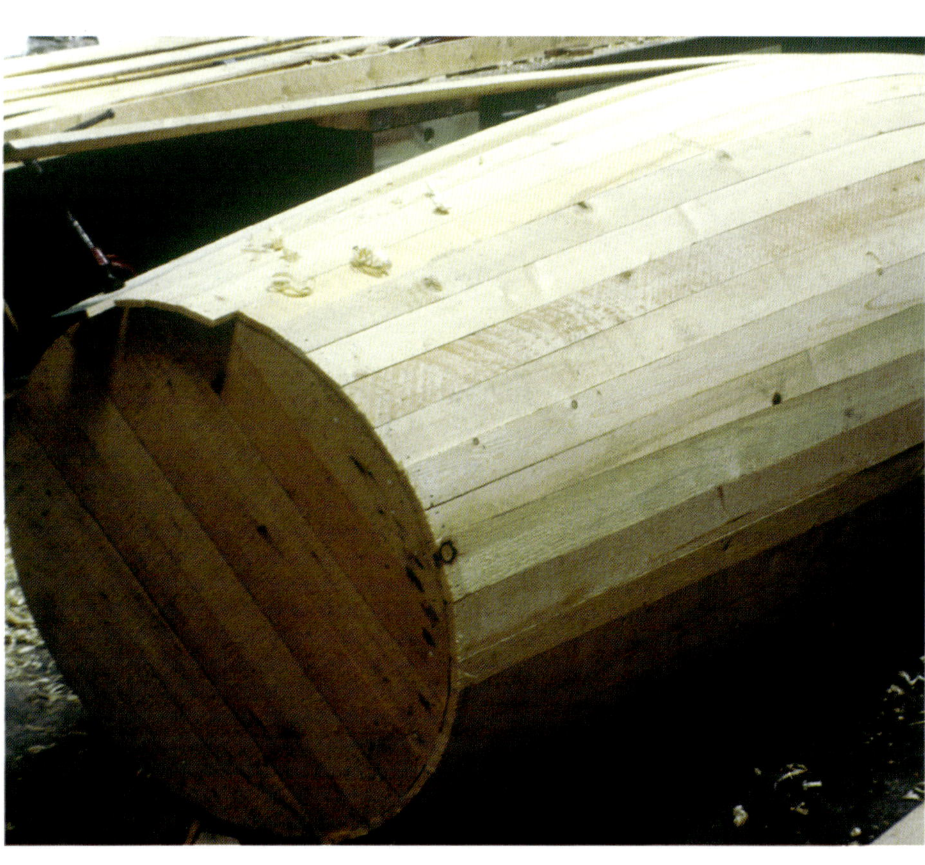

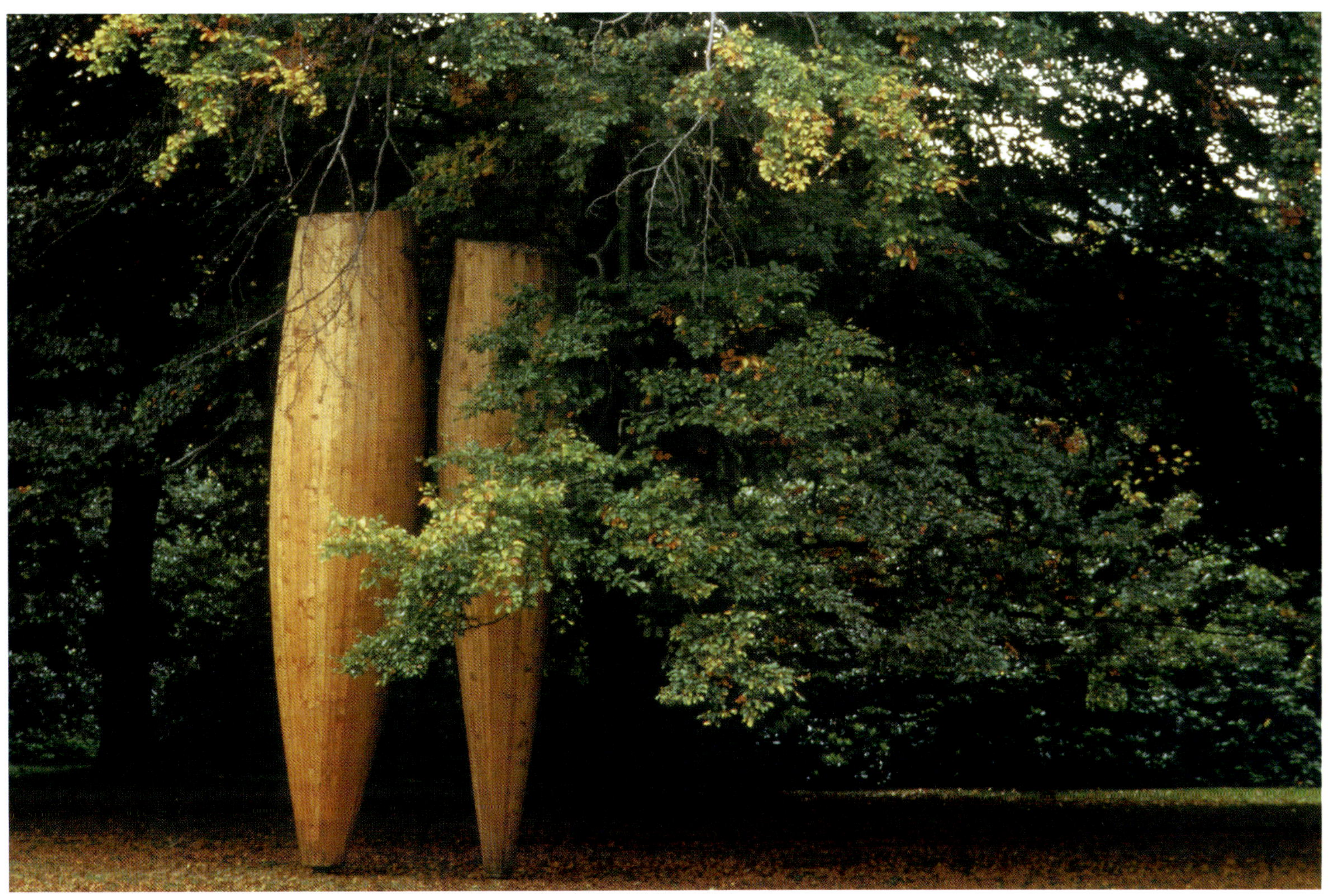

Dancing Drums are two tapering vertical drums, perhaps the musical instruments of a giant, left behind in a forest glade. They hint at containers, at funerary urns, and yet they are discrete objects, closed off from the forest around them, yet made of the materials of the forest, of wood. Because they are a duo, and one is taller than the other, they also seem like sentinels, both a gateway perhaps and a couple, suggestive of an alliance: giant – over 3 metres high – but intimate, both in their relationship to each other and to the surrounding forest.

The outdoor pieces of the 1980s and early 1990s often deliberately explored the ramifications of a visual experience that is original – and magical. Colin Rose has made sculptures, often anchored by the tree which frames them and holds them, to be seen by both night and day. In the day sunshine glints on the painted steel of *Ting* (nearly 12 metres in diameter) or the aluminium of *Night and Day* – an aluminium sphere held in its tree by a jagged line – a moon or sun or possibly hills on a horizon. By night moonlight, starlight, or human and mechanised traffic pick up these ghostly glints of geometry invading nature.

A 20 ton granite ball brings us down to earth: it is called *Meteor*. We have not however seen it land; rather when we come upon it, it looks as though it has emerged from the forest floor. *Meteor* is surrounded by birches in a clearing whose floor consists of the soft debris of pine cones, leaves, the moultings and sheddings of trees as they prepare for further growth. It is as though a strange new and giant creature is pushing up from underneath the earth. But this work allows for ambiguity: far from emerging from within *Meteor* has fallen down to earth, and is burrowing beneath it.

Pine Ball though is indeed up a tree: is it a grotesque overgrowth? a tumour? Or is it simply a joyous decoration, an exuberant bauble? Is it the observer's mood that will decide whether *Pine Ball* is destructive or celebratory?

Creative contradictions inform much of these sculptures: there is both paradox and ambiguity in these geometric figurations, the non-objective world, nestling, nesting, invading, parading in trees and forest. On the shores of the Black Loch, in Dumfries and Galloway, that part of Scotland near to the Irish Sea, there is a 9 metres 'eye' made of split quarry tiles. It is a carefully constructed structure, a spire dwarfed by the landscape, yearning towards limitless sky, yet, reflected in the water it is doubled, looking both upwards and down into depths. It is indeed an eye, providing imagery which punctuates and underlines and intensifies our apprehension of landscape. The contrast of the seeming artlessness of the landscape – however an understanding of ecology tells us how profoundly it is affected by human activity – and the absolute man-made nature of the eye, which serves no practical function but to make us see more – and thus feel more – is intensely satisfying.

Pineball (in progress)
90cm Ø

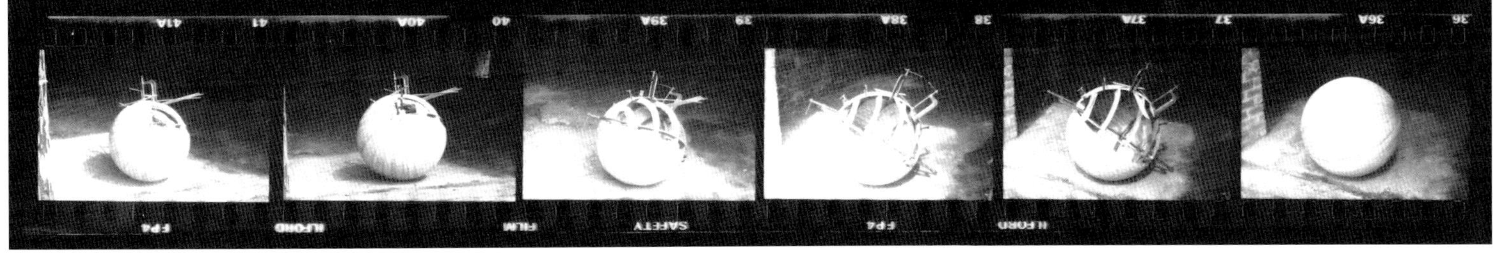

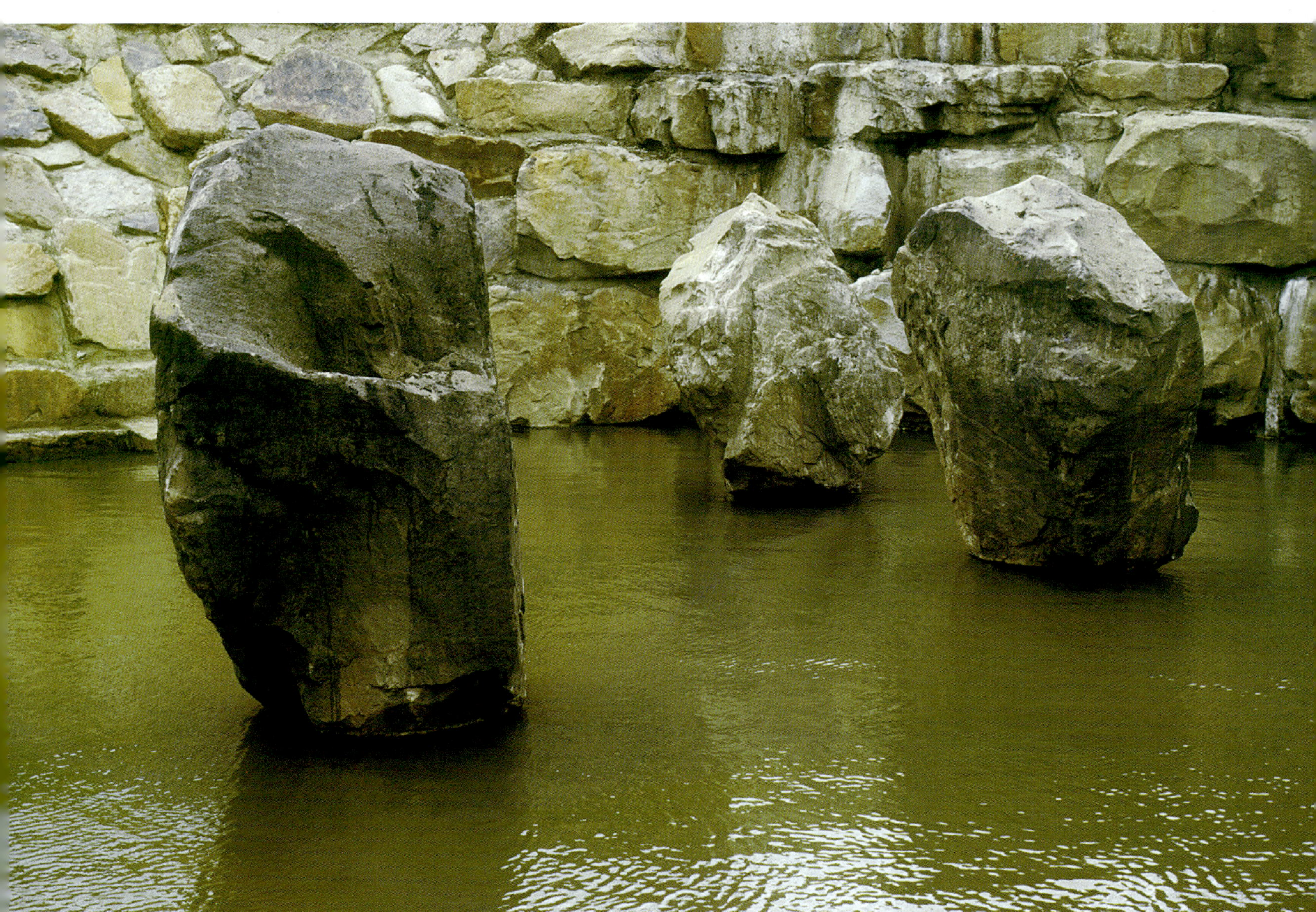

One piece which sums up in its own distinct and individual
way Colin Rose's beguiling obsessions is *Floating Rocks*.
This was a massive undertaking for an aesthetic result
which is fascinating and absorbing, beautiful, tranquil and
yet with something that is characteristic of Rose's art: a
distinctly disturbing yet subtle edge. There is something
that is unexpected, whether it be geometric shapes afloat
in trees, circular meteors which never could exist naturally
come to earth. Are these surprises of a gentle, entrancing
nature? Or is there something menacingly alien? These
are structures which appear inevitable, at ease. But have
they come to dominate, or are they simply gentle and
welcome strangers?

In the world of Colin Rose, things are always given an
unexpected twist, so that our eye and mind is startled –
but not frightened. These are not works based on fear, but
on acceptance: an acceptance of the strangeness of the
ordinary, the life that surrounds us that we do not really see.
So we are sensitised to our surroundings, but more, we see
things that do not appear to be real, but are: embodiments
of visual fantasies, of gravity defying artifacts, visitors
either from outer space, but in fact realisations of the
imagination, of inner space, of the non-objective world.

Floating Rocks is just that, a labour intensive work that is
the result of hard won technical solutions, so that we see
– but can we believe it? Here are boulders, not emerging
from the water, but floating. The sculptures defy all our
instincts about the natural world and our place in it. Rose
manages to get us to suspend our disbelief because what
informs his art is his own journey from the domestic to
the public, the practical to the imaginative. From those
transformations of domestic objects, turned inside out,
stretched every which way, to interventions in landscape,
he has made the possible appear from the realm of the
impossible. Or rather he has made the impossible tangible.

In parallel to these highly imaginative excursions, there
has been an urban practice, the industrial monumental
and minumental in tandem with sculptures in forests,
woods, lakes and the patchwork wilderness of our islands.
A later work, *Ship*, a huge red steel slice curves through
a city space in Jarrow, hints at the monumental. It is as
though Ellsworth Kelly had suddenly turned towards the
art of memory and commemoration. Some 12 metres high,
it indicates the bow of a ship, stylised, extracted, refined
and powerful. A huge sliced through red disc is nearby – a
fragment of machinery that symbolises a ship's propeller
The work by the water marks a dying industry, resonant
with its own past. Rose's use of materials are always
appropriate to the intent: building materials for structures;
metals for free floating geometries; wood, stone and rock
for landscapes. The journey from the domestic to the
public has thus been informed by both the architecture
of the town and the architecture of the natural, the found,
the landscape – although always acknowledging the
manipulation of the landscape by human intervention.
In this process over several decades Colin Rose has used
the various vocabularies of modernism expanded and
codified in the past century to create a communicable
visual language of his own – visible, entrancing, powerful
and memorable. It is a corpus of work infused by a quiet
heroism, a successful determination to find an individual
voice amongst a plethora of possibilities. It is a voice
unafraid to draw attention to other voices, to show us
the spaces of landscape, and the spaces of the built
environment, to punctuate and underline. In so doing,
it is quietly shocking in its subtle confidence: less truly is
more, much more.

Floating Rocks 1996 (detail)
Watergate, Whickham, Tyne & Wear

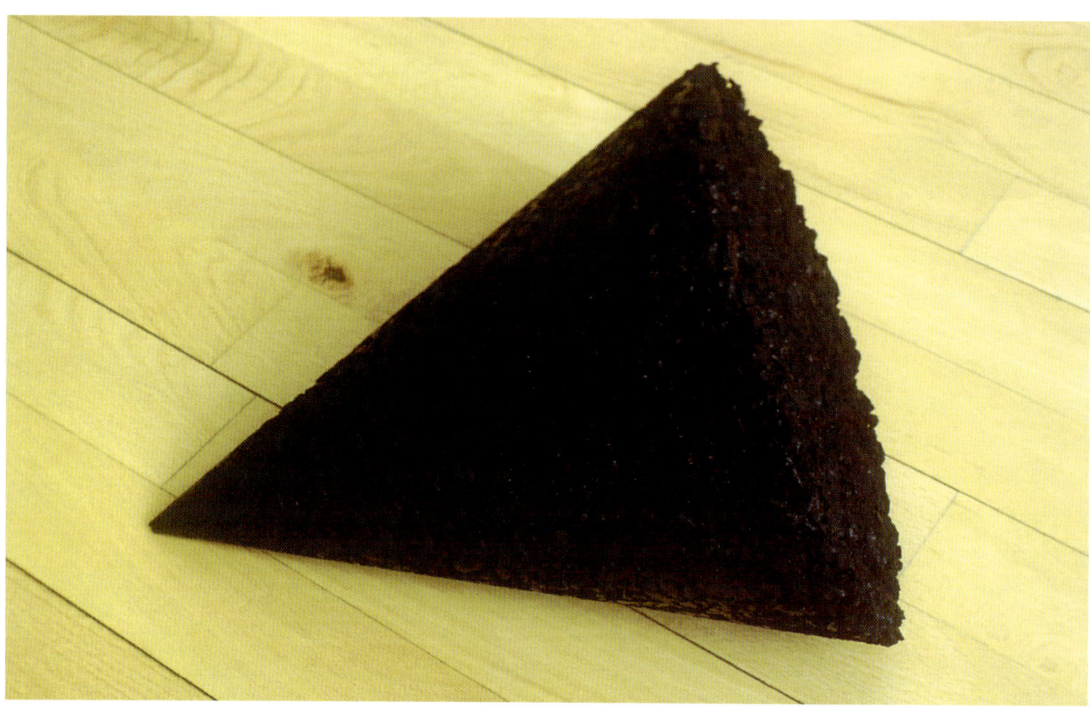

Opposite: **Cone** 1996
Charcoal
25 x 40cm

Right: **Untitled** 1996
Aluminium
30 x 12cm Ø

Following pages: **Passage** 1979
Plaster
Approx. 1.2m Ø

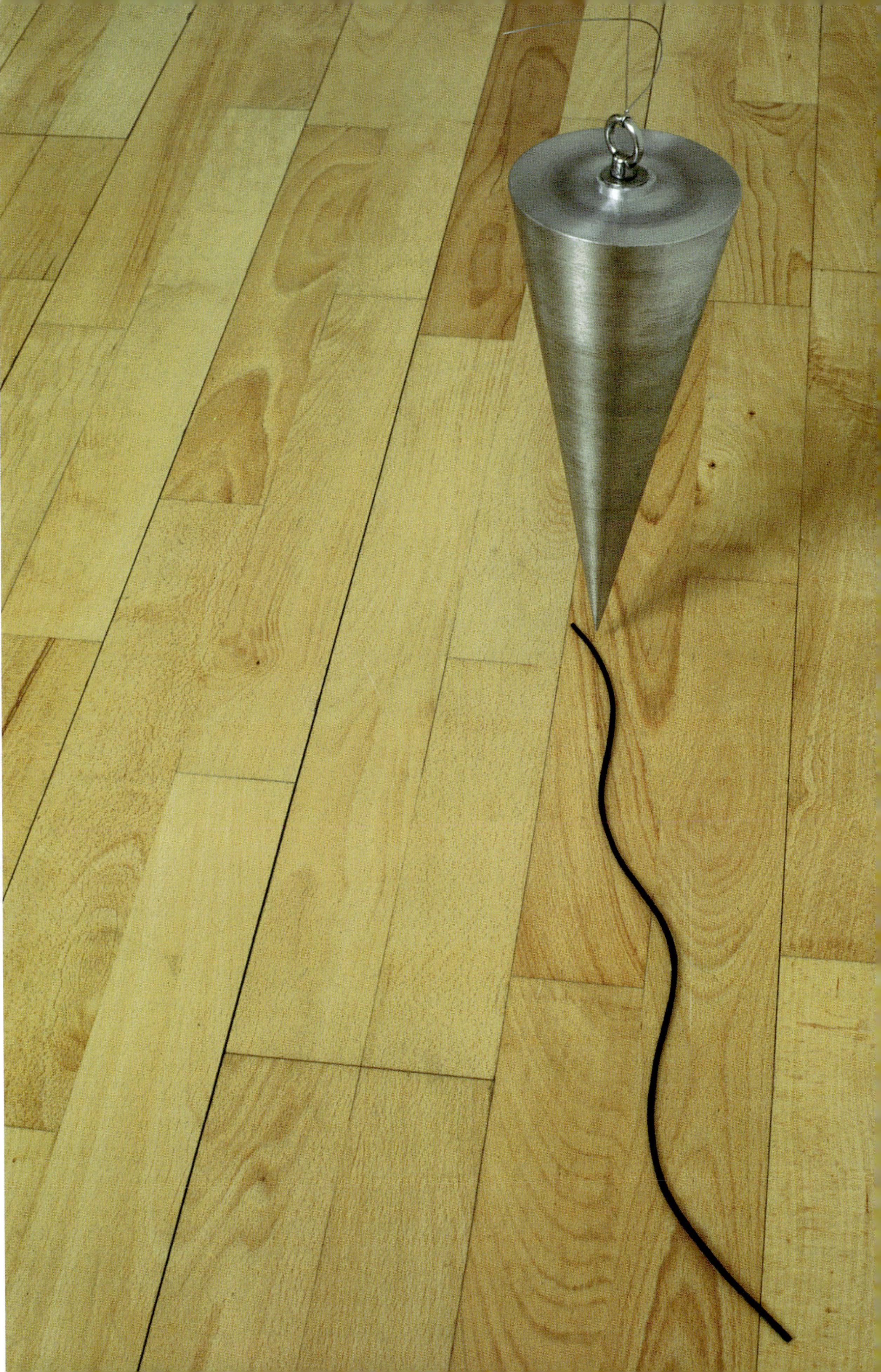

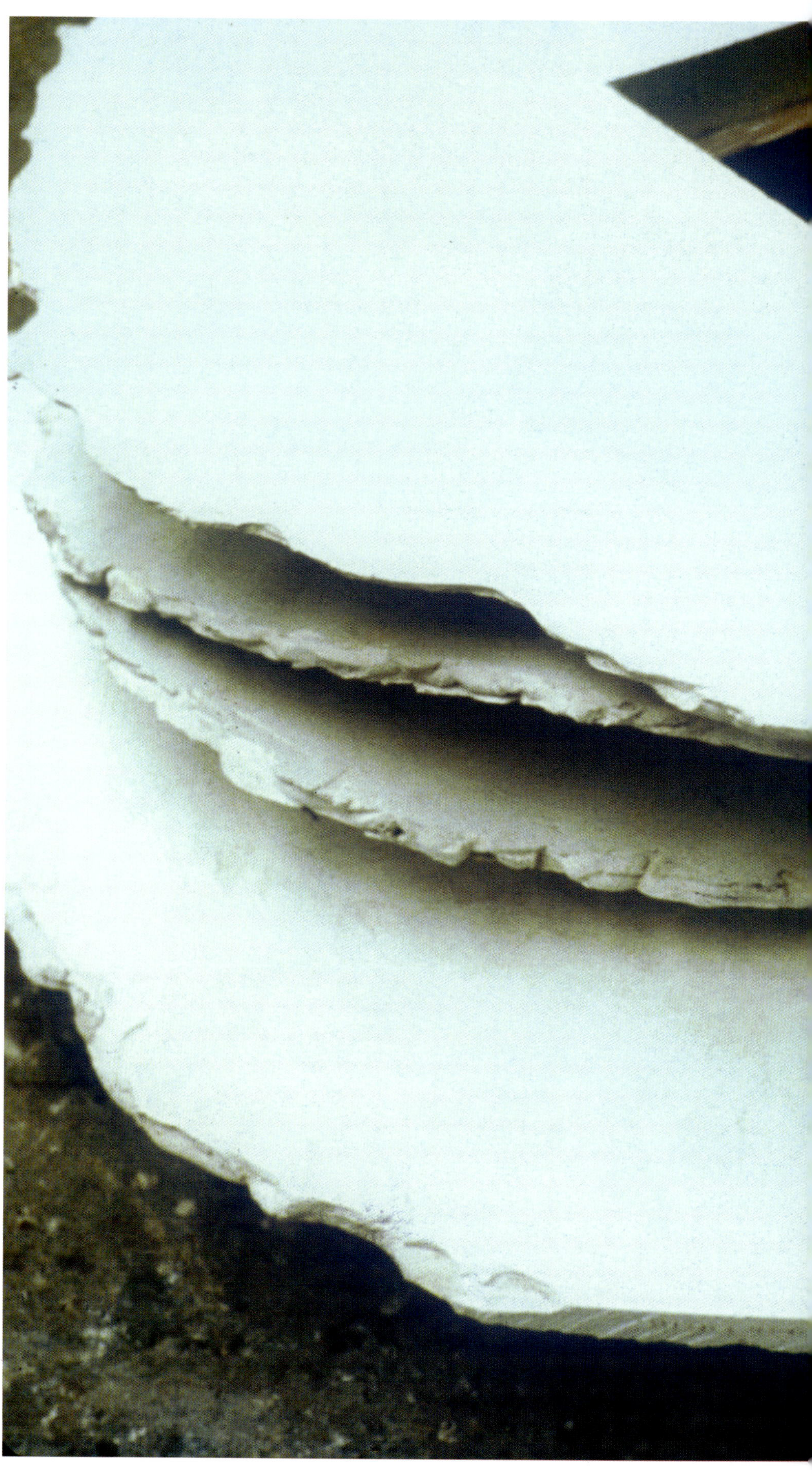

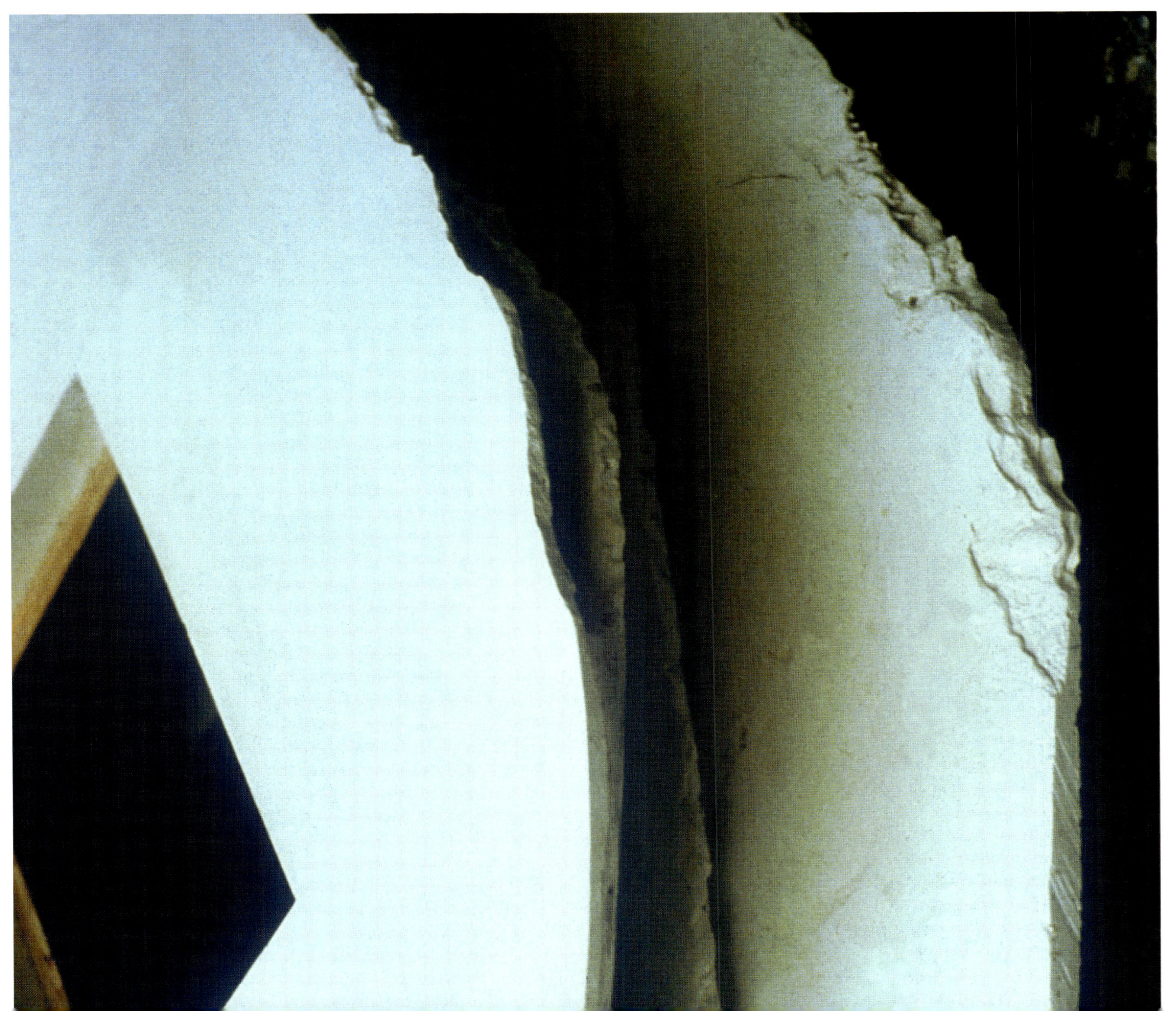

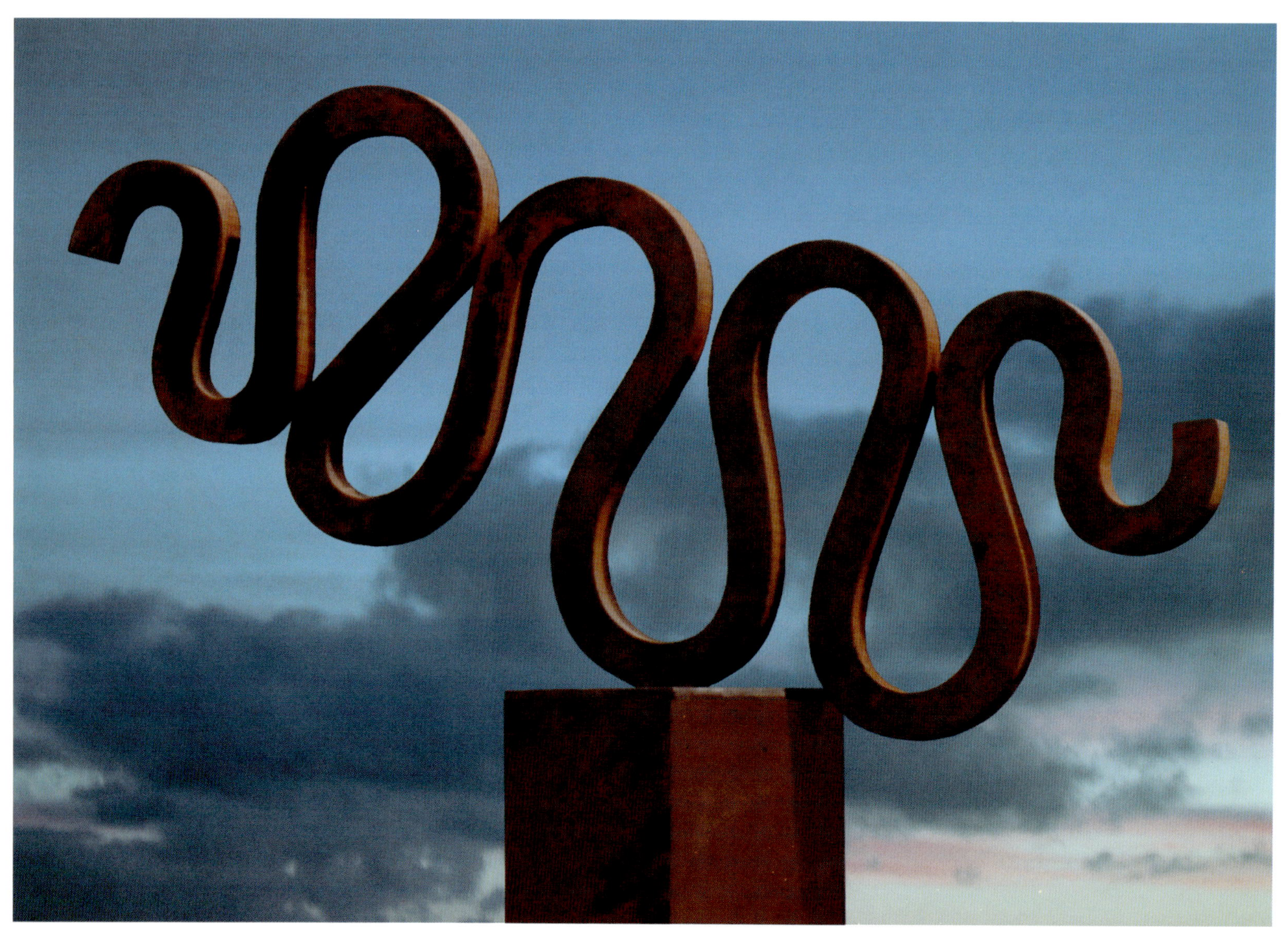

Opposite: **Little Wriggle** 1991
Steel
60 x 120cm

Below: **Untitled** 1991
Aluminium
50 x 40 x 15cm

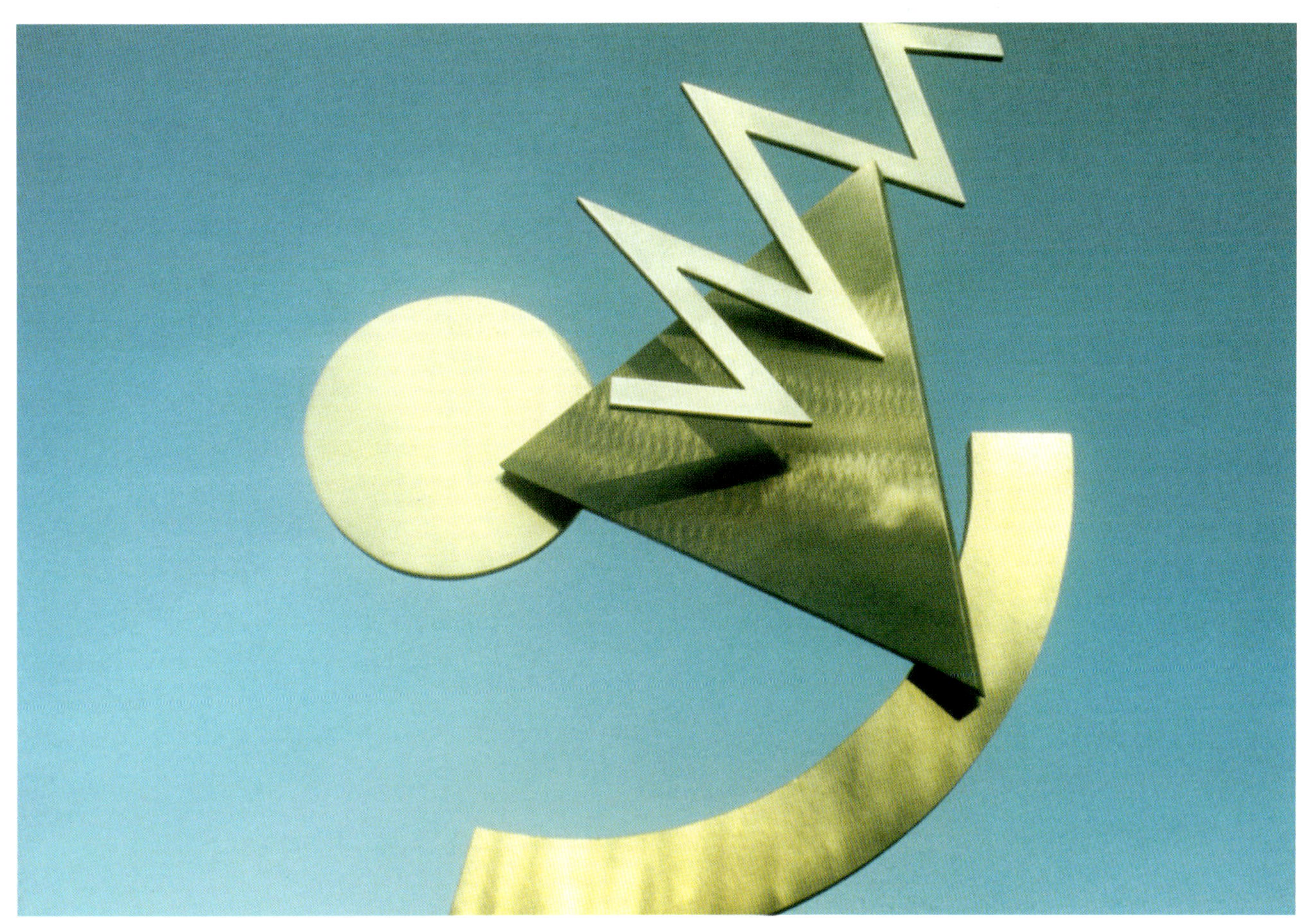

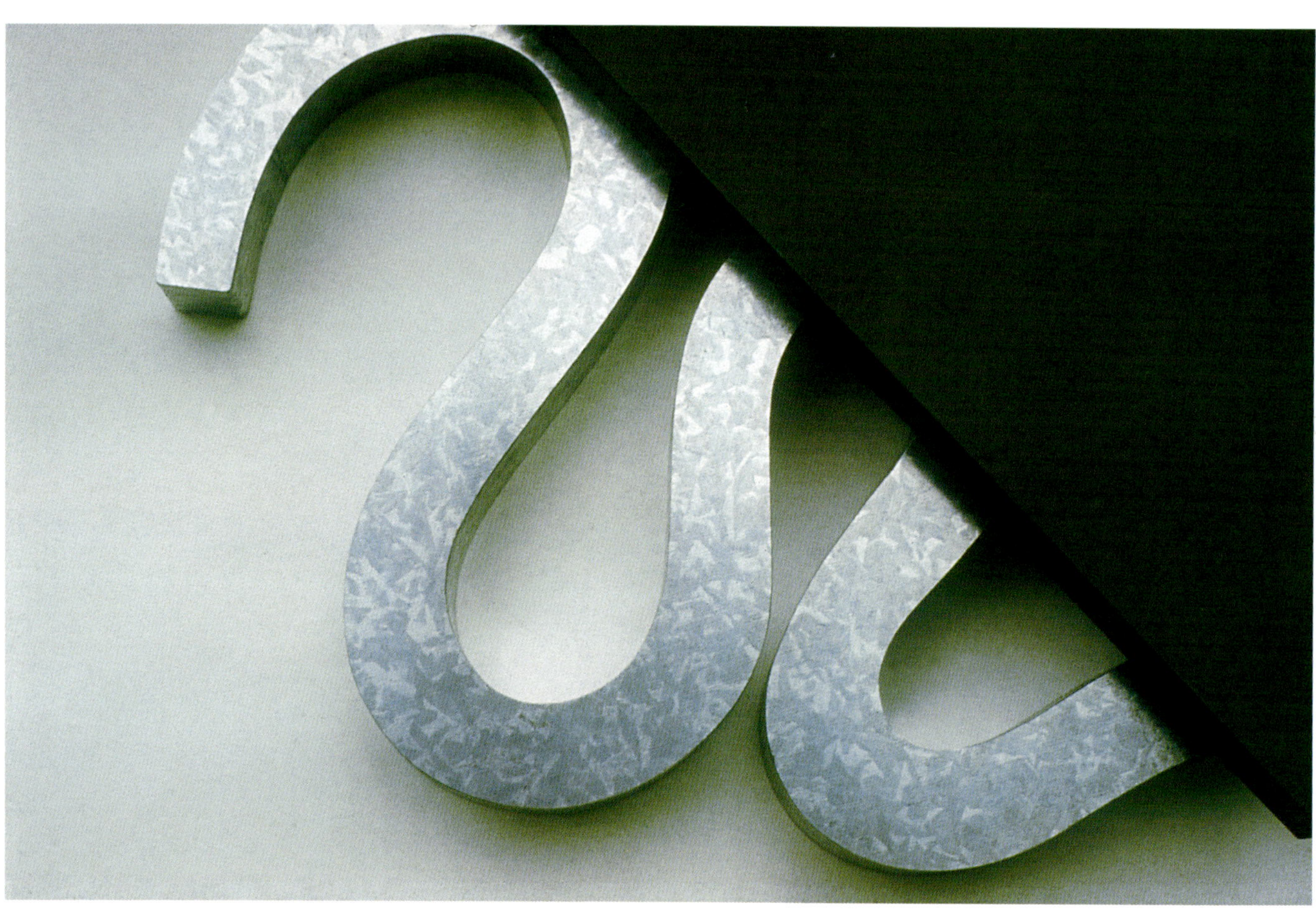

Opposite and right: **Little Cracker** 1992
Zinc, steel resin and lino
70 x 70cm

Middle: **Apple Pie** 1991
Ink on paper
(100m proposed inflatable)

Bottom: **Untitled** 1991
Zinc, wood and resin
60 x 30cm

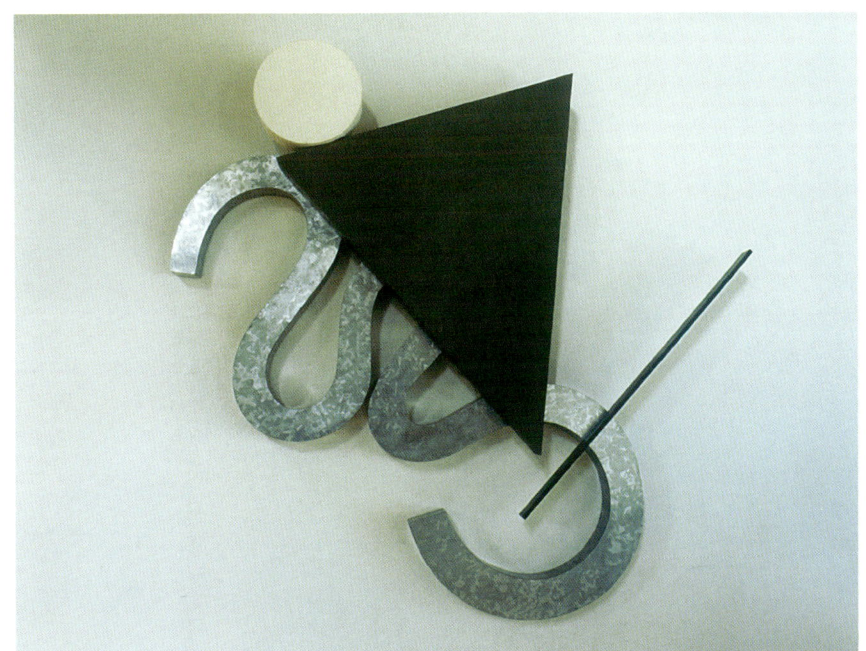

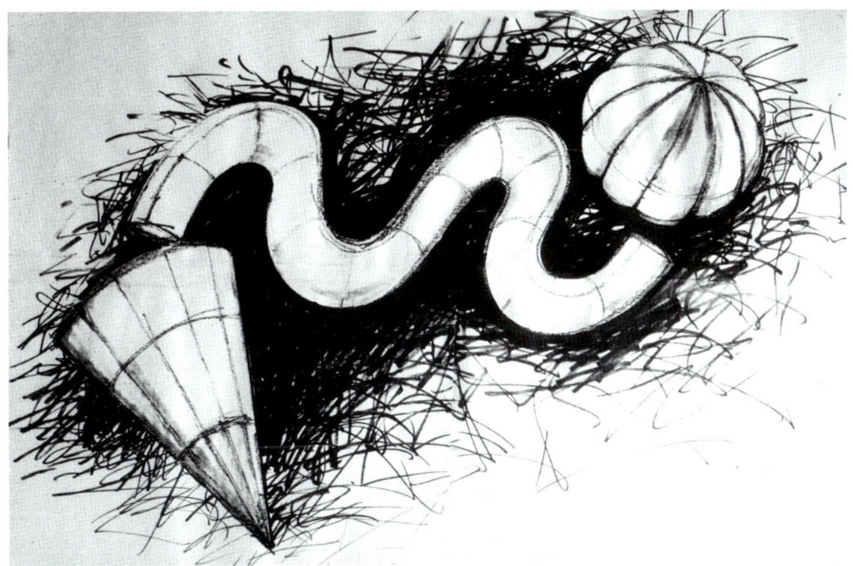

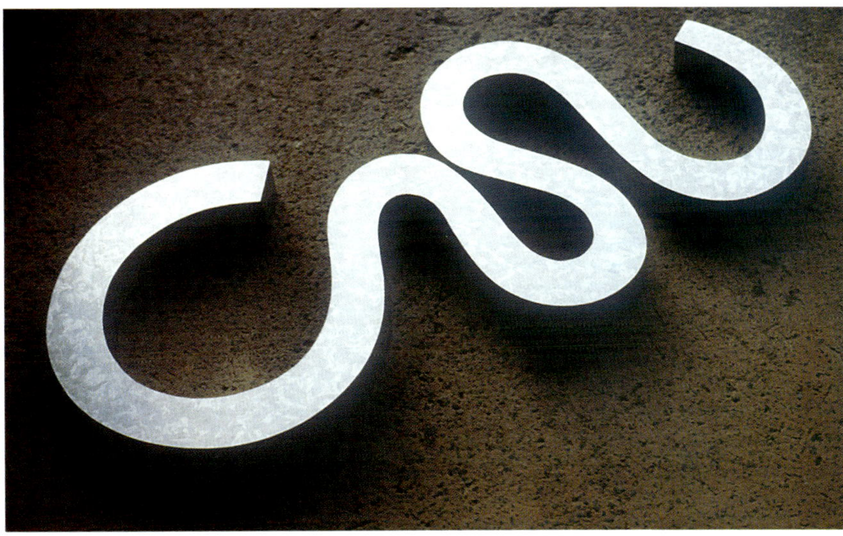

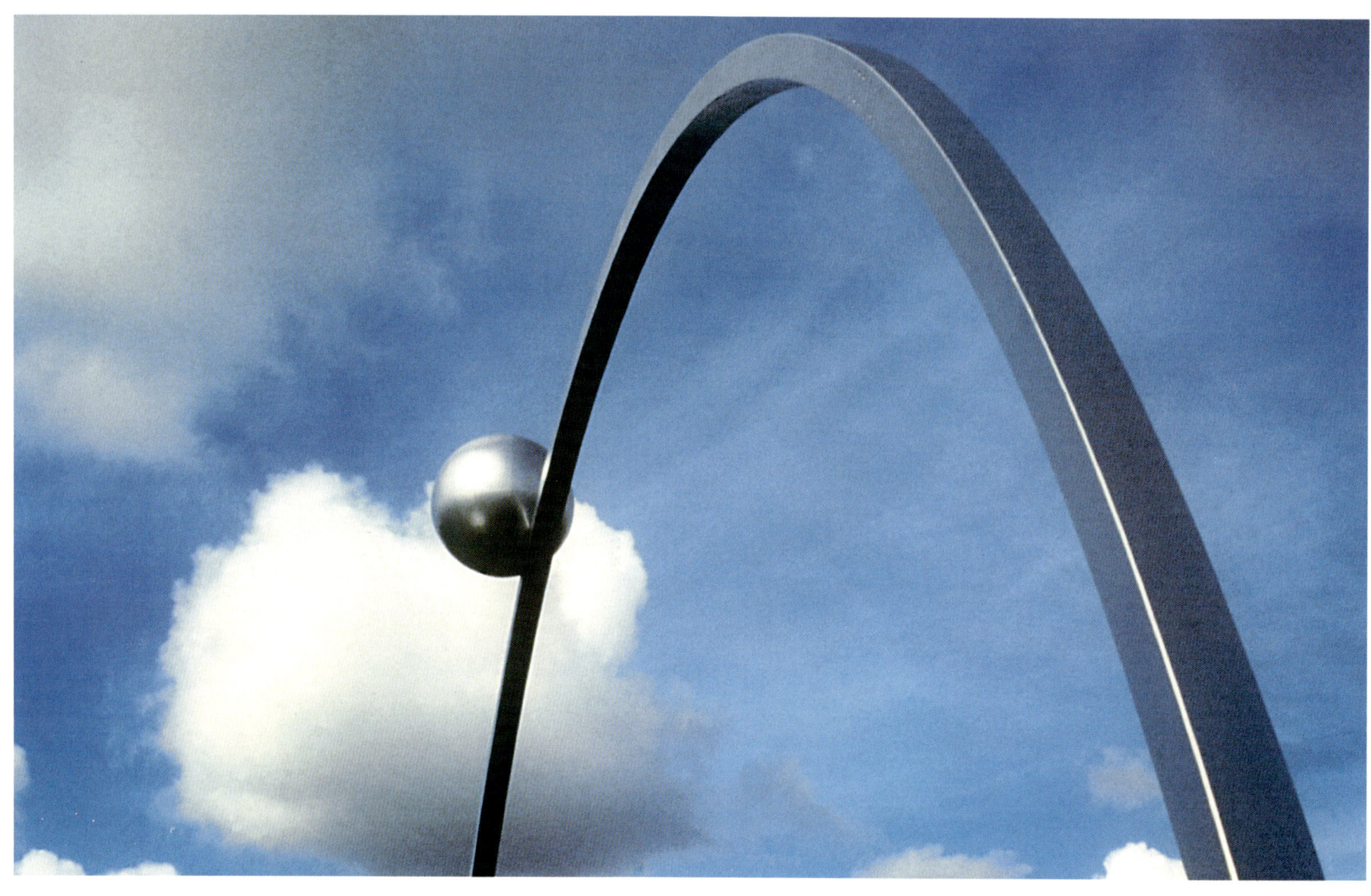

Working in the Landscape: Playfulness and Precision Precarious Motion

Ian Thompson

One of my earliest conversations with Colin Rose took place on the A 74, in a car full of officers from Gateshead Metropolitan Council. Colin had been commissioned to provide a sculpture to complement the garden and pavilion which Gateshead was building at the National Garden Festival, held in Glasgow in 1988. This work was *Rolling Moon*, a silvery steel arch upon which a spun-steel ball seemed to be in precarious motion. The piece had been selected for its inherent dynamism, for the way in which its simple form would be reflected in the ornamental pool which it would span, and for the way in which it would act as a foil for Gateshead's glass pyramid. My part in this, as a landscape architect employed by the council, was to supervise the construction of the garden and to share in Colin's anxieties about swinging a sculpture, which was 10 metres high with a span of 25 metres, into place beside the unforgiving waters of the Clyde.

As we sped back towards Tyneside, Colin seemed transfixed by the traffic on the dual carriageway. When I asked him why, he answered that he couldn't get over the amount of stuff there was in the world. There were mountains of it, filling and consuming our lives. From this beginning our conversation veered off into cosmology and philosophy. Colin had immersed himself in these subjects while still an art student, while I had read philosophy as an undergraduate, turning to the earthy profession of landscape architecture as a remedy for too much rumination. Colin's ontological view seemed to be a sort of monism. There might be all sorts of stuff, and a hell of a lot of it, but behind this apparent diversity there was a unity. All of this stuff was somehow the same stuff.

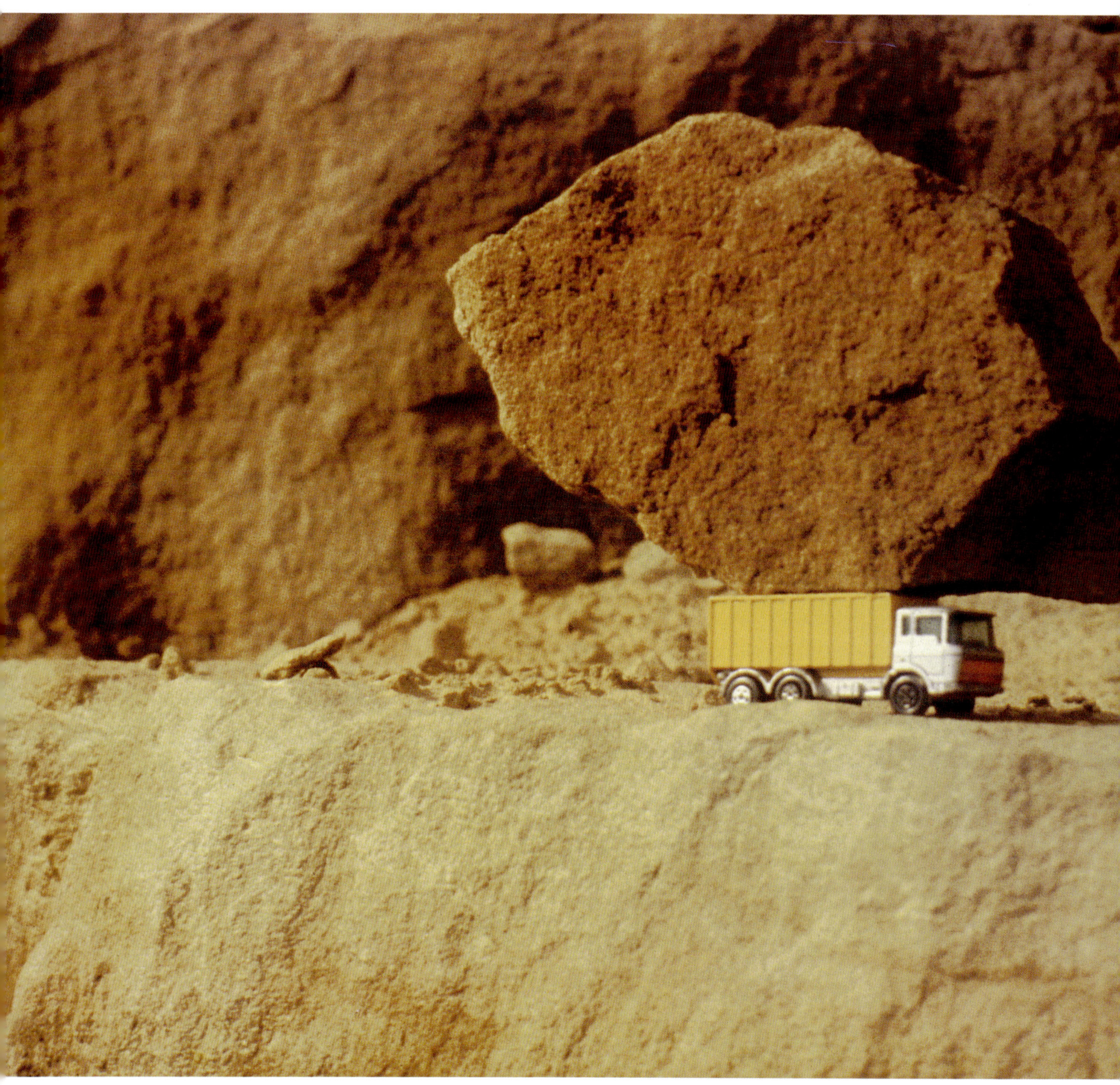

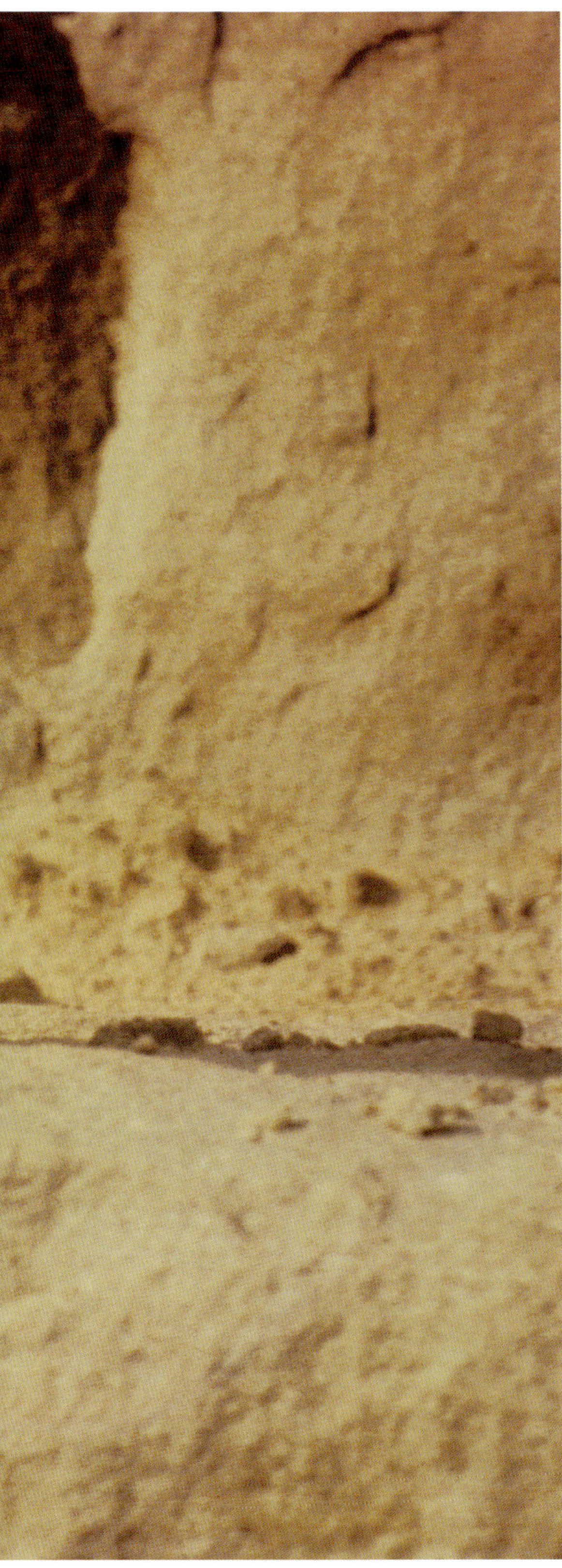

These themes, the fecundity of matter, its multiform but unitary nature, its transport and its transformations, are woven throughout Colin's work and his development as an artist. This became clear when I invited Colin to talk to a group of town-planning and urban design students about his work in public places. His first slide showed a "Dinky" truck carrying a lump of rock.

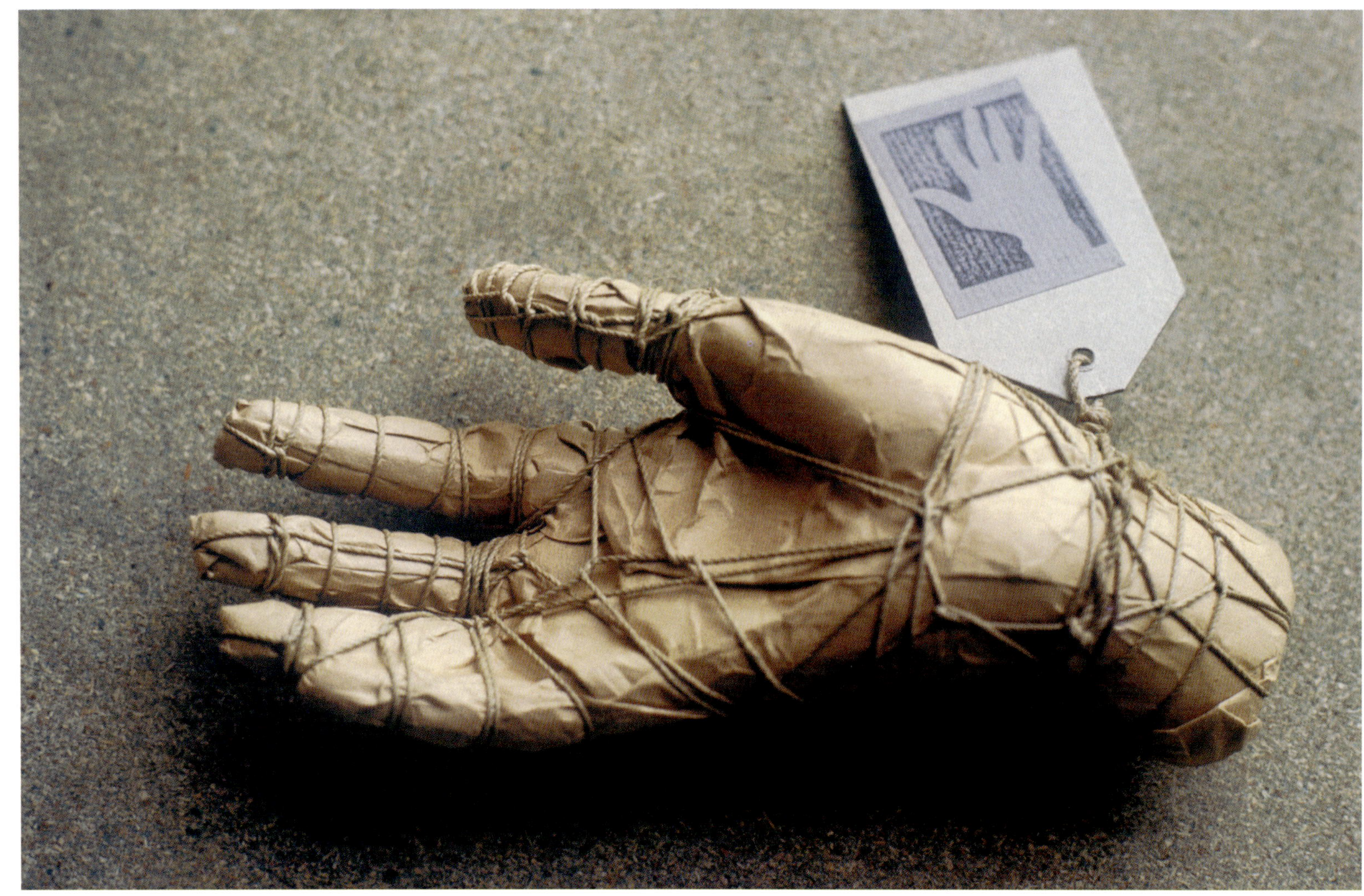

Above: **Parcel** 1981
Right: **Little Rock 'n' Roll** 1996
Basalt
25 x 20 x 20cm

This work, *Rock*, 1976, was made when Colin occupied a studio at a quarry on the Northumberland coast about 20 miles north of Tynemouth. Considered on its own, *Rock* is a visual joke, made from the combination of a child's toy and a fragment of stone that was close to hand. With the benefit of a perspective on the artist's whole life, it becomes more significant. It indicates the emergence of significant themes, such as the fascination with transport and delivery which appears in quite another way in postal works like *Parcel*, 1981, and the delight in startling juxtapositions, particularly between natural and man-made materials, which is so evident in *Ting*, 1984, and in the *Swirl* and *Wriggle* series, 1992. Jumping ahead 20 years, it is easy to see how *Rock* was revisited in the rocks-on-castors pieces, *Blasted Rock*, *Rock 'n' Roll* and *Little Rock 'n' Roll*, all 1996.

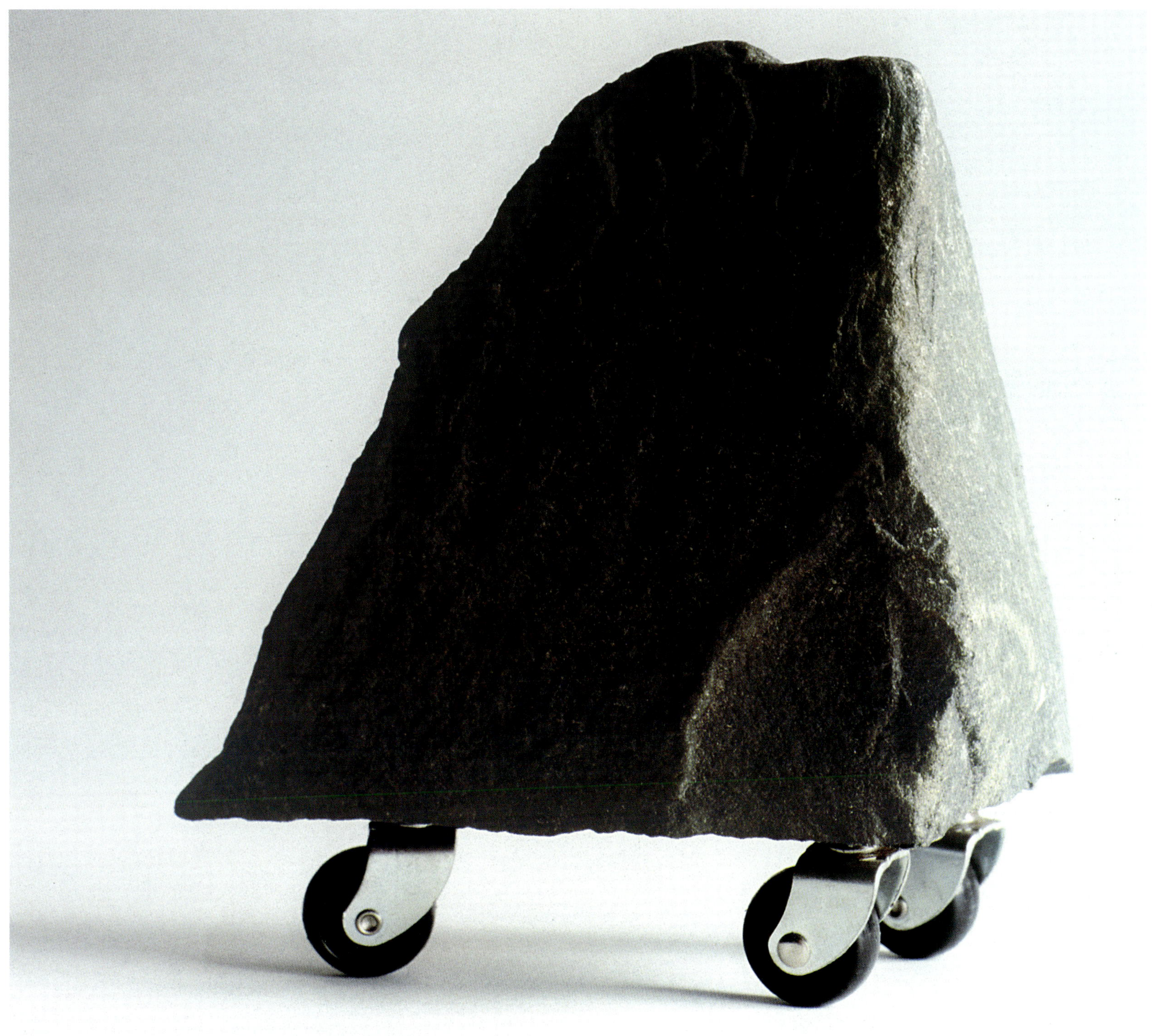

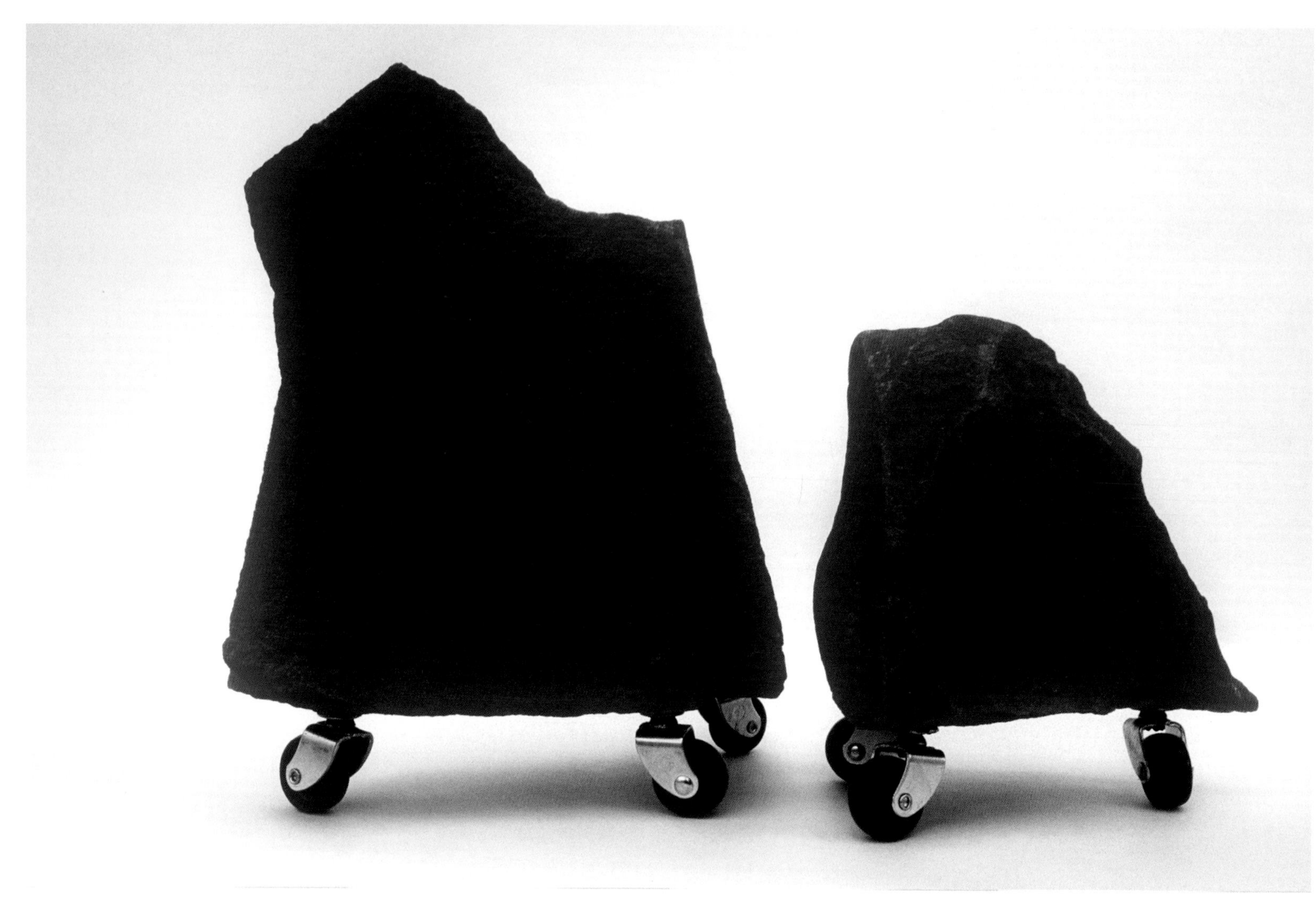

Rock 'n' Roll 1996
Rock and castors
35 and 25cm high
(part of sequence)

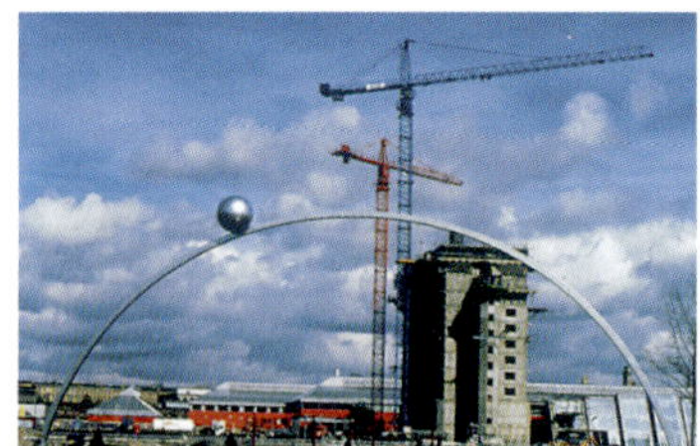

Left: **Rolling Moon** 1988
Glasgow

Right: **Map** 1976
120 x 120cm
Bleanau Ffestiniog (slate mine)

One of the issues with which my students and I have wrestled is whether sculpture that is put into public places should be interpreted in the same way that much gallery art is. The gallery-going public are generally aficionados. They are likely to see themselves as part of an art world, to read books and watch documentaries about art, to buy exhibition catalogues, read the critics and so on. They know a lot about art and generally know what they like. Curatorial policies vary, but it is likely that a visitor to a gallery will get some help in interpreting what is on show. Exhibitions will often include biographical notes explaining how the works displayed fit into an artist's development. Maybe they will include quotations from the artist giving some insight into thought processes during the making of the work and, if all else fails, visitors can usually visit the gallery shop and buy a book about the work. Rightly or wrongly, there is rarely this kind of support for work which is made for public places. Coming upon *Rolling Moon,* for example, in its current position on the Gateshead riverbank, will a member of the public realise that it is by the same artist who made *Window,* 1986, about half a mile away on Bensham Bank, even though there are strong similarities in materials and the visual language used?

Maybe such a connection can be made, but wider connections to cones or hoop-like sculptures in distant forests or earth-drawings made in Australia are unlikely to be. With my students, I had the benefit of hearing Colin discuss his work, and, in the process, explain his life. It was gratifying to see how positively these students, who were not themselves aspiring to be artists, responded to his story. In part this essay is an attempt to share my understanding of these autobiographical seminar presentations with a wider audience.

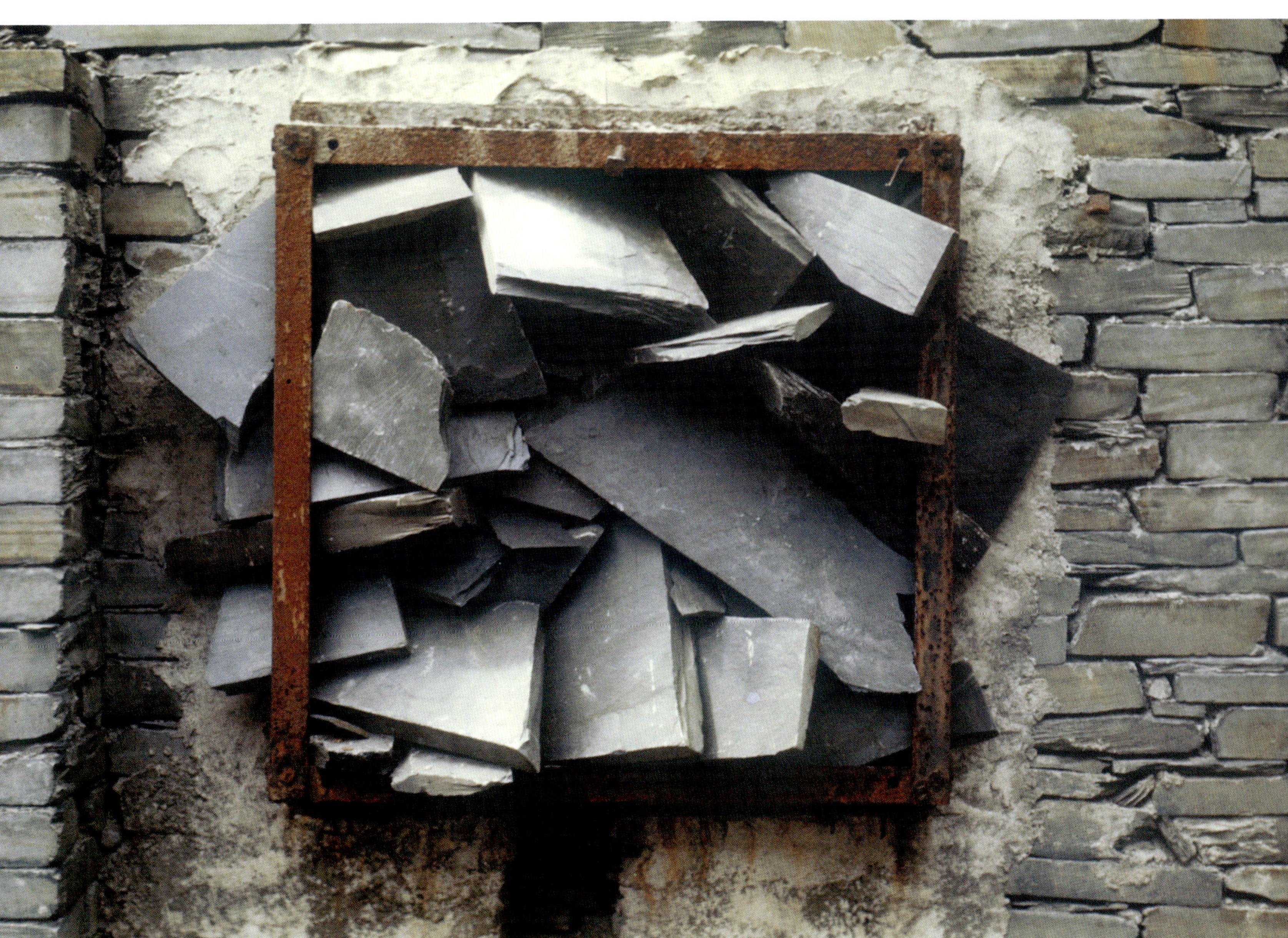

In Place and Out of Place

One of the early themes in Colin's work was the idea of belonging. We don't just take material and process it; we make it into objects, and, once made, these have a rightful place in the world. It is for this reason that we have shelves and cupboards and drawers. Some of Colin's early works express a fascination with this ordering of the world. For the work known as *Shelf*, 1976, for example, he re-cycled old crates into new objects, including the fruit-like forms which would later re-emerge in the *Pineball* series, 1988. He placed these on a high shelf, where they nestled snugly into a corner. For the rest of his career, Colin would concern himself with ideas of place, and notions of where things belong. Travelling to his studio he would pass harvested fields where the straw had been rolled into the huge drum-like bales which are now a familiar sight in the landscape, but at the time were a new phenomenon. The simple rolling process was held visible in the created form. One could roll up a field and take it away on the back of a lorry! Colin's response to this was the straightforwardly titled *Sandbox*, 1977, which consisted of a rectangular outline on the studio floor and a small box of sand. The quantity of sand within was just sufficient to cover the area within the rectangle, which could then be swept up and put back into the box.

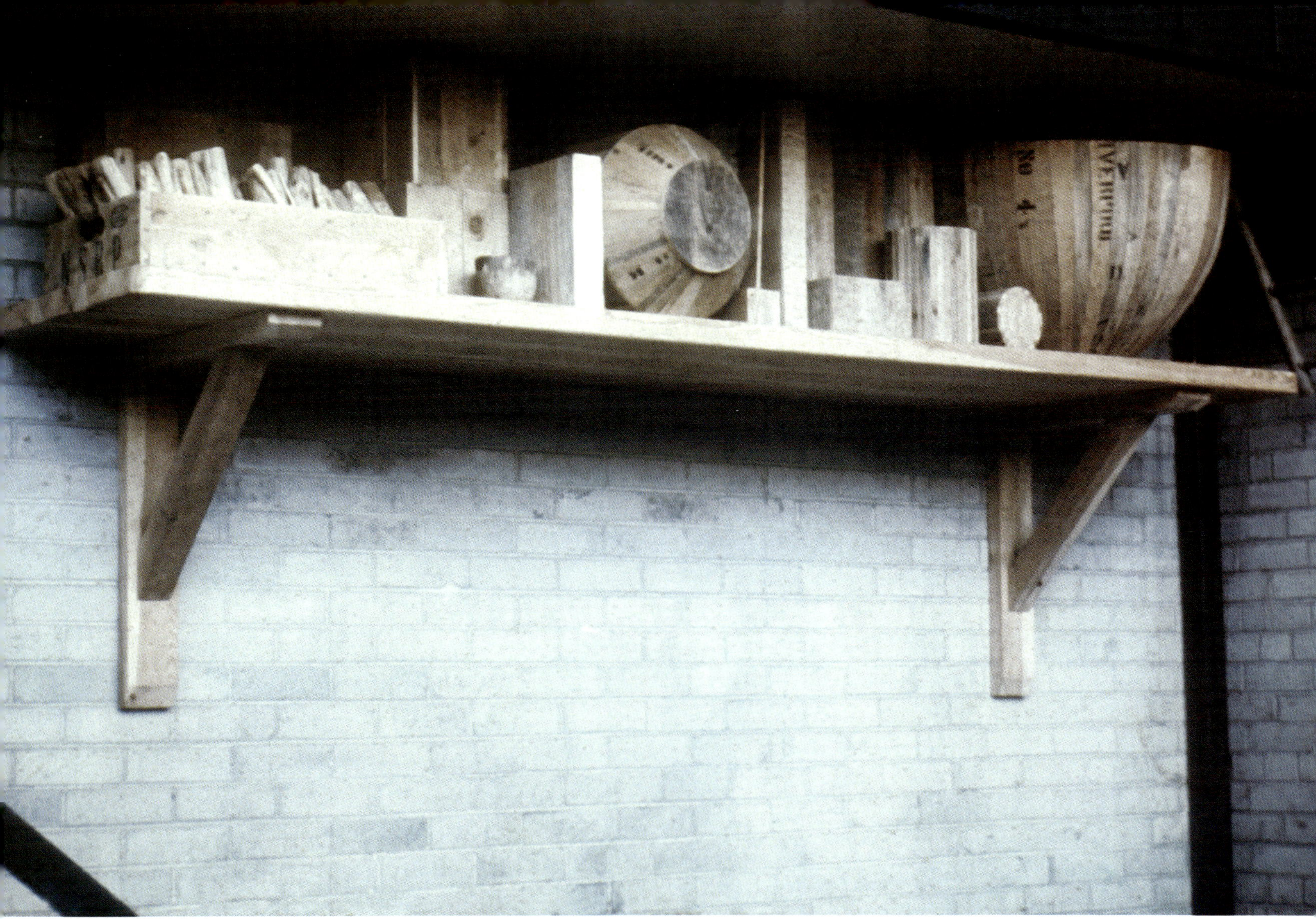

Above and following pages: **Shelf** 1976 (detail)
Wood
180 x 60 x 300cm

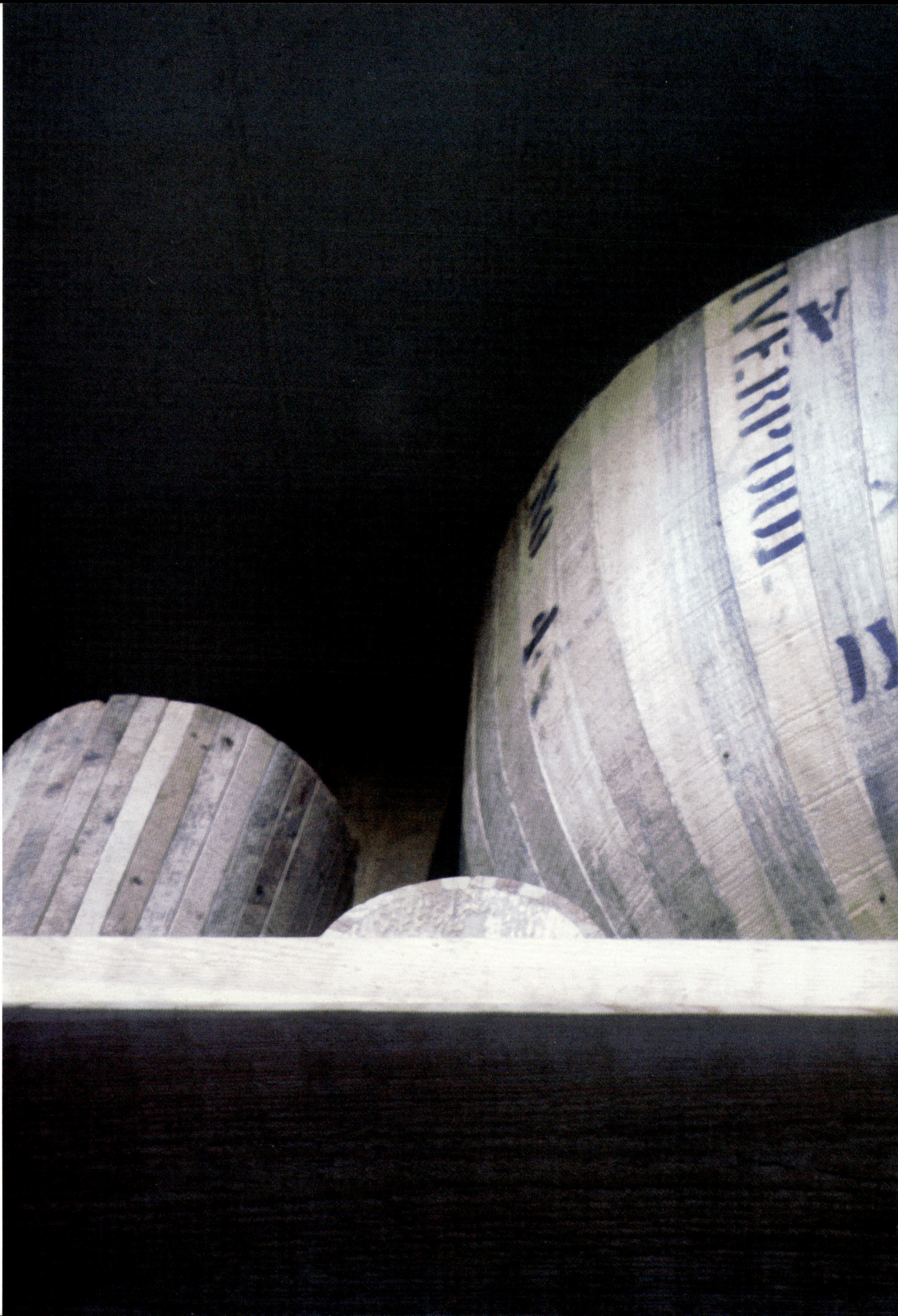

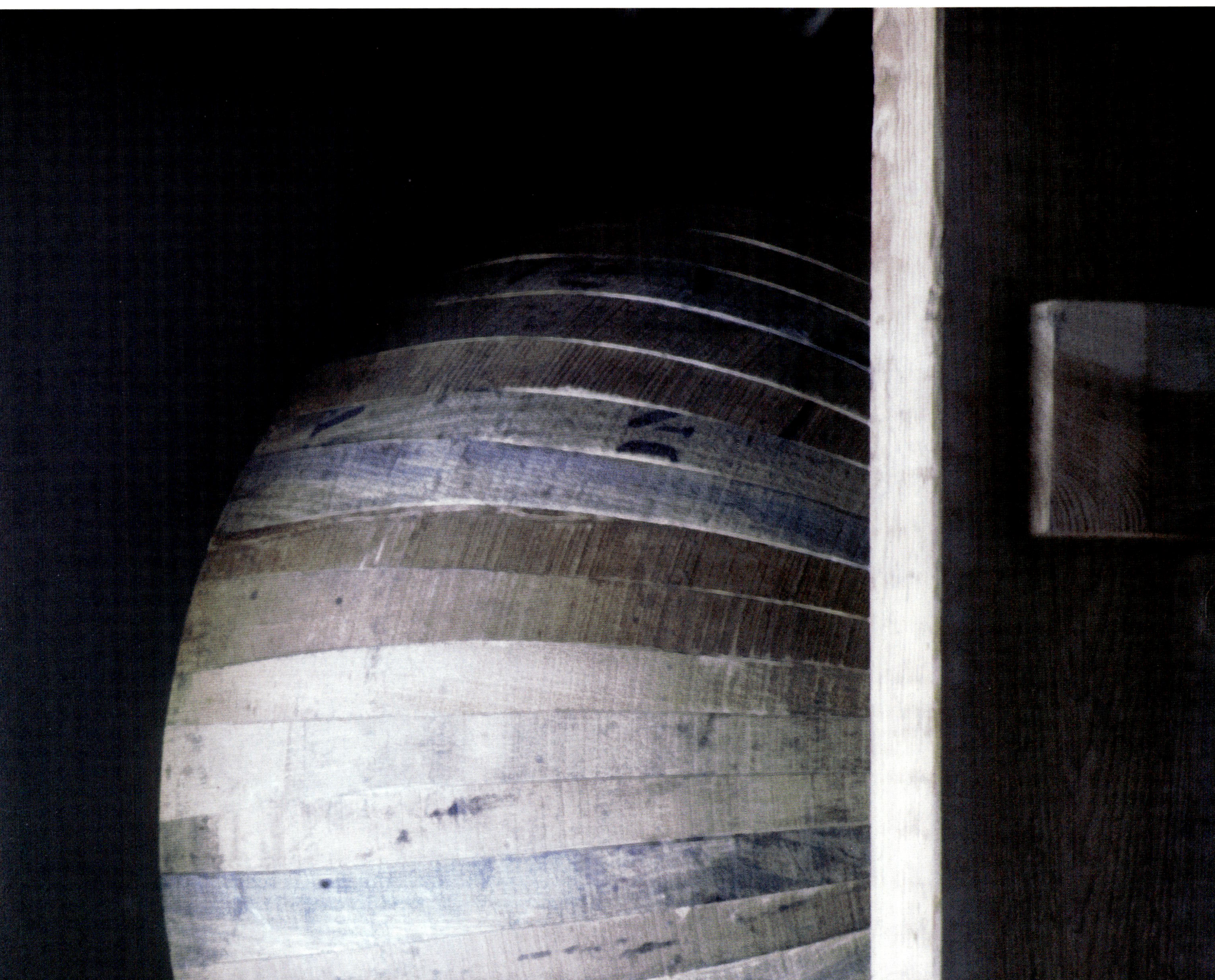

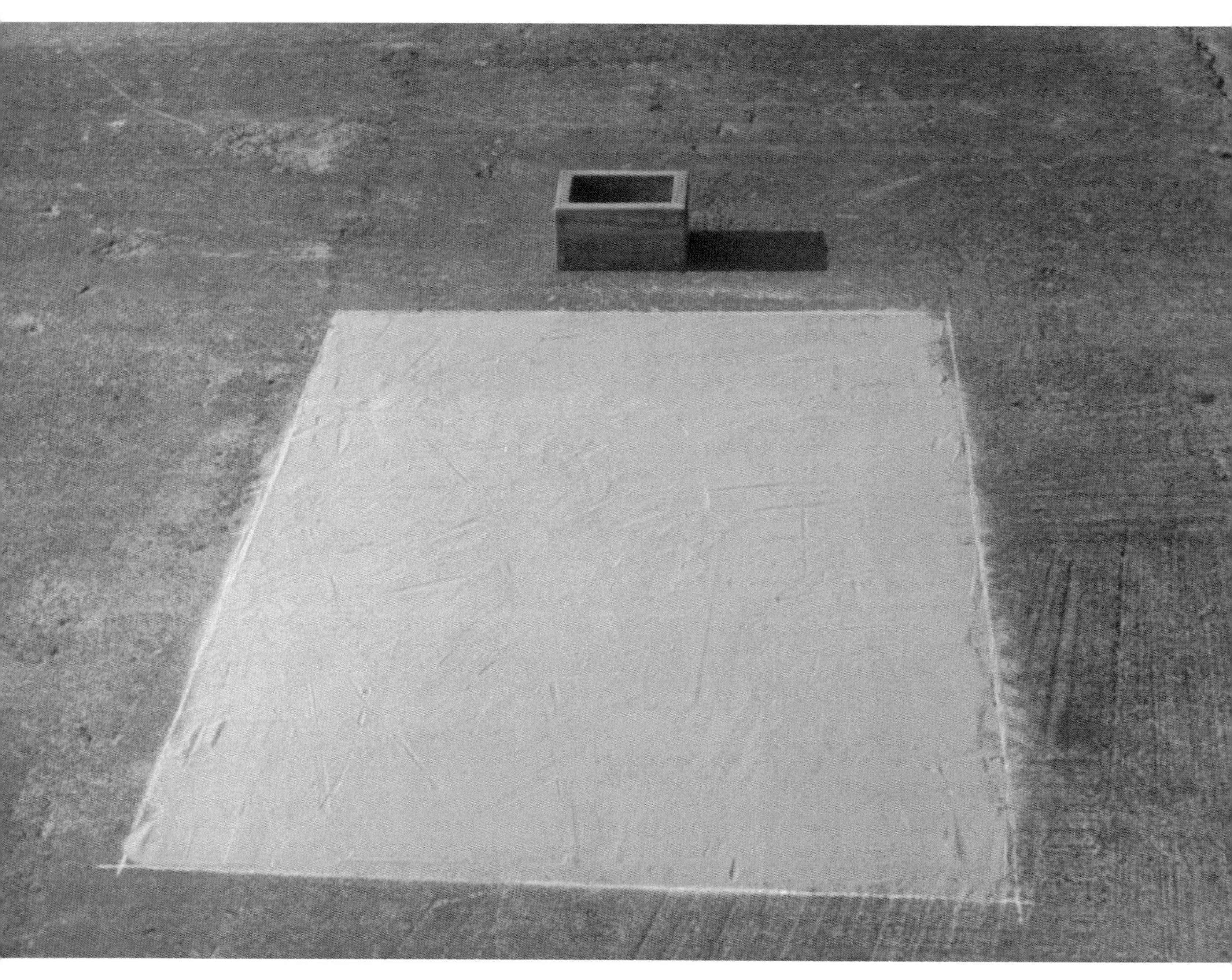

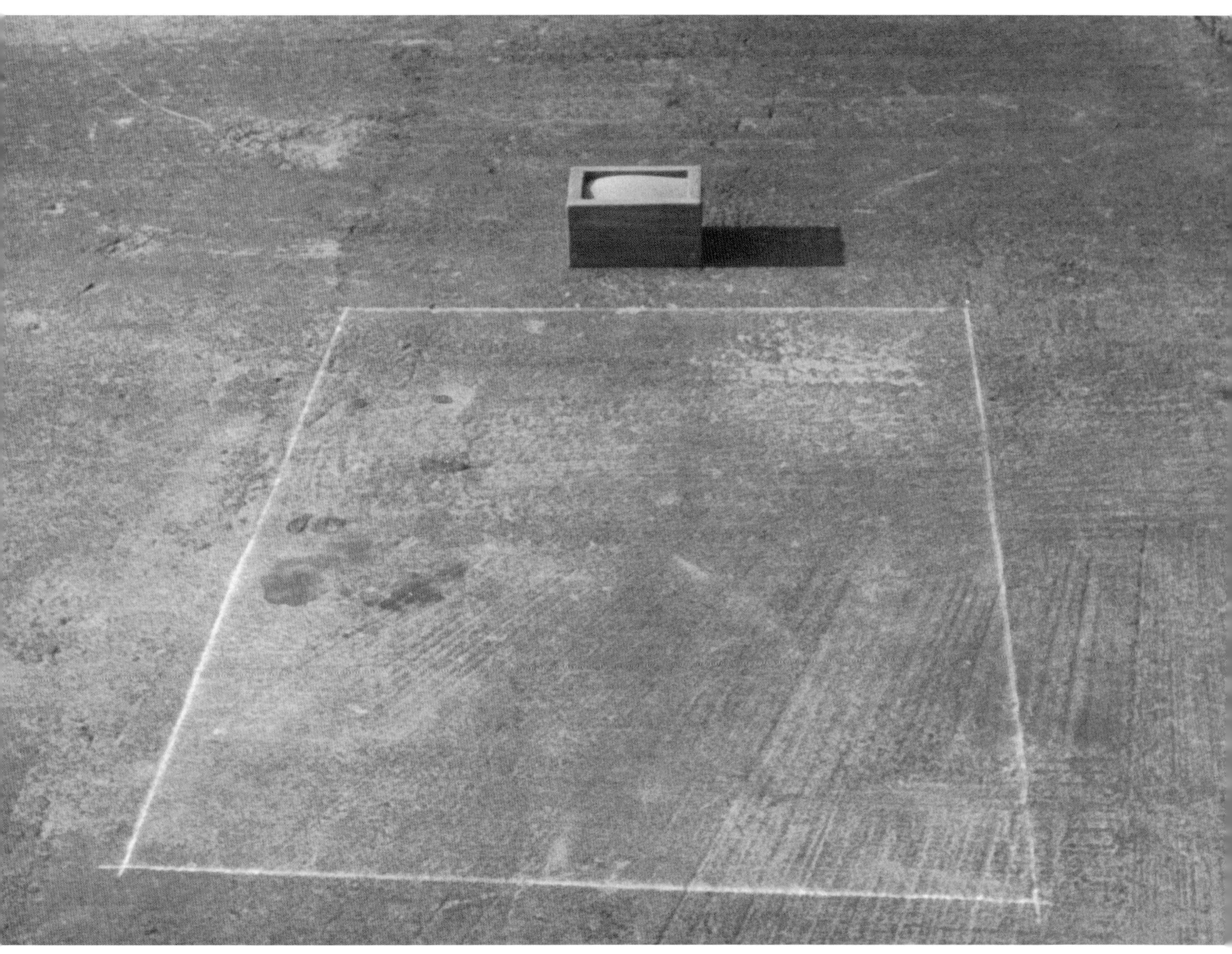

Sandbox 1977
Ash and sand
13 x 25 x 18cm

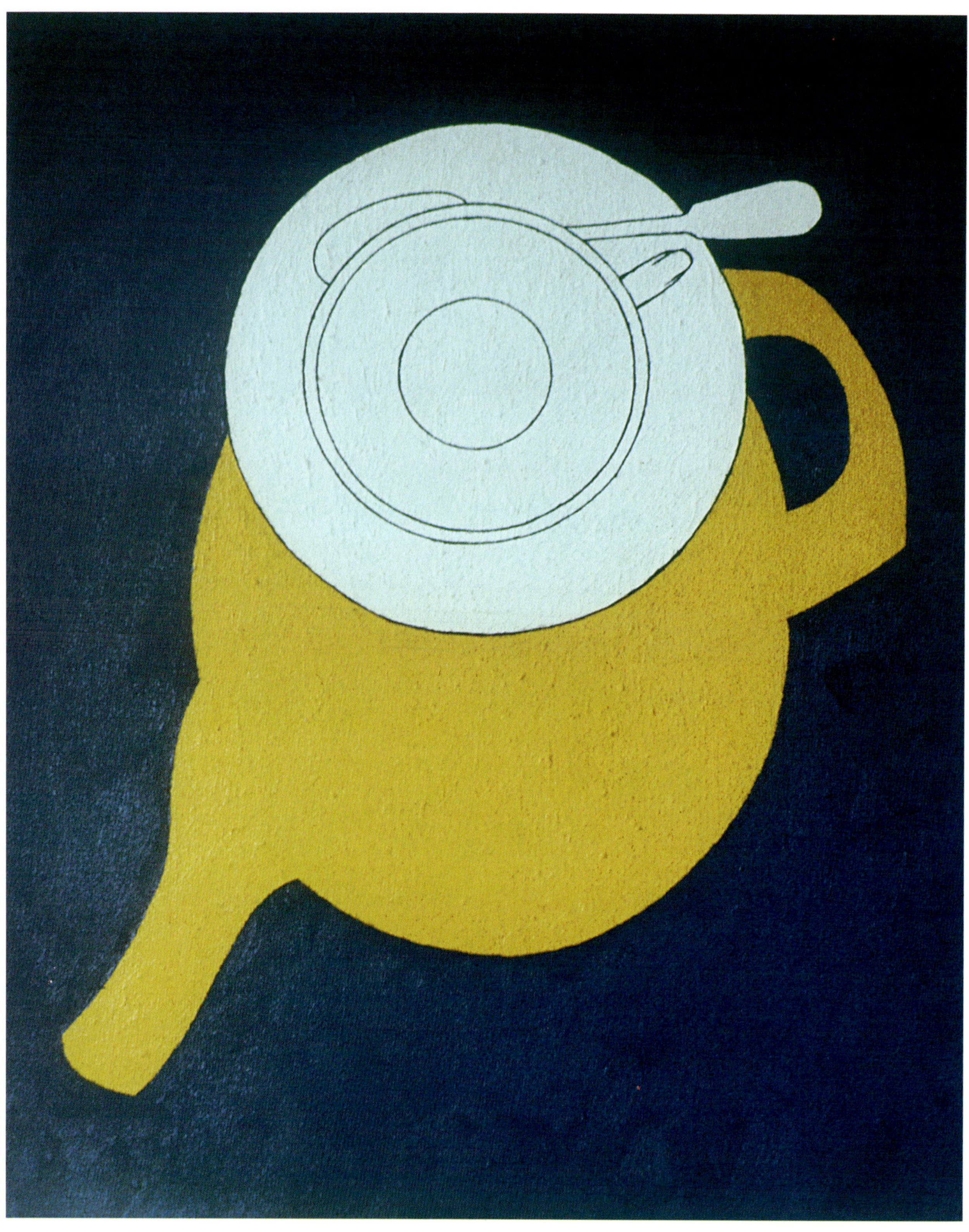

Left: **Cup Dreaming** 1979
Oil on canvas
30 x 23cm

Following pages: **Flying Pan** 1976

There is a tension in Colin's work between the artist's wish
for order and an anarchic playfulness. On one hand we have the
Platonic discipline of pieces like *Stone Cone*, 1995, *Peaks*, 1998
and *Eye*, 1999, but on the other we have works which might be
categorised as 'objects behaving badly'. The artist admits that he
has a penchant for puns, both visual and linguistic, so the 200
tea cups which dangle from the branches of a tree, *Tea*, 1997,
have become 'tea-leaves', while the pan which has flown up to
the studio roof has earned the title *Flying Pan*, 1976. In dishing
out their puns, these objects also seem to be thumbing their
noses at us. The cup in *Cup Dreaming*, 1979, does not want to
be constrained to its rightful place in the world. It has grander
ideas about its identity.

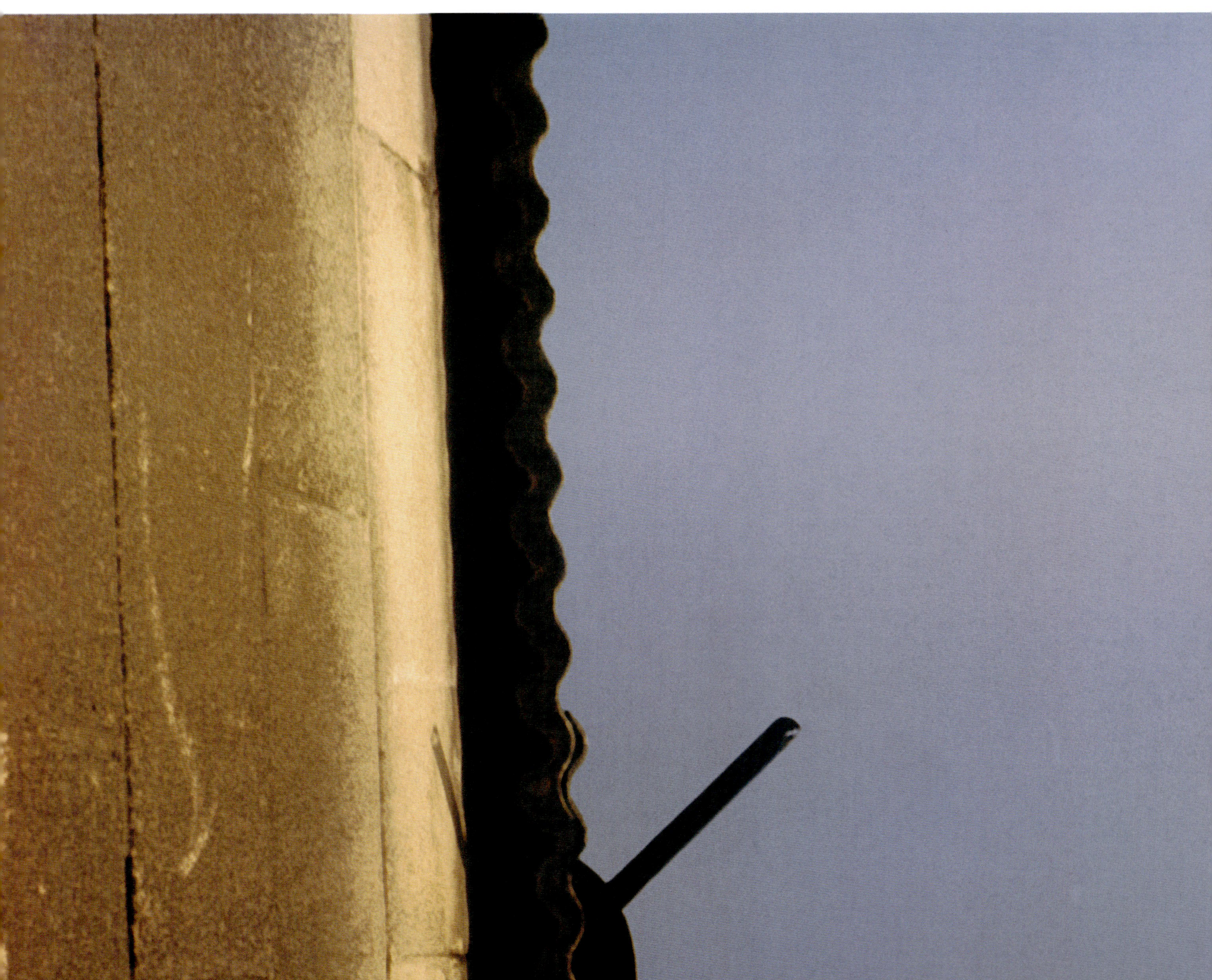

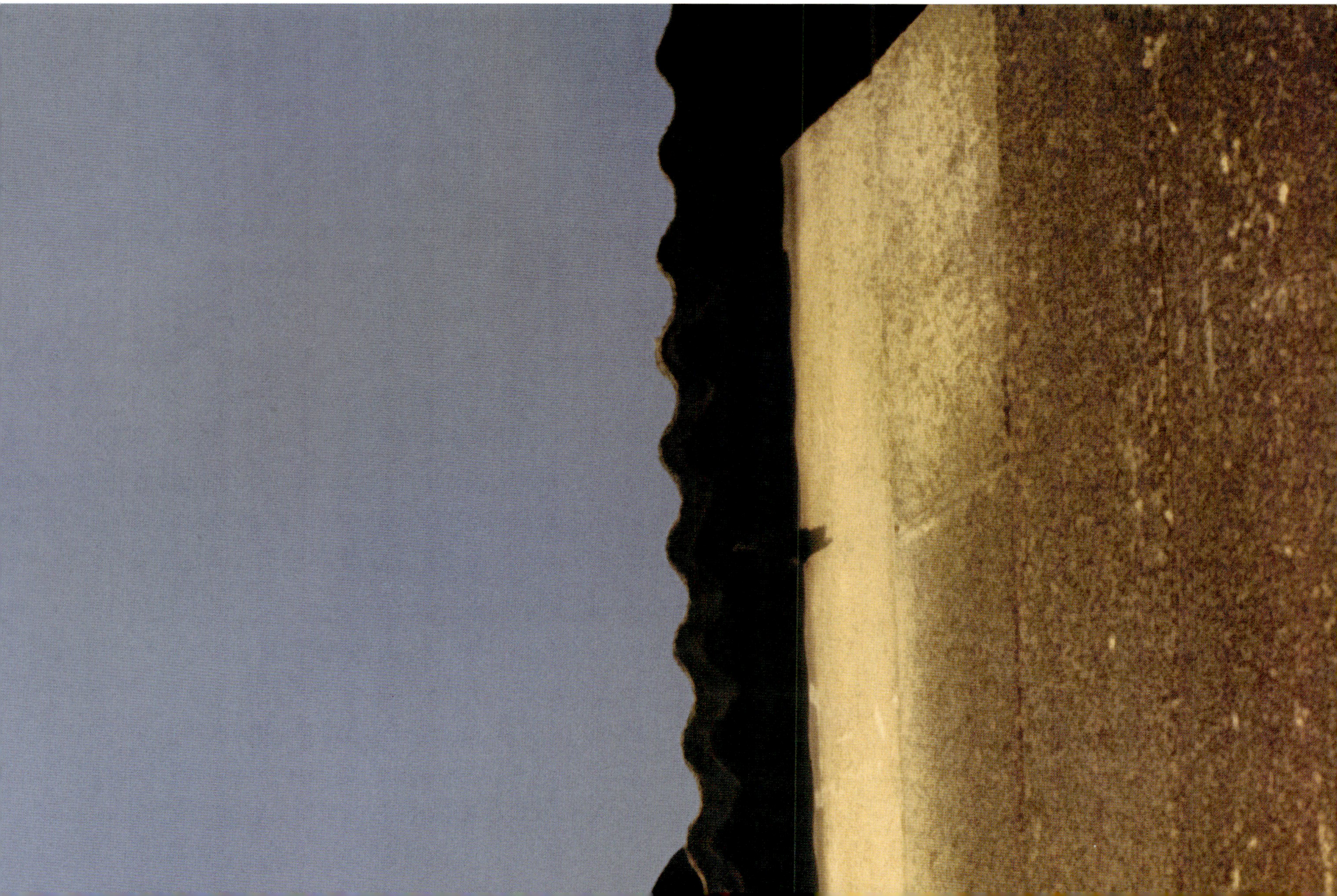

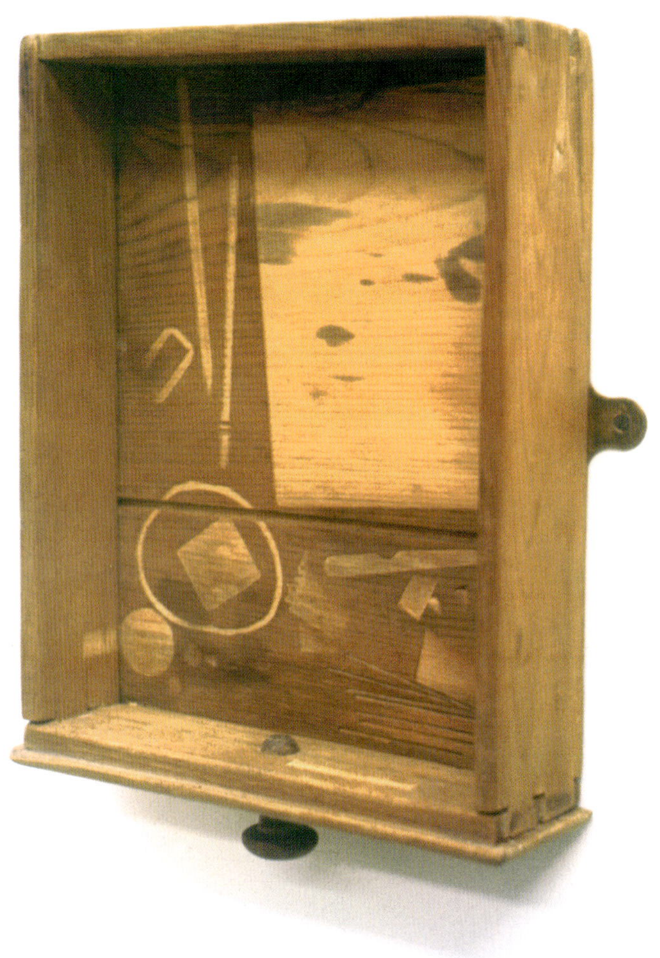

This tension is reflected again in the series of furniture works.
There are well behaved pieces, such as *Draw*, 1978, where the
contents of a wooden drawer – a nail file, a rubber band, a screw
and some ink bottles – have their traces sunk into the wood itself,
revealing the construction of the furniture. It is also an allegory of
the landscape with its strata and layers of vegetation, its animal
tracks and accumulation of details, all of which seem to have a
sense of belonging.

Draw 1978
Pine
36 x 30cm

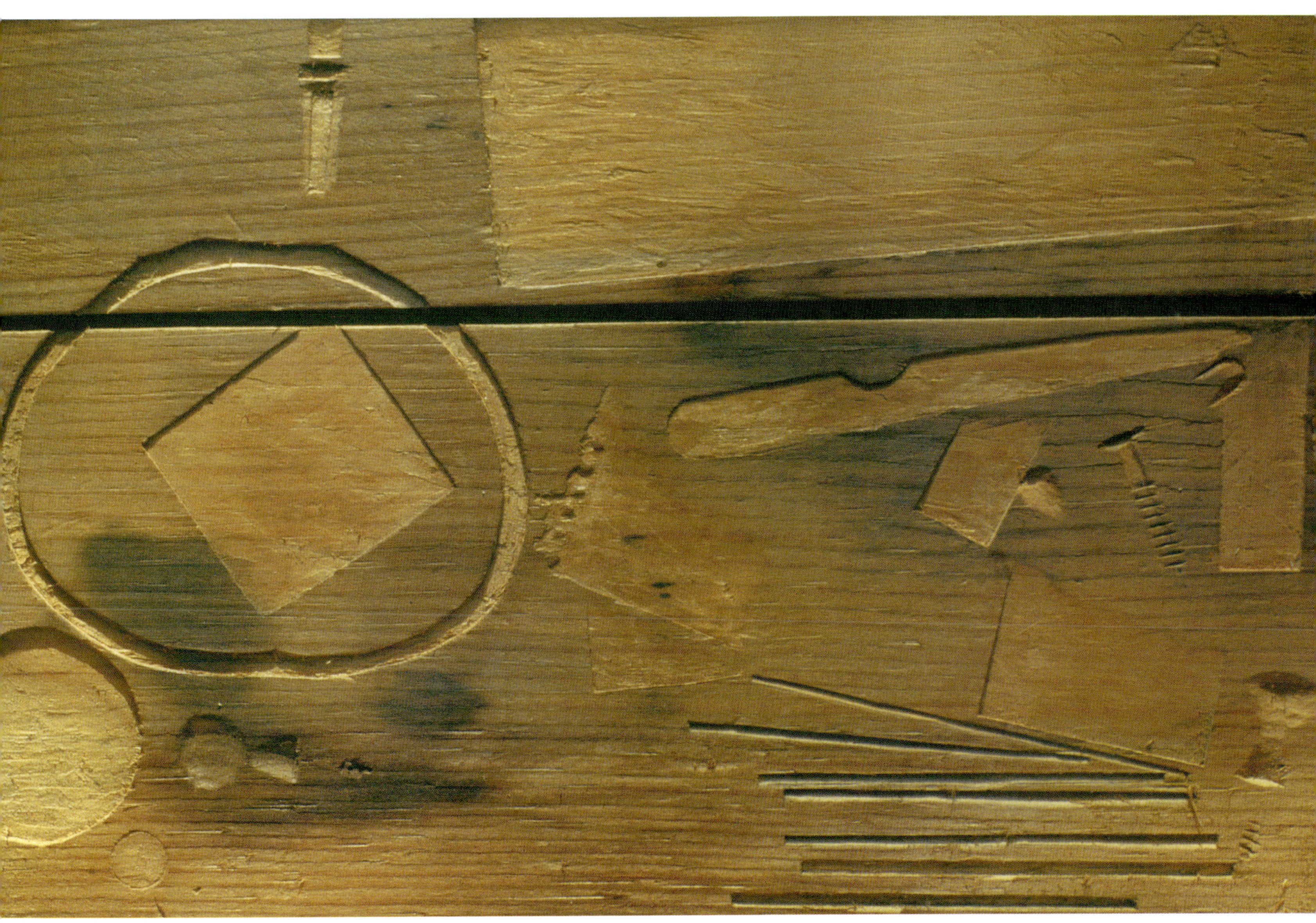

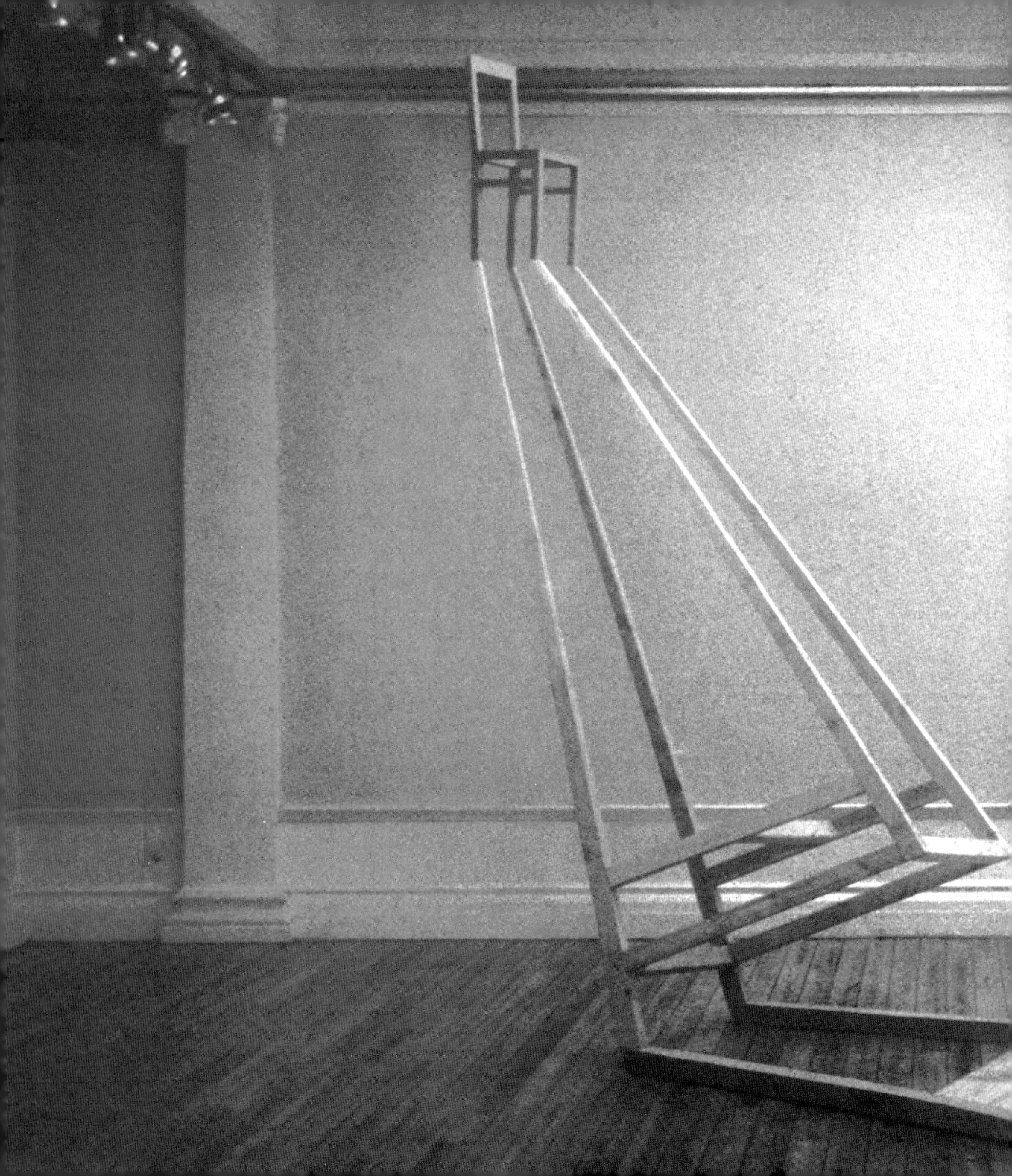

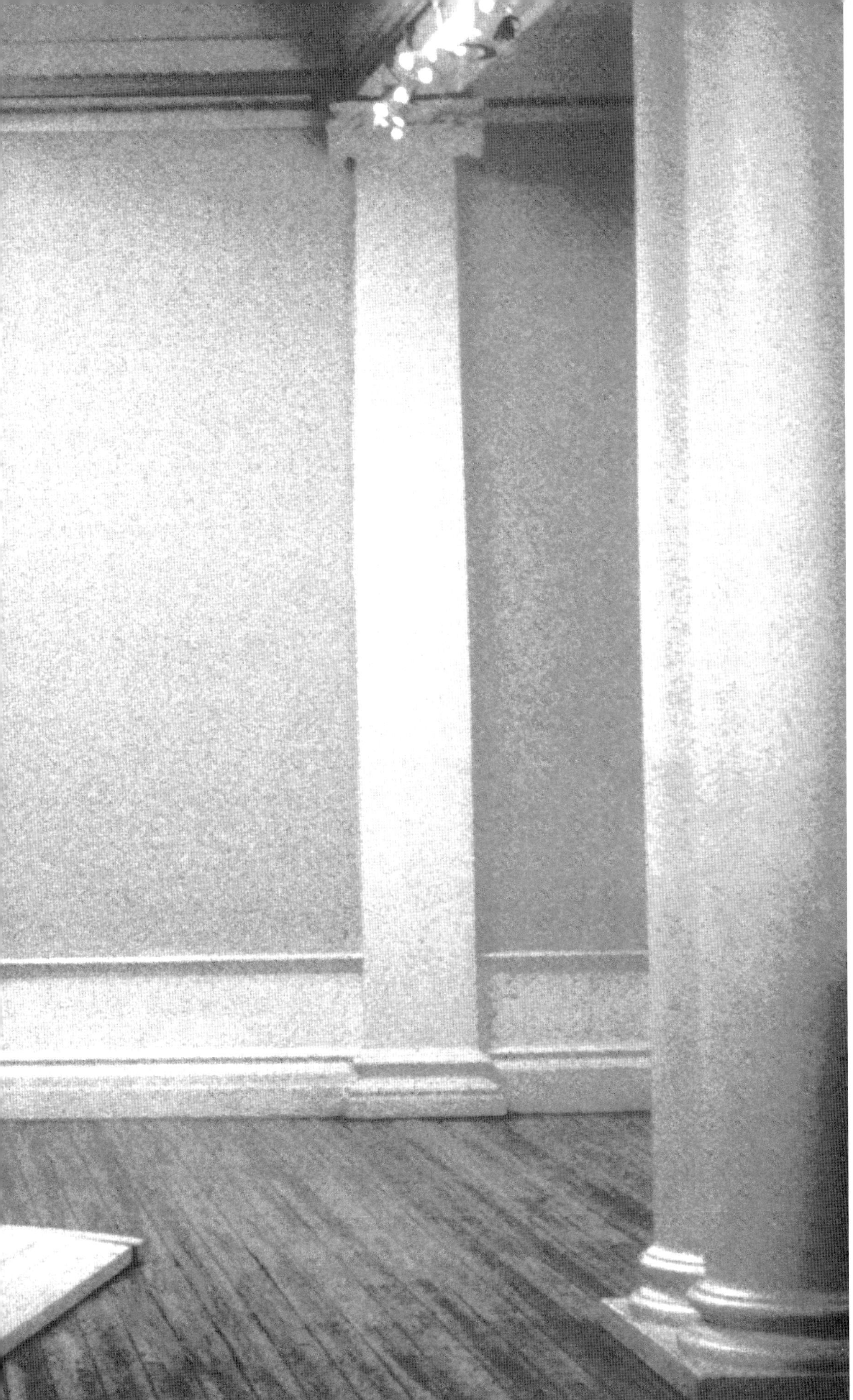

Anonymous Shadow 1979
Wood
450 x 200 x 150cm

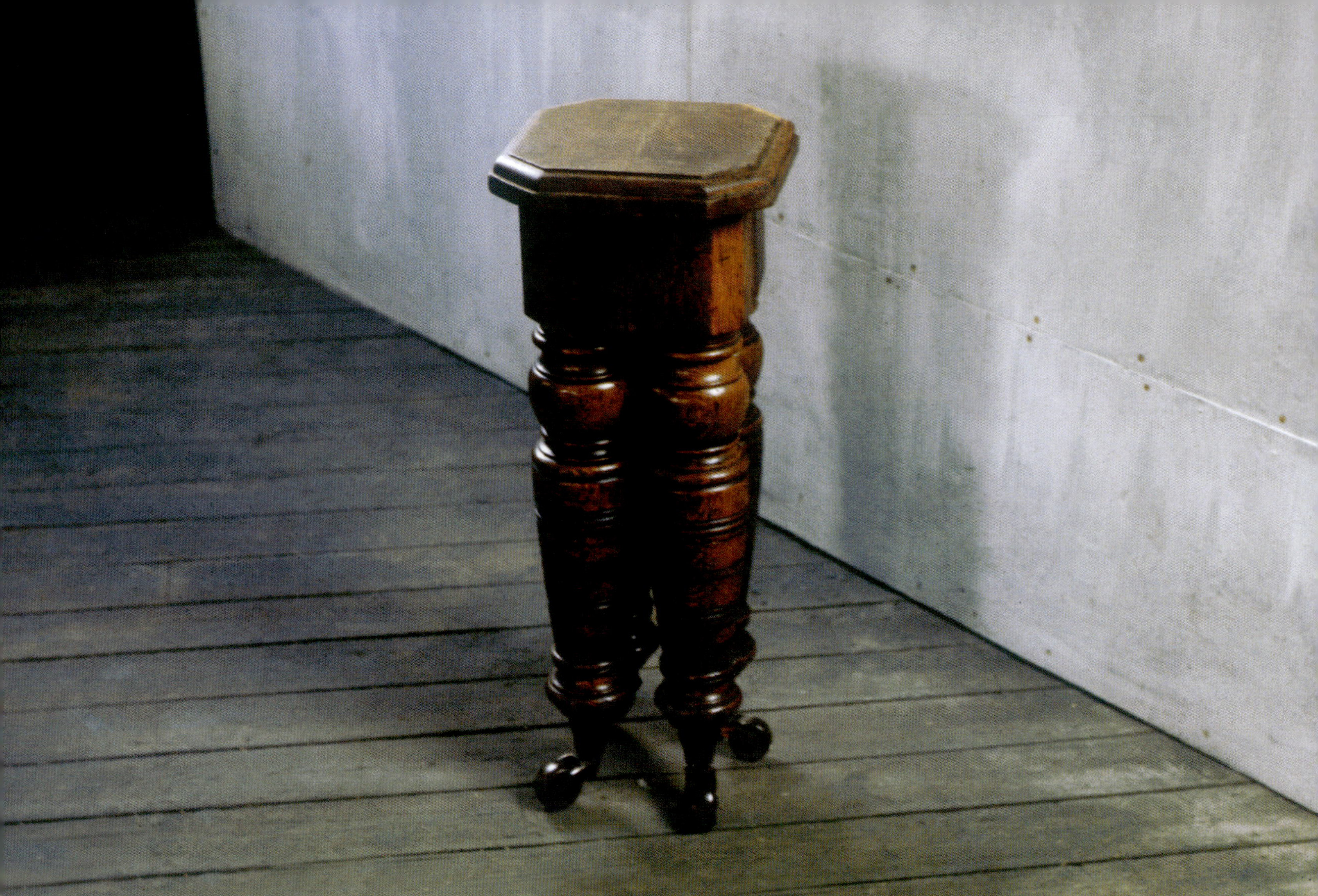

But what are we to make of *Oak Table*, 1980, which seems to be intent on going somewhere, or *Potted Palm*, 1979, the plant stand which is already halfway through the gallery wall? Then there is the mad little *Table*, 1980, cannibalised from a larger piece of furniture, which seems to contain so much compressed energy that one expects it to go skittering around the gallery on its erratic castors.

What too of later pieces, like *Pineball, Moon*, 1986 or *Whirling Beans,* 1992. What about this predilection for incongruous objects in trees? Which side of Colin Rose's nature has the upper hand here? Are these objects carefully positioned in appropriate places, or are they misbehaving? They are not tame or complacent objects, but equally they don't seek to confront. Paradoxically they acquire their sense of rightness by being out of place.

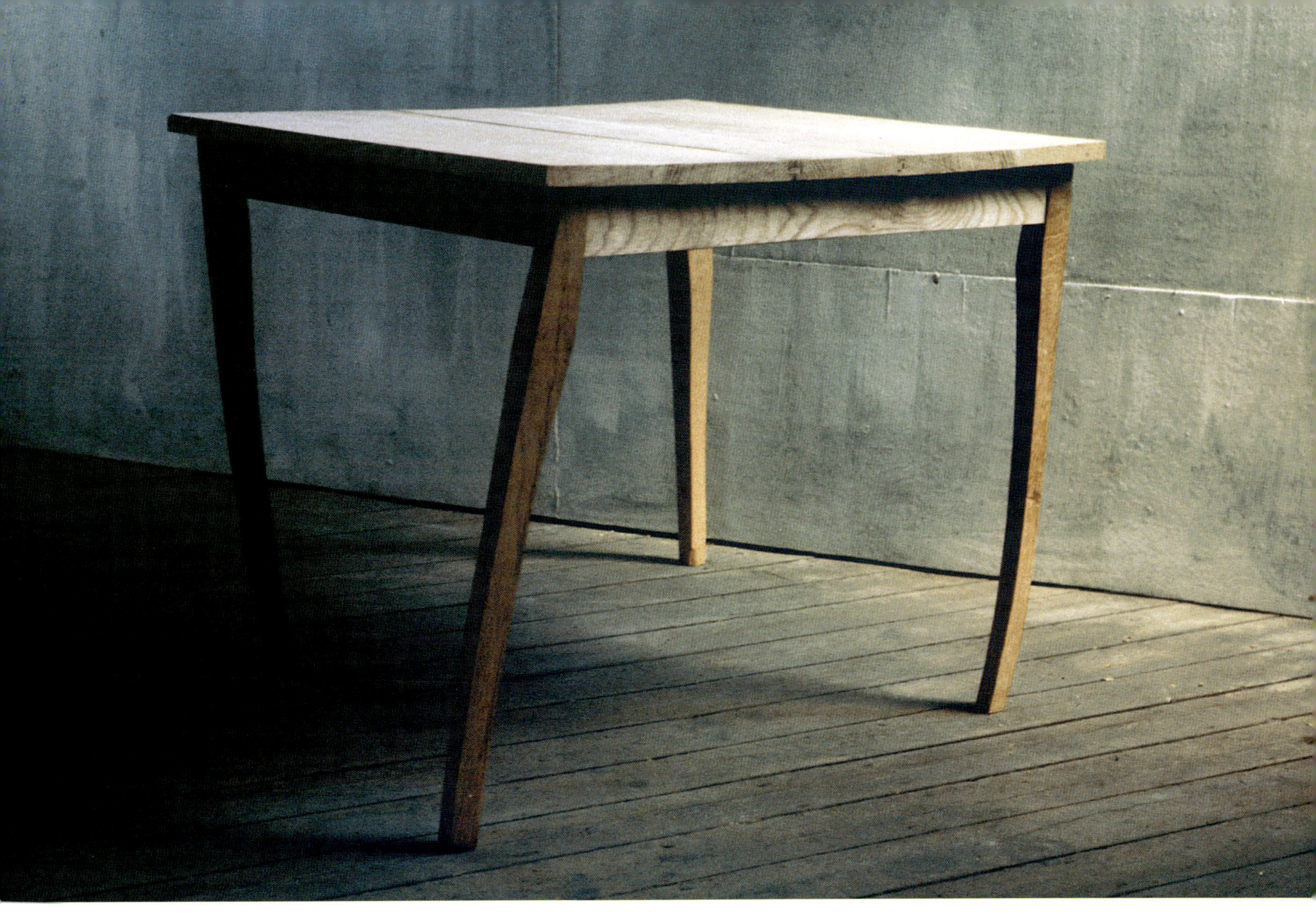

Below: **Mirror With Nothing In It** 1981
Oak
Approx. 100cm Ø

Right: **Potted Palm** 1978
Oak
120 x 45 x 45cm

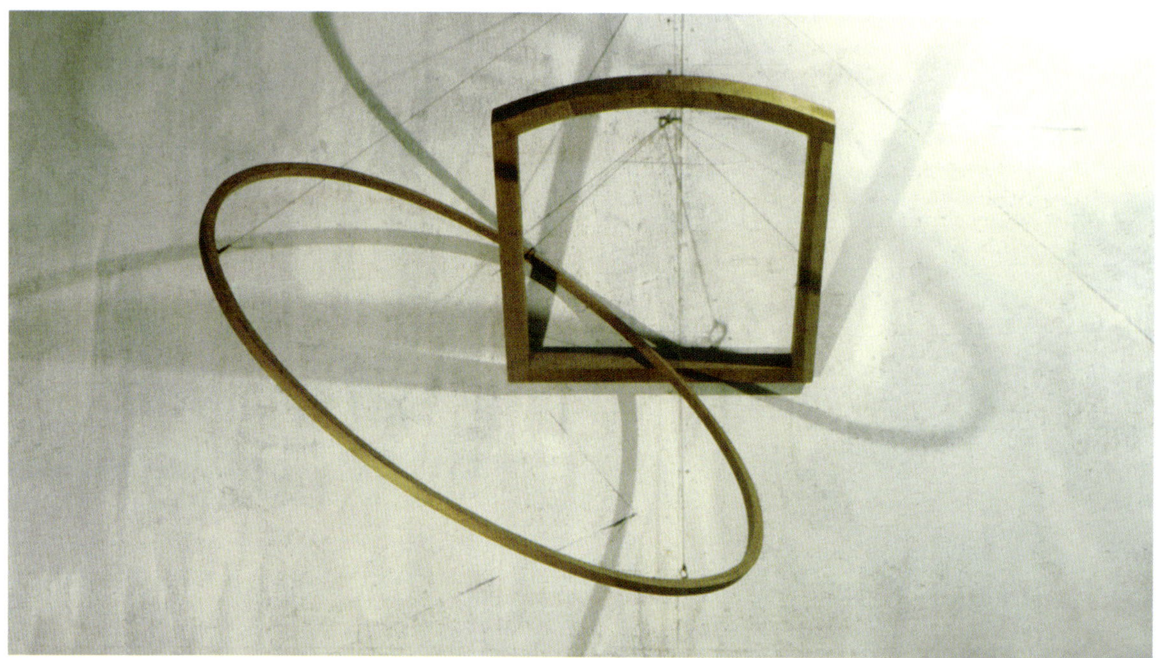

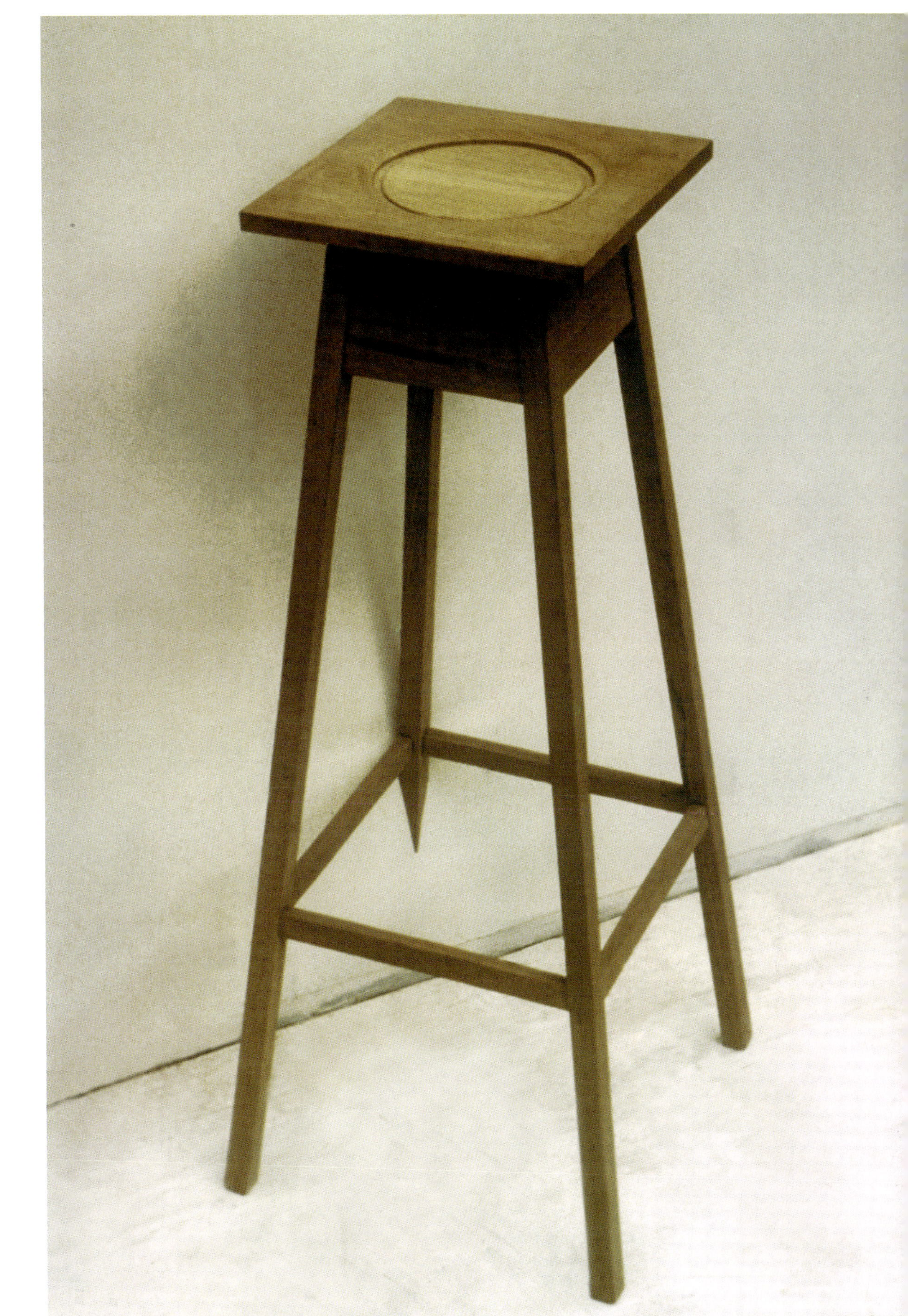

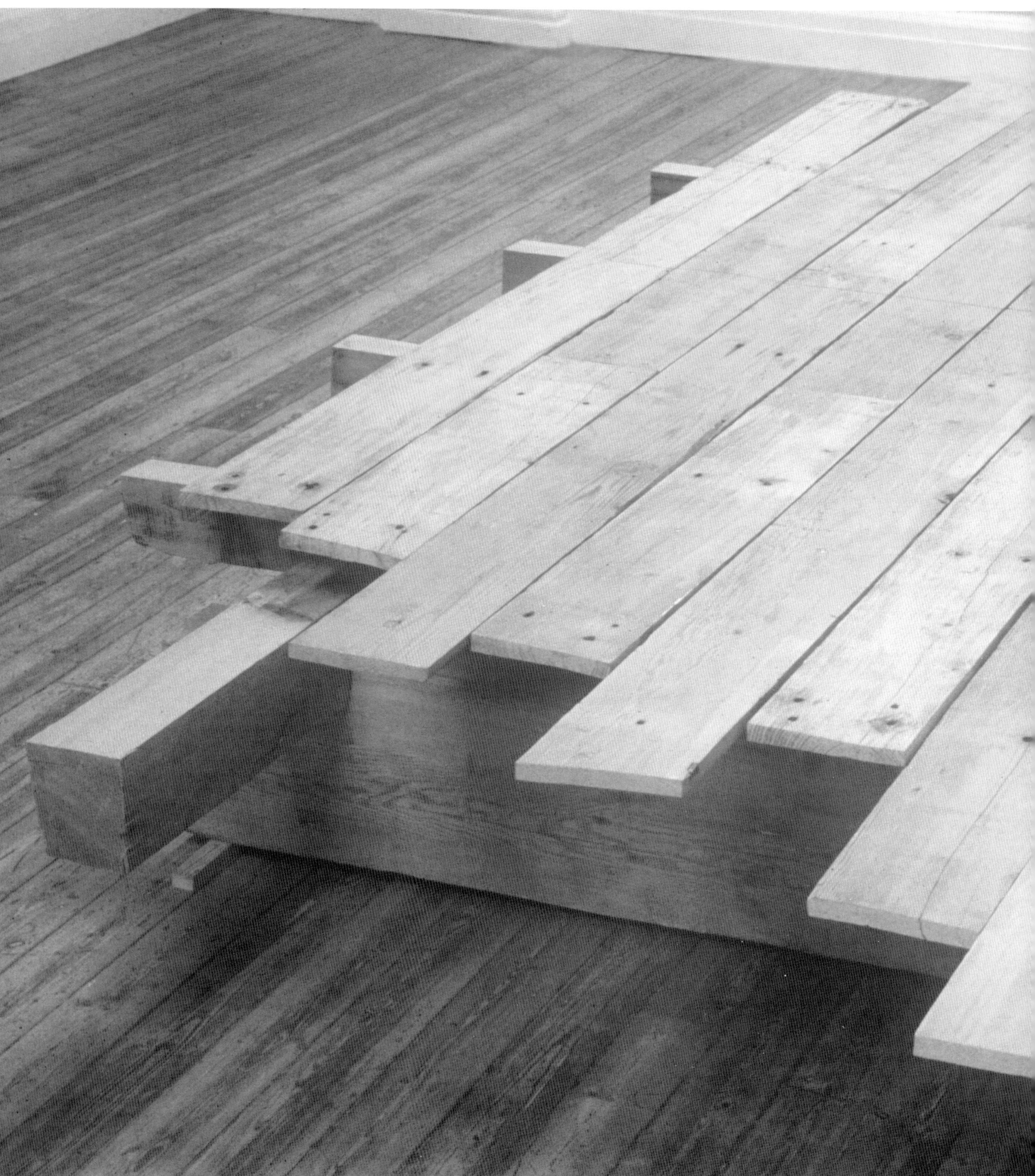

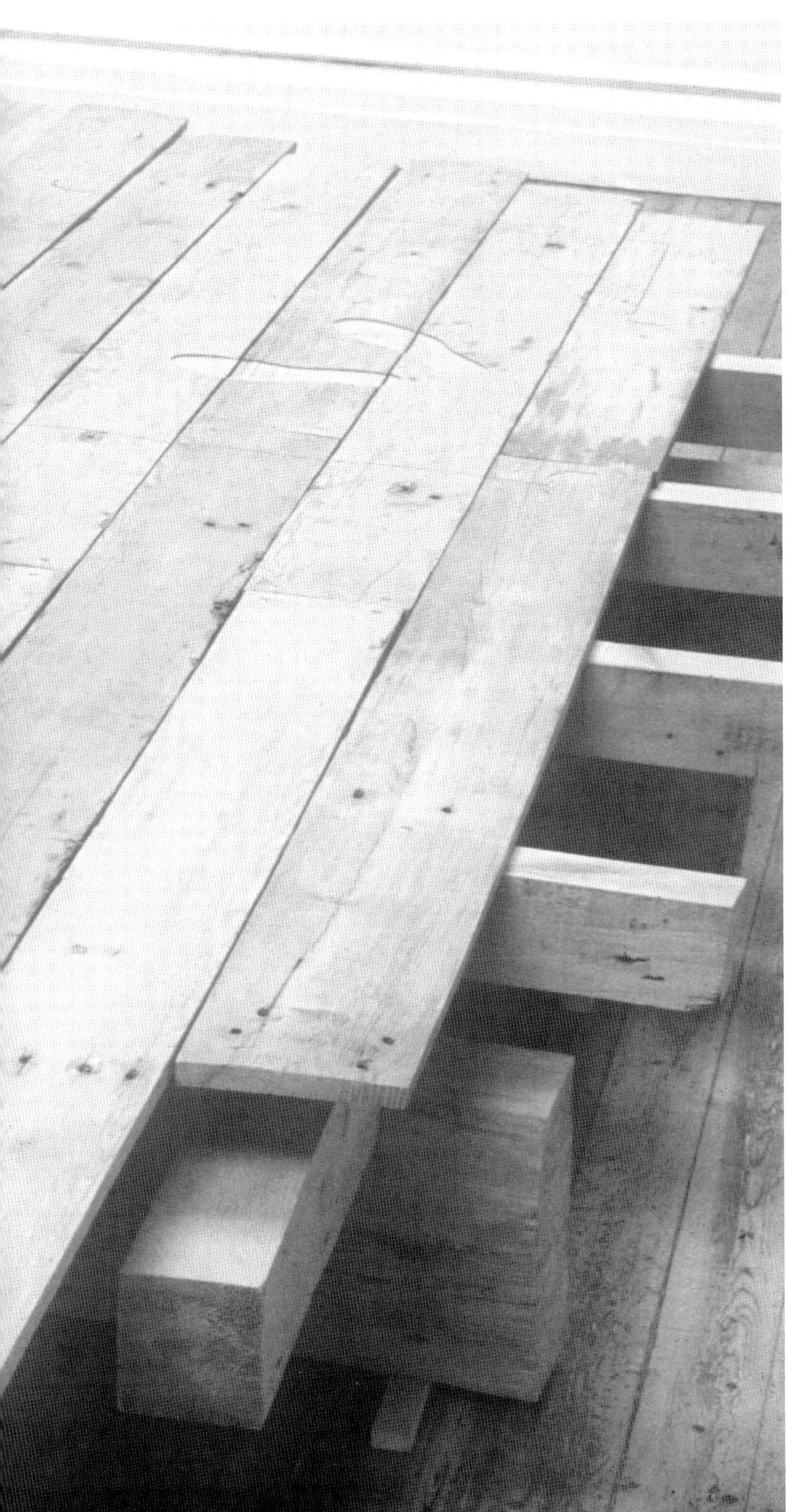

The Other Room 1979
Wood
400 x 240cm

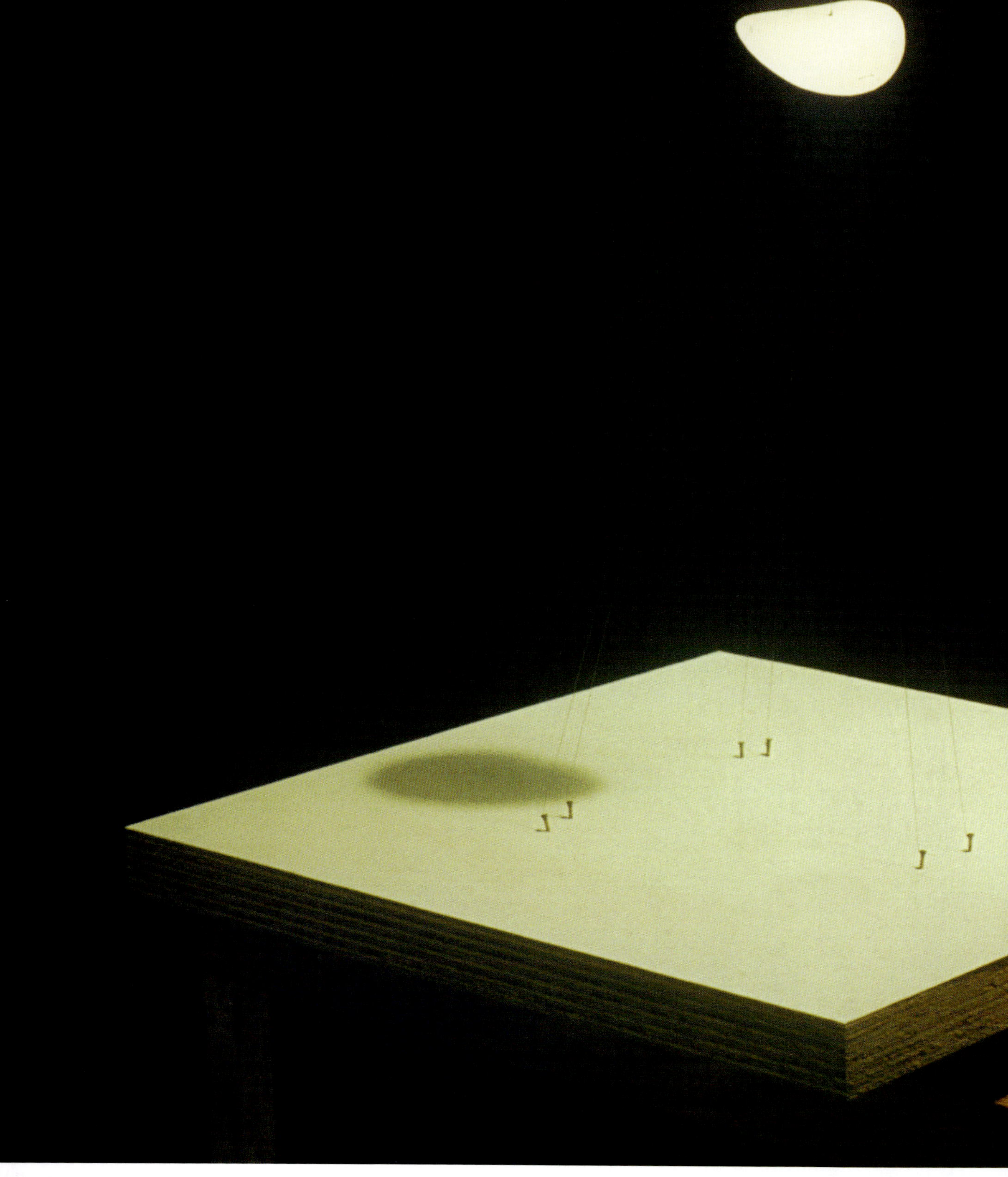

Left: **Shadow of a Kiss** 1982
Paper and wood
150 x 26 x 26cm

Following page: **Moon** 1986
Painted wood
120cm Ø

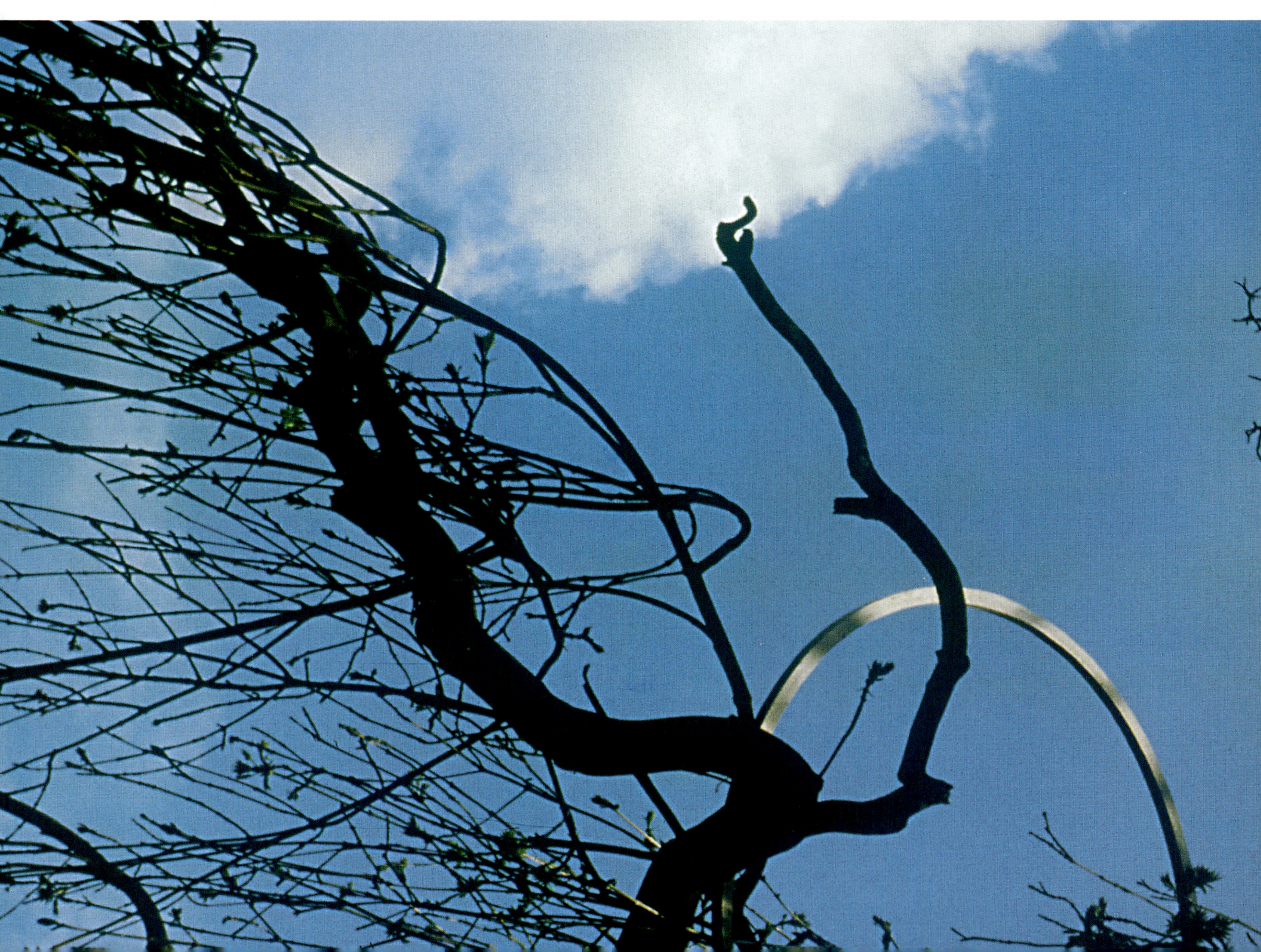

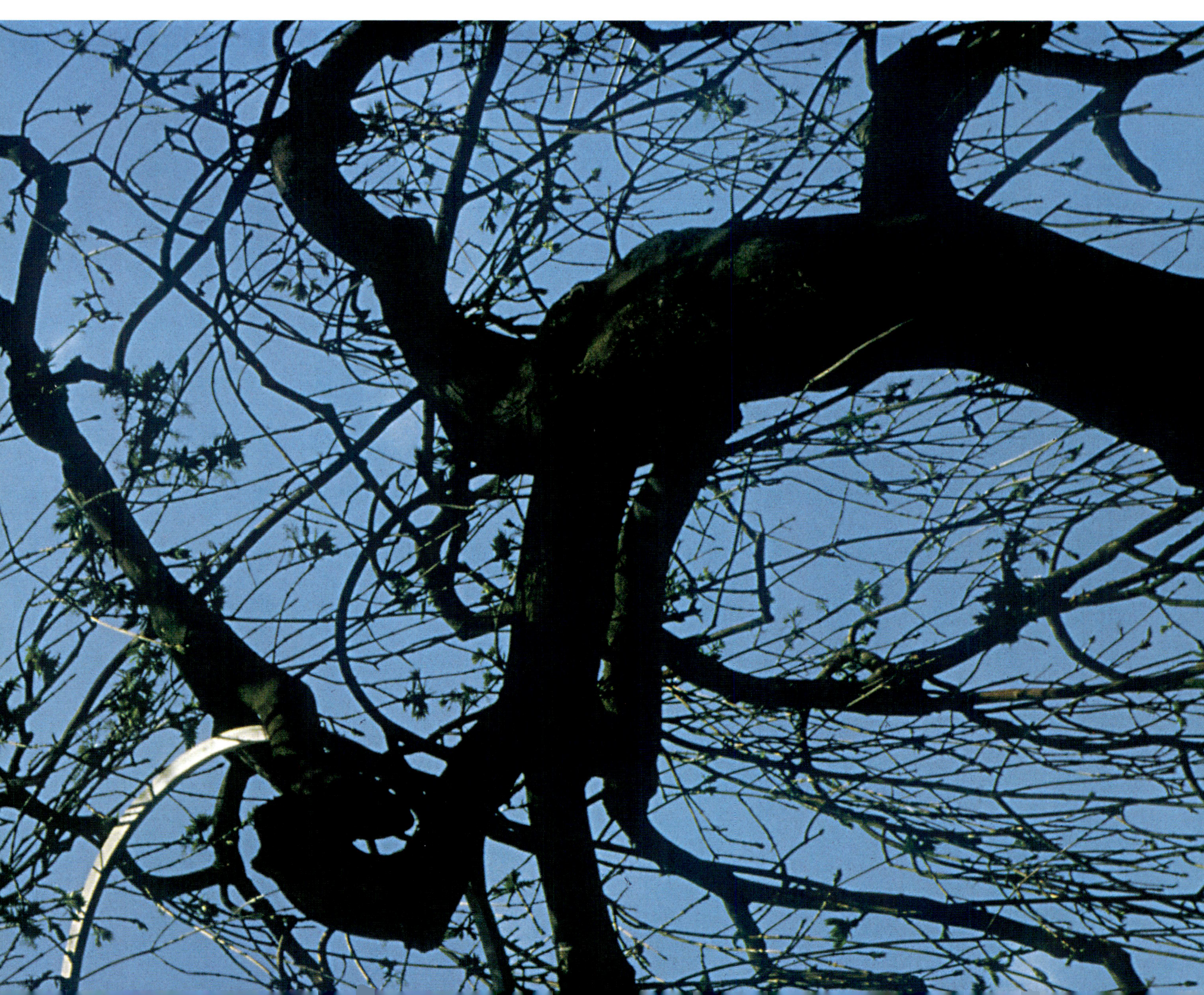

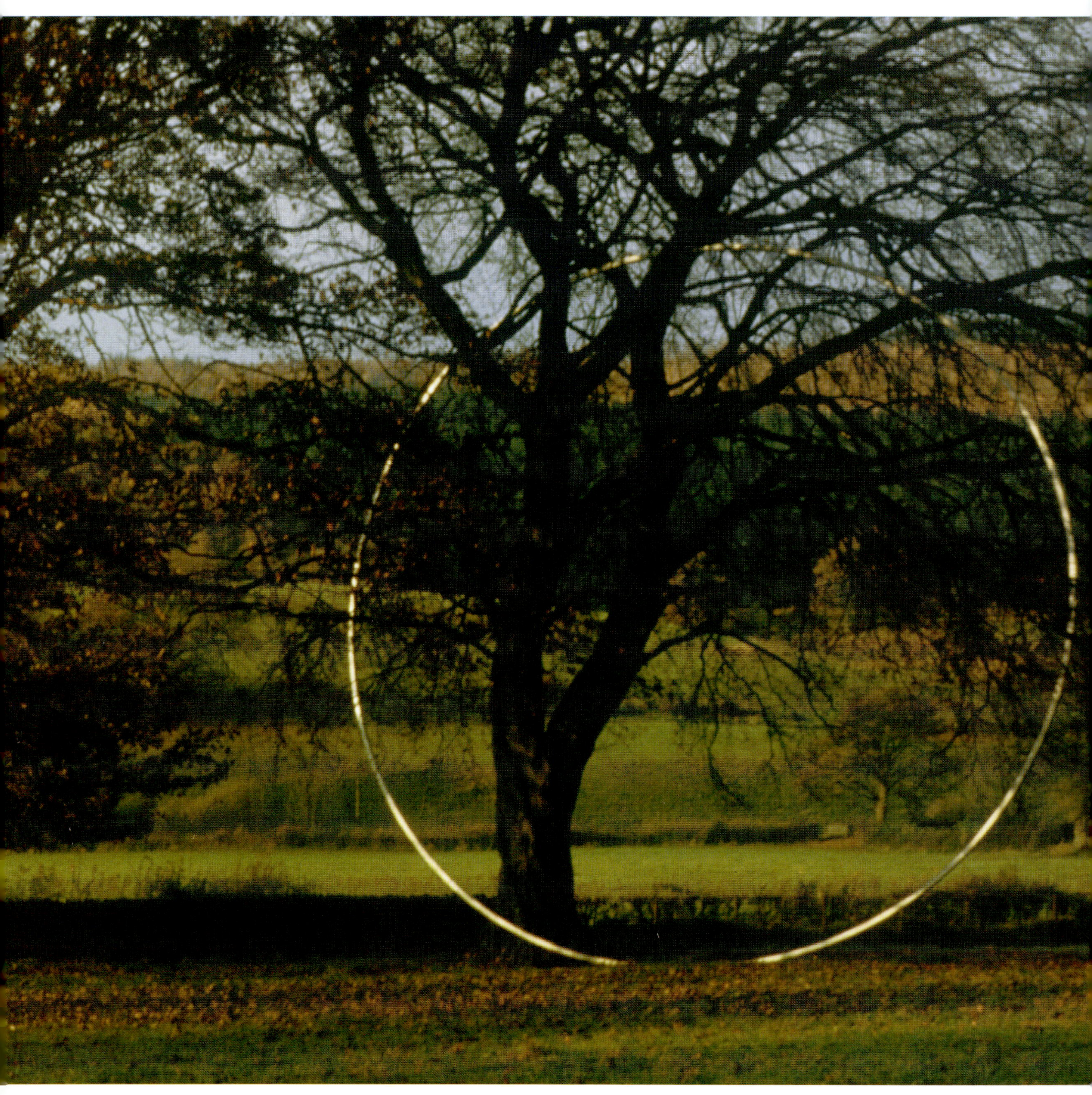

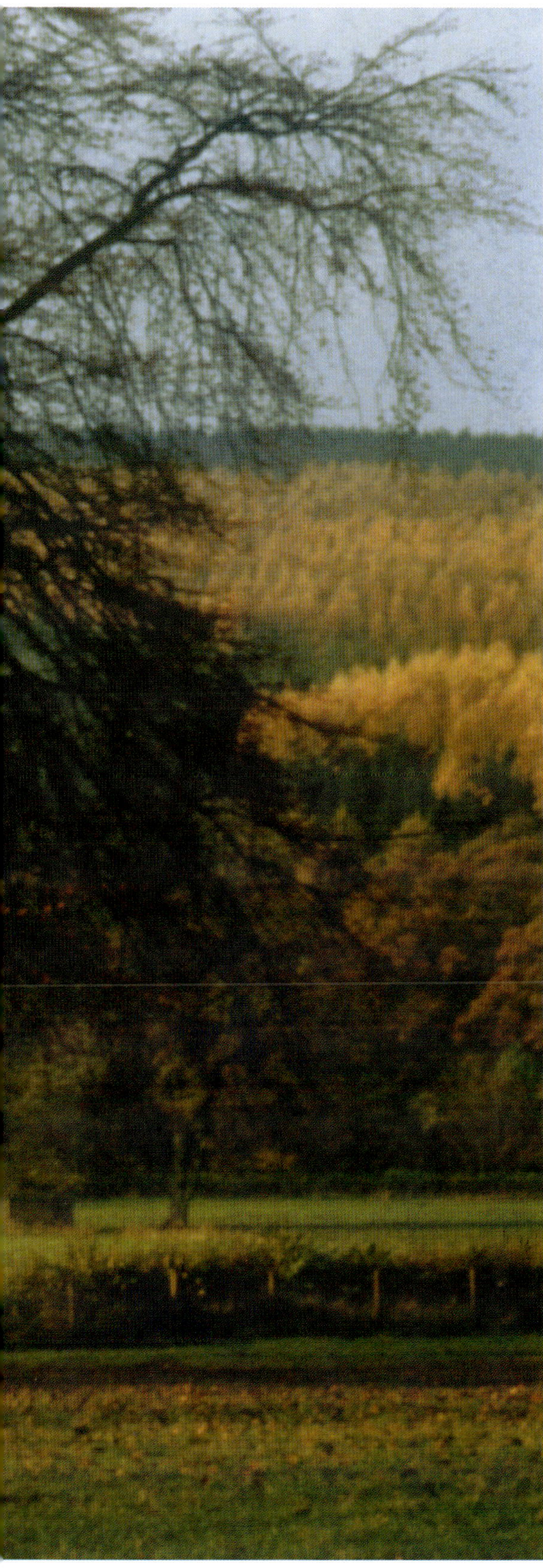

If we exclude the dangling tea cups, it was in the early 1980s when Colin became seriously interested in placing objects in trees. Of these it was the first, *Ting*, 1984, which attracted the most attention and controversy. The piece is a circle of painted steel, some 13 metres in diameter, which is fastened within the canopy of a copper beech. The bottom of the hoop rests on the ground, the top is securely but inconspicuously fastened to one of the branches. Colin first showed this piece at Yorkshire Sculpture Park but a more permanent home would be found for it at Grizedale Forest in Cumbria. Other sculptors who had worked in Grizedale, such as Richard Harris, Andy Goldsworthy and David Nash, had worked with timber or stone found locally. Their work was thus seen as respectful of the character of the place. In time most of these works would degrade; it would be as if they had never existed. Colin was the first to introduce a man-made material (square-hollow-section steel) into the forest and for some it was a step too far. Originally he had wanted to site the piece deep amongst the trees, but there was opposition to this. Eventually he approached a farmer whose fields included some old parkland close to the woodland edge, and the sculpture went ahead. In its present position, the sculpture can be taken in at a single glance. Had it been sited in the woods, as the sculptor originally intended, this would not have been possible.

Ting 1984
Painted steel
13m Ø
Grizedale Forest

Following pages: **Ting** 1984
Yorkshire Sculpture Park

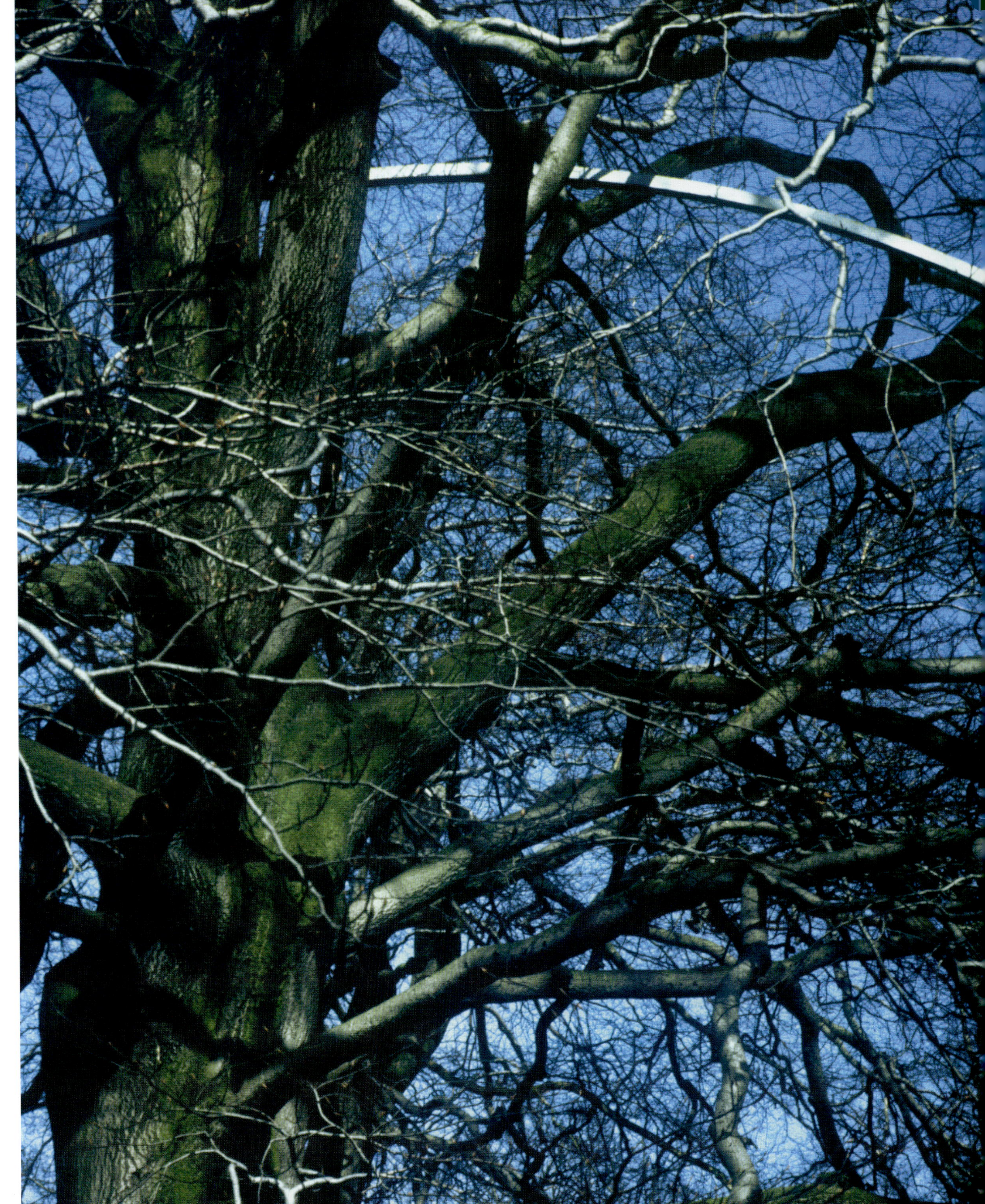

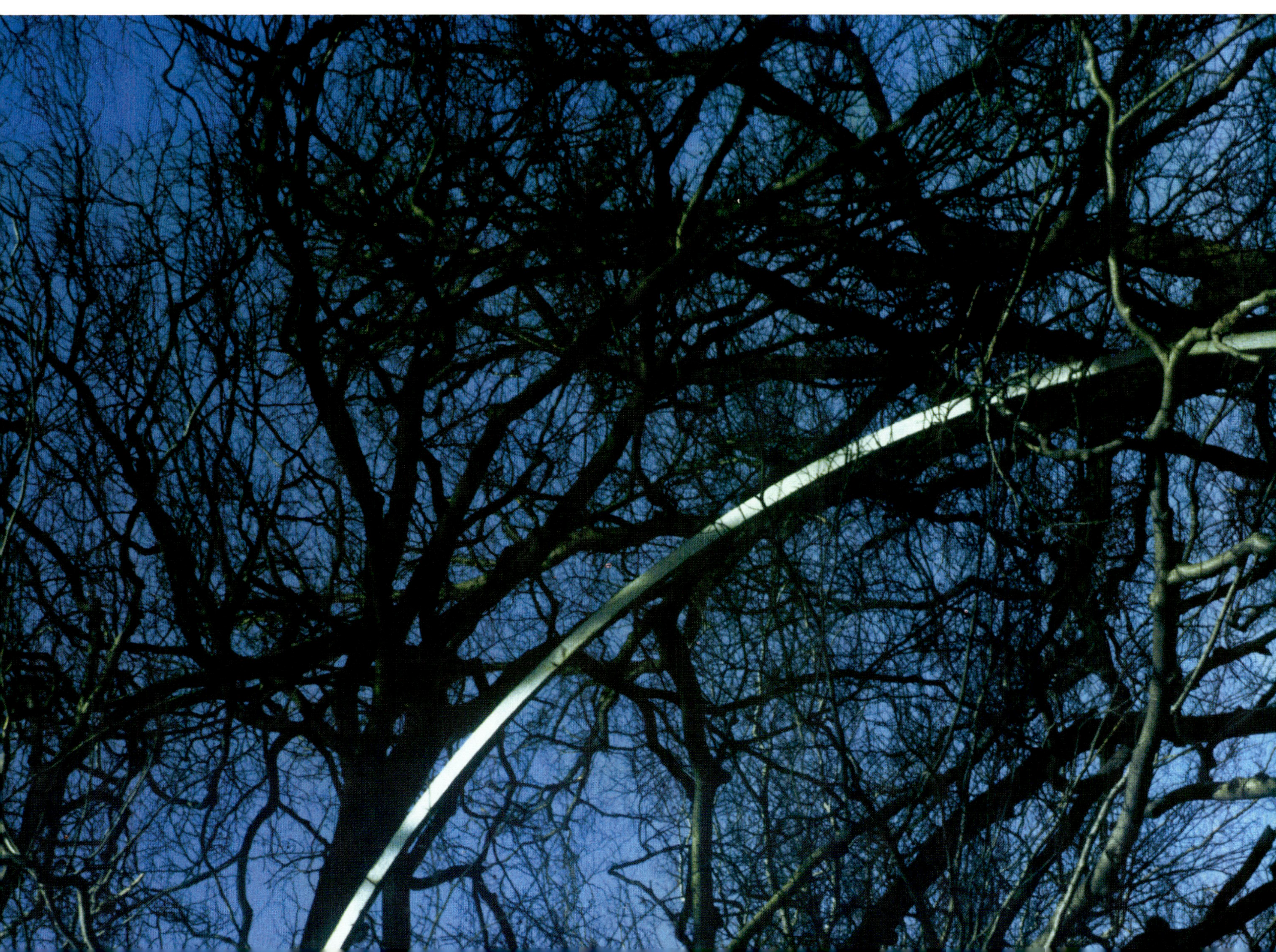

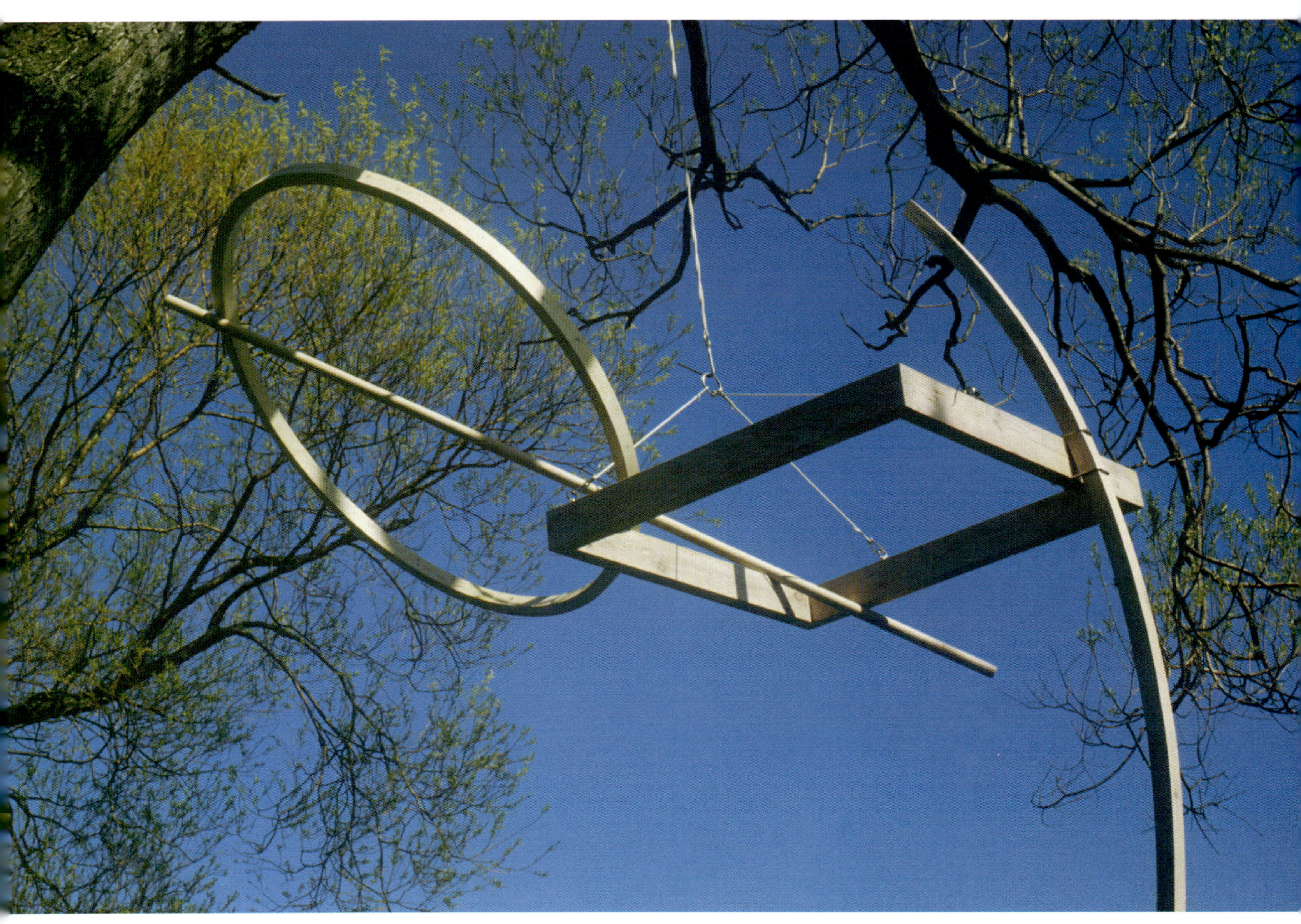

Far from seeming an alien or ugly intrusion, *Ting* has a lightness and grace, and its once perfect form (for it has sagged a little with the years) was an ideal foil for the fractal geometries of the tree's branching patterns. This is not an object in the wrong place; it is perfectly decorous. There is no aggression in the piece, indeed almost the opposite. Colin explains that at the time he had become intrigued by the idea that every object, including natural objects like twigs and leaves, has its own sound. Imagined thus, the countryside is not a quiet place. A woodland is a cacophony. *Ting* was conceived as a quiet refuge in the centre of this natural racket. As the name suggests, its own sound was pure, clear and gentle.

Another theme which enters into Colin's work about this time is the symbol of the moon. He recalls a sense of wonder at seeing both a daylight and a night time moon from the same place within 24 hours, and the piece called *Two Moons*, first made in 1983, but reiterated in 1991, is an attempt to capture this experience. The presence of the grid linking the circular and crescent forms is a reference to human rationality. Science has helped us to understand and to measure these astronomical phenomena and thus to bring them within our ideas of order. Later versions of *Two Moons* were also placed in trees, as was the single hoop of *Moon*, 1986, and suspended over water, perhaps in recognition of the effect the moon has upon the tides. Colin also feels that the reflected image, paradoxically, approached a kind of Platonic perfection that the constructed piece itself could not obtain, for although Plato might have thought that a reflection was at one further remove from the ideal world of 'Forms', it was less easy to notice the compromises of jointing and fixing in the reflection than in the piece itself. *Rolling Moon*, Colin's piece for Glasgow Garden Festival, echoed these themes, and it too was placed over a pool.

Left: **Two Moons II** 1991
Painted wood and stainless steel
120 x 270 x 480cm

Below: **Two Moons I** 1983
Wood
Approx. 150 x 200cm

Following Page: **Two Moons III** 1984
Painted wood and stainless steel
360 x 480cm

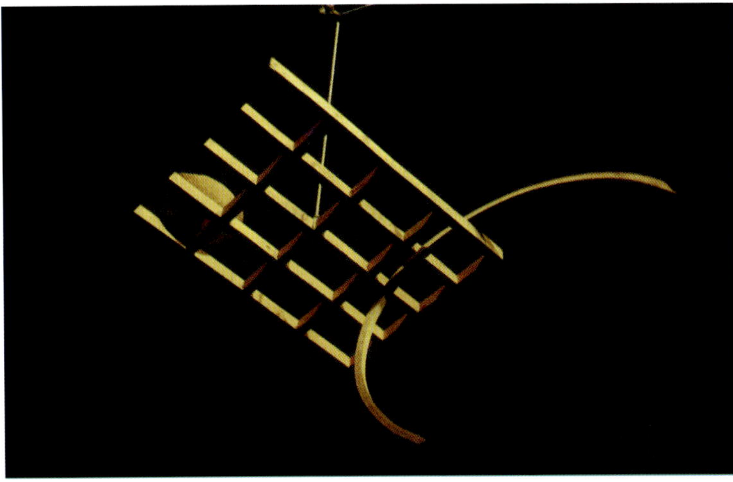

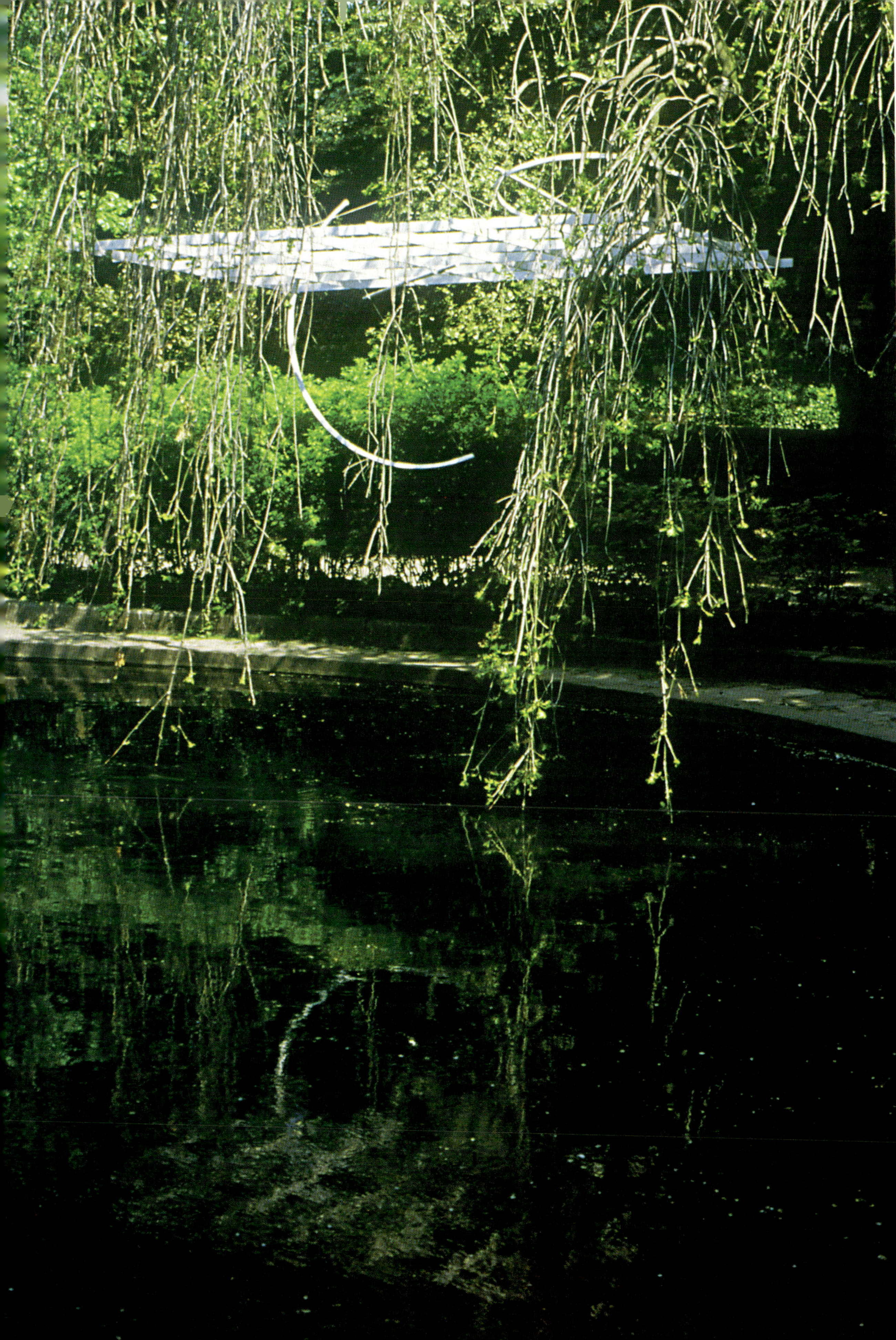

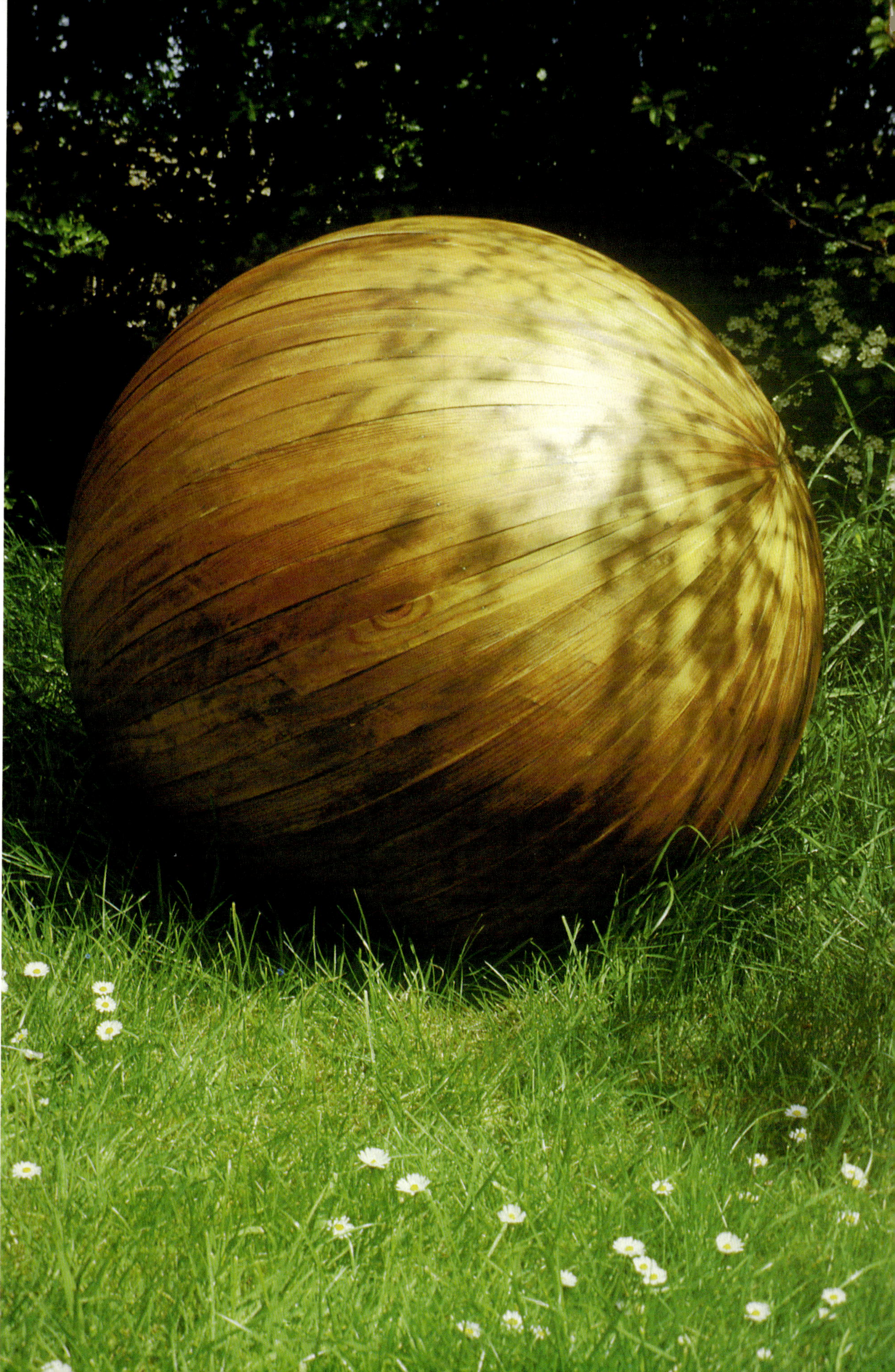

Precision Fruits

It is evident that language is an important influence upon Colin's work. His short unpretentious titles are carefully considered. Just as the onomatopoeic "Ting" was chosen as the exact sound-equivalent of his 13 metre hoop at Grizedale, so too is "Moon" the word which most economically captures the essence of this later work. In a sense his titles are clues to interpretation, but their very simplicity leaves ample scope for viewers to form their own associations and connections.

In the mid 80s Colin recognised that his work had become very cool and linear and he had what he describes as "a thirst to work again with volumes", so, as he has often done, he progressed by first taking a step backwards, in this case by again working with the bulging pumpkin-like forms he had first used in *Shelf*. He had drawn the original inspiration for these from observing the work of coopers and boat-builders on Tyneside, but he was also intrigued by the hydraulic notion of pumping a fruit up until the skin was in such tension it might burst. The result was *Pineball*.

Having experimented for so long in placing objects as diverse as teacups, steel hoops and reflective spirals into tree canopies, it seemed entirely natural to want to do the same with these new fruit-like forms. At the time there was much discussion within artistic circles about the issue of site-specificity, and a general feeling that pieces made in, of, or for particular places were somehow to be preferred over pieces that were bought off the shelf. The derogatory term 'parachute art' had been coined for work which appeared to have been dropped arbitrarily into a site, with no apparent connection to place or reason for its being there. Colin's work defies these polarised categories. Like *Ting*, *Pineball* has been shown in different places, so it cannot strictly be called site-specific; yet equally it has always been placed with great respect, care and deliberation. Colin believes that there are sites which are too obvious and easy, places which already had such positive qualities that they do not need an artwork to enhance them. He has always preferred sites where the artwork would become a focus, where the addition of a made object would turn a mere space into a meaningful place. His idea was that in placing the work into the landscape he would be giving something back, so that the made object was only half of the artwork and needed to be completed by the landscape into which it was set.

Initially *Pineball* was sited in a weeping elm tree in a public park; it was placed to ensure that the viewer would have a sense of surprise and recognition, as one had to be right under the tree before one discovered this huge fruit tucked beneath the canopy. Four years later the same piece was shown at the Yorkshire Sculpture Park, where it nestled on top of a spray of branches in a cedar tree. The artist particularly enjoyed the inversion whereby the ball was made of the inside of a tree, but was found perched on the outside of one. In purely sensory terms the complementary relationship between the orangey glow of the pine wood against the blue-green foliage of the cedar is hugely pleasing. Again there is the familiar play between positive and negative values.

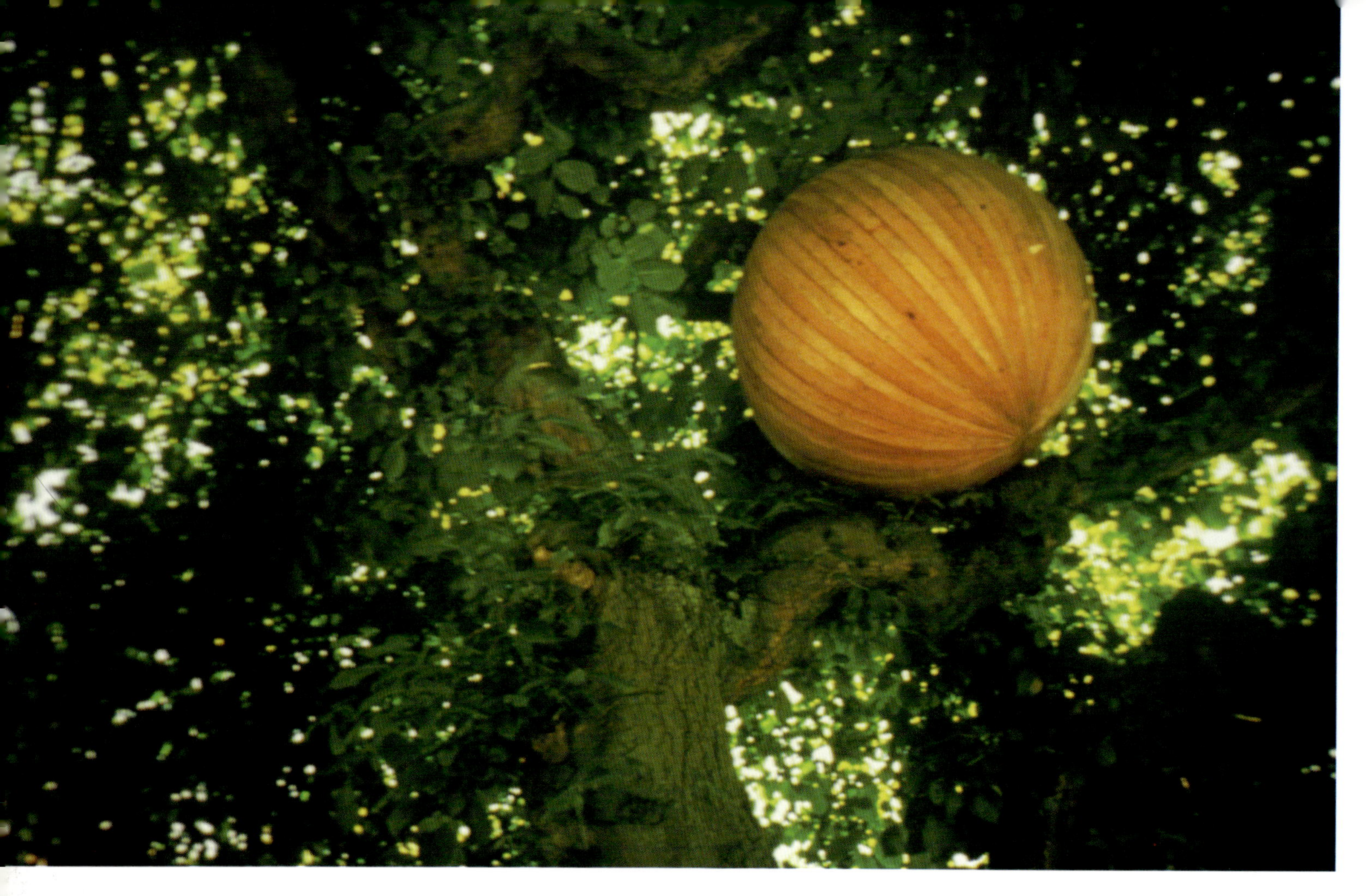

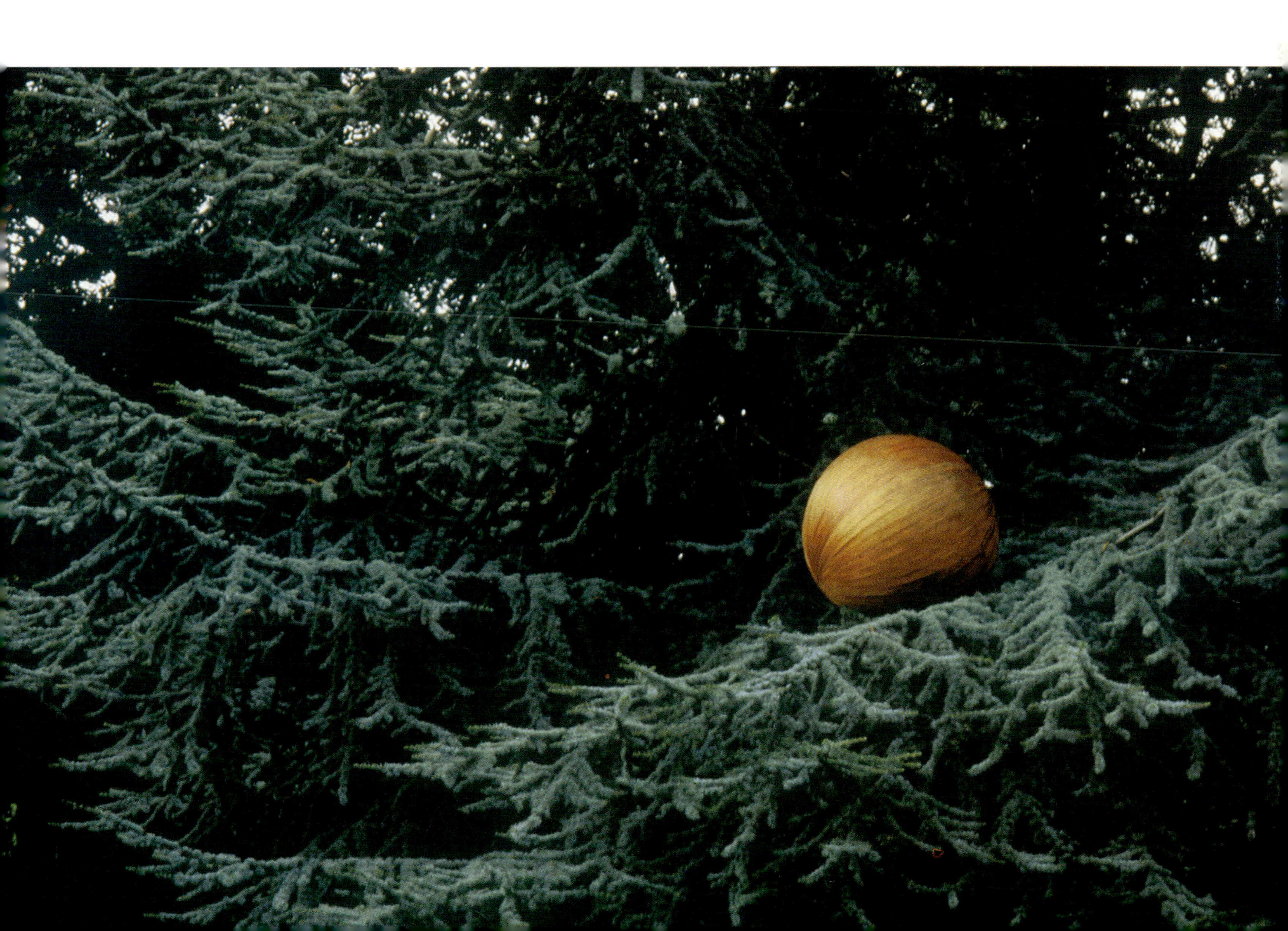

The early 90s were a productive period for Colin. In 1991 he had been given a Henry Moore Foundation Bursary to develop work for exhibition at the Yorkshire Sculpture Park. The *Whirling Beans* series was a product of this period, and one in which Colin's enthusiasm for gardening, his engineer's delight in precise geometries and his love of trees converged. He tells a story which has a bearing upon these pieces. For days he had been aware of a small object caught up in the lining of his jacket which he worked at with his fingers but could not free. Then, while waiting in a supermarket queue, he dislodged it and discovered that it was an apple pip. To him it was a moment of epiphany; the object which had been teasing him for so long was a seed. Unwittingly he had been carrying the idea of a tree around in his pocket. The moment passed unnoticed by everyone else in the supermarket.

As with much of Colin's work, the simplicity and purity of his ideas gives one little inkling of the technical and physical difficulties involved in their realisation. The prototype rope balls for *Whirling Beans* were made with bamboo and rope, but Colin could not obtain the desired tightness of form. The solution was to cast a resin sphere around a steel armature, then to wind the rope on top. In this work anarchic playfulness once again gets the upper hand. Colin likens throwing the beans back into the trees to kids throwing bicycle tyres over lampposts, although the process was actually much more careful and controlled. It involved using a machine with a hydraulic arm. Colin was anxious that no harm should come to the tree, and at Yorkshire Sculpture Park this concern was heightened by the existence of a Tree Preservation Order. The beans, which each weigh over a quarter of a ton, are tied into the tree rather than bolted into the wood, but this brought with it new worries, as squirrels are fond of gnawing through rope.

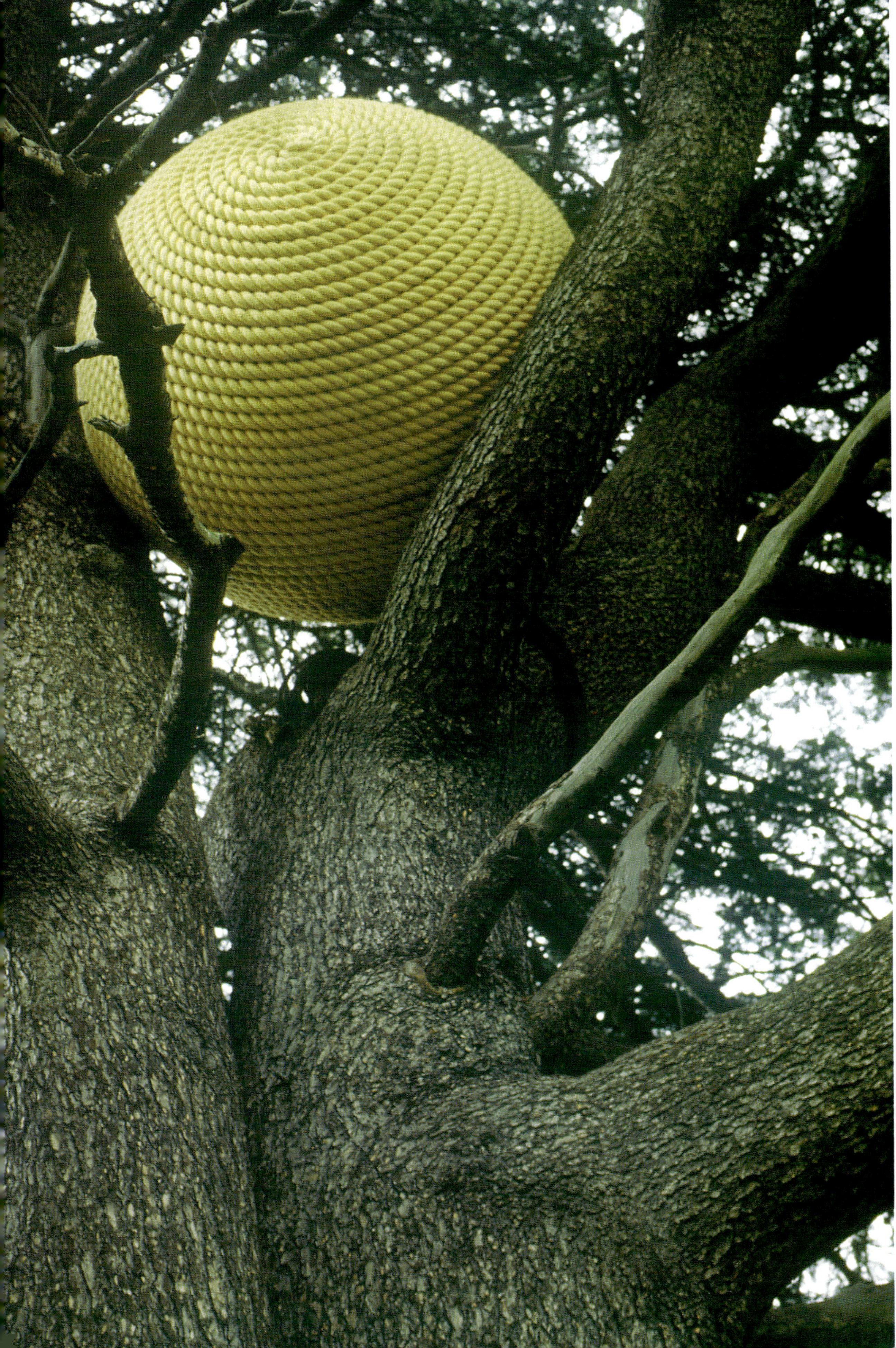

Left: **Rope Ball** 1992
Rope, resin and steel
150cm Ø
Yorkshire Sculpture Park

Following pages: **Whirling Bean** 1991
Resin and tarred rope
38cm Ø

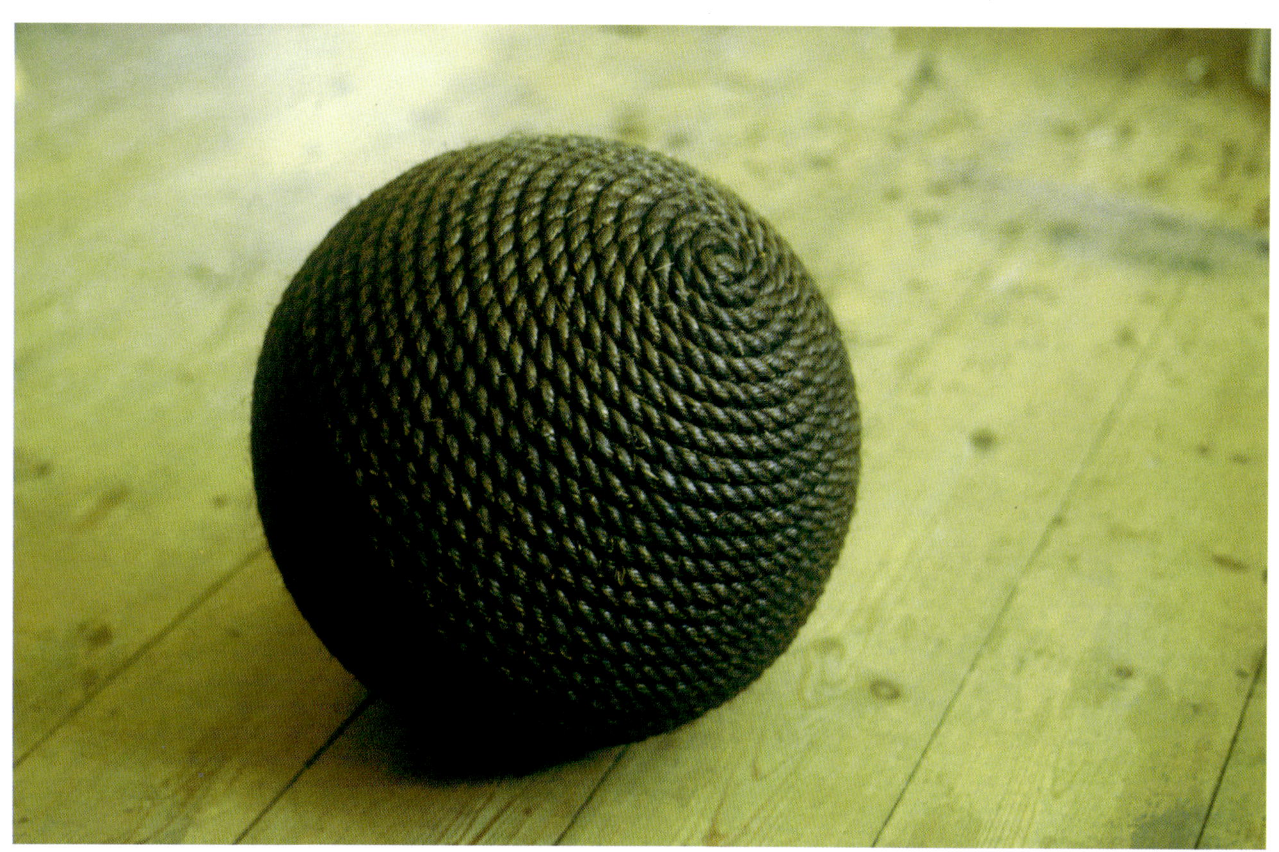

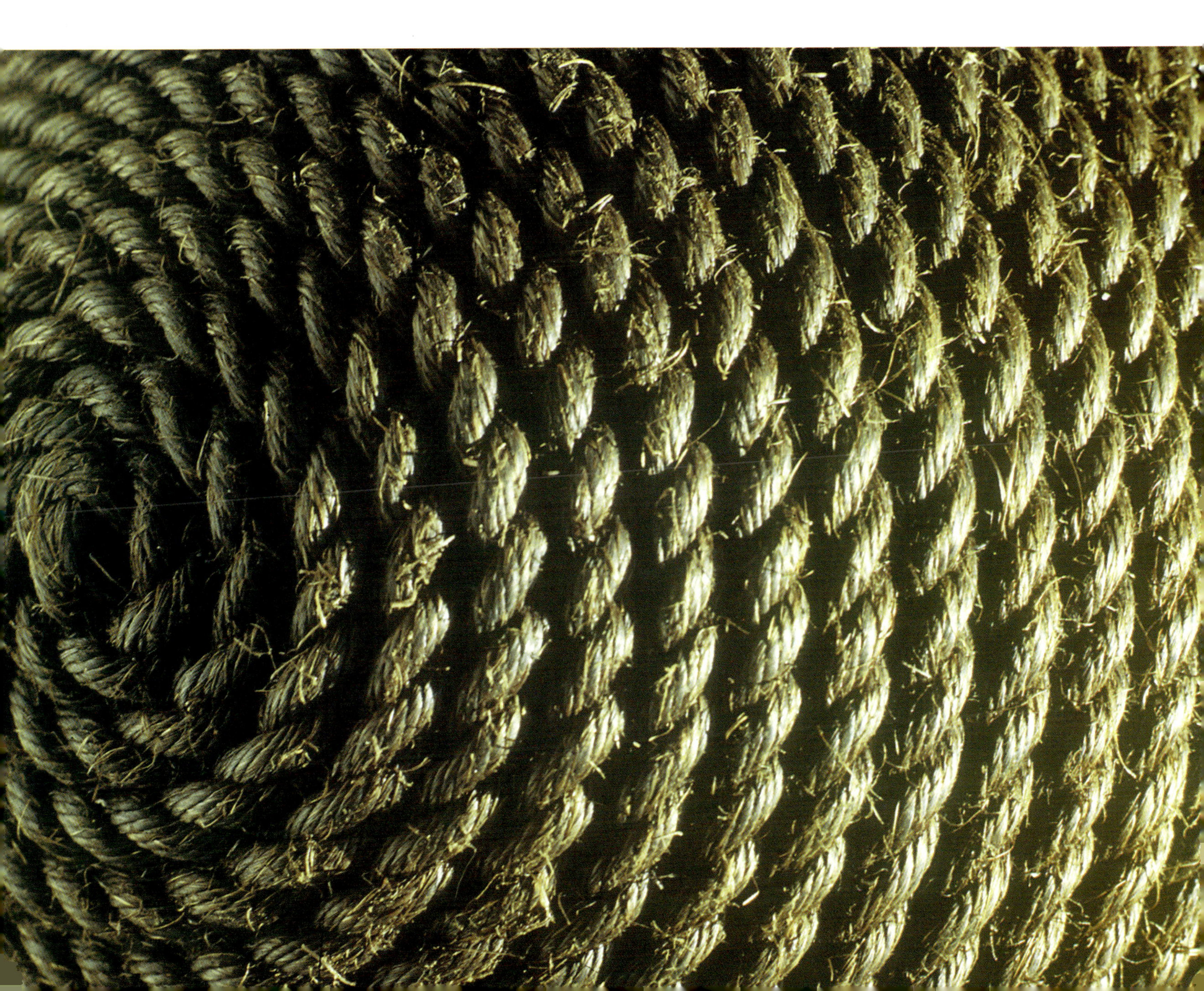

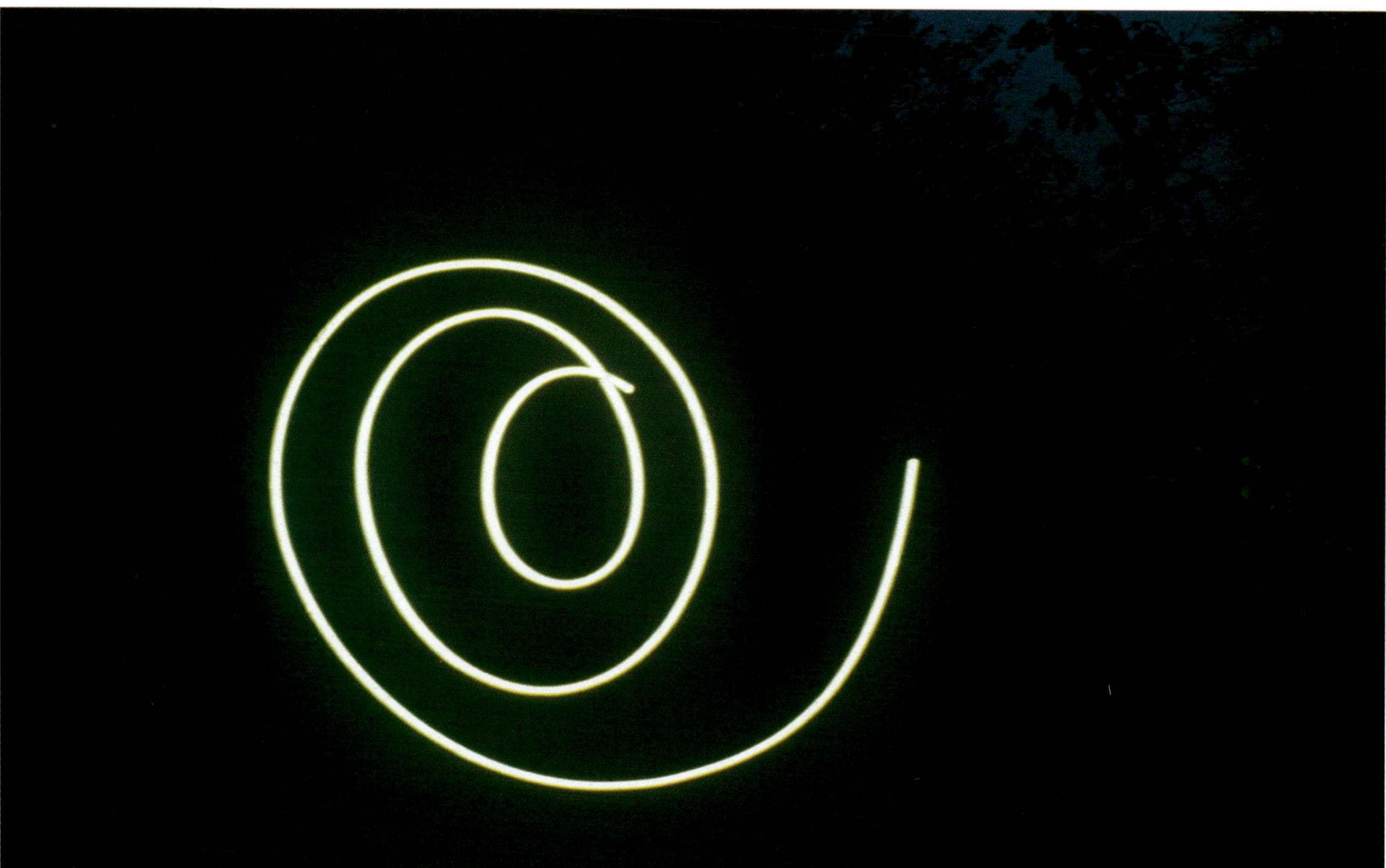

Colin has always had a capacity for refreshing his practice by switching between media. In 1991 he began to make a series of graphite drawings, amongst which was *Pool*, which started as a process of abstraction from natural elements experienced on the beach near the Northumbrian farm where he then lived, but which soon developed into a personal language of forms. These forms, in turn, fed back into his sculptural practice. At the same time Colin had been experimenting with reflective materials, cutting up traffic cones to make direction markers. Living in a farm some distance from main roads, evening visitors were having difficulty in finding him. This activity, both playful and pragmatic, was the origin of the *Swirl*, *Wriggle* and *Ripple* pieces, which began life as signs in hedgerows, their shapes furnished from the *Pool* sequence. Versions of these found their way into the trees at the Yorkshire Sculpture Park, along with pieces like *Night and Day*, 1991, which is at once a development from *Moon* but also related to the graphite drawings. With sponsorship from Alcan UK and 3M, Colin was able to cover some of these pieces with the reflective material used for road signs. Subtle and inconspicuous by day, they would become startlingly vibrant when illuminated at night.

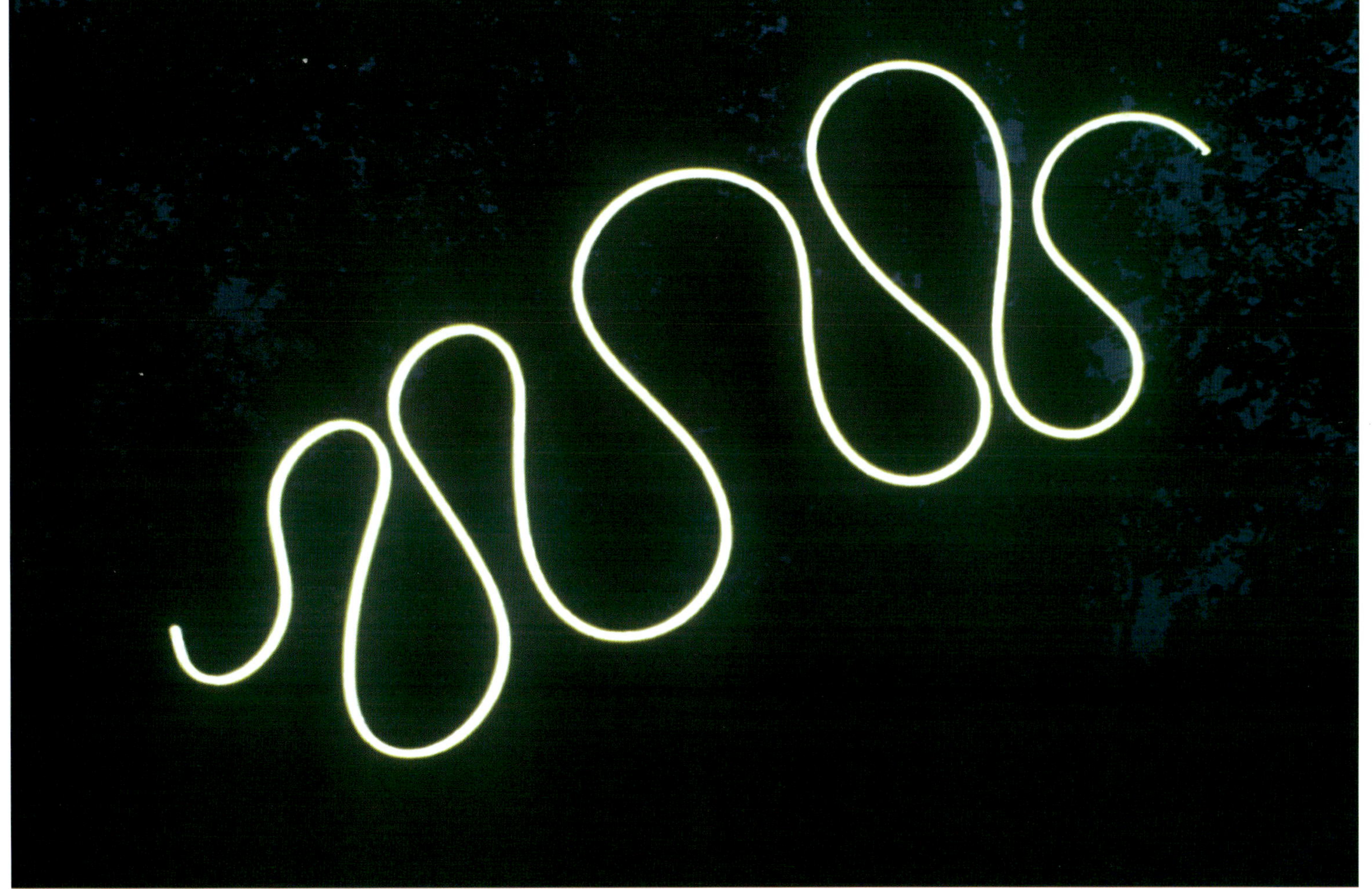

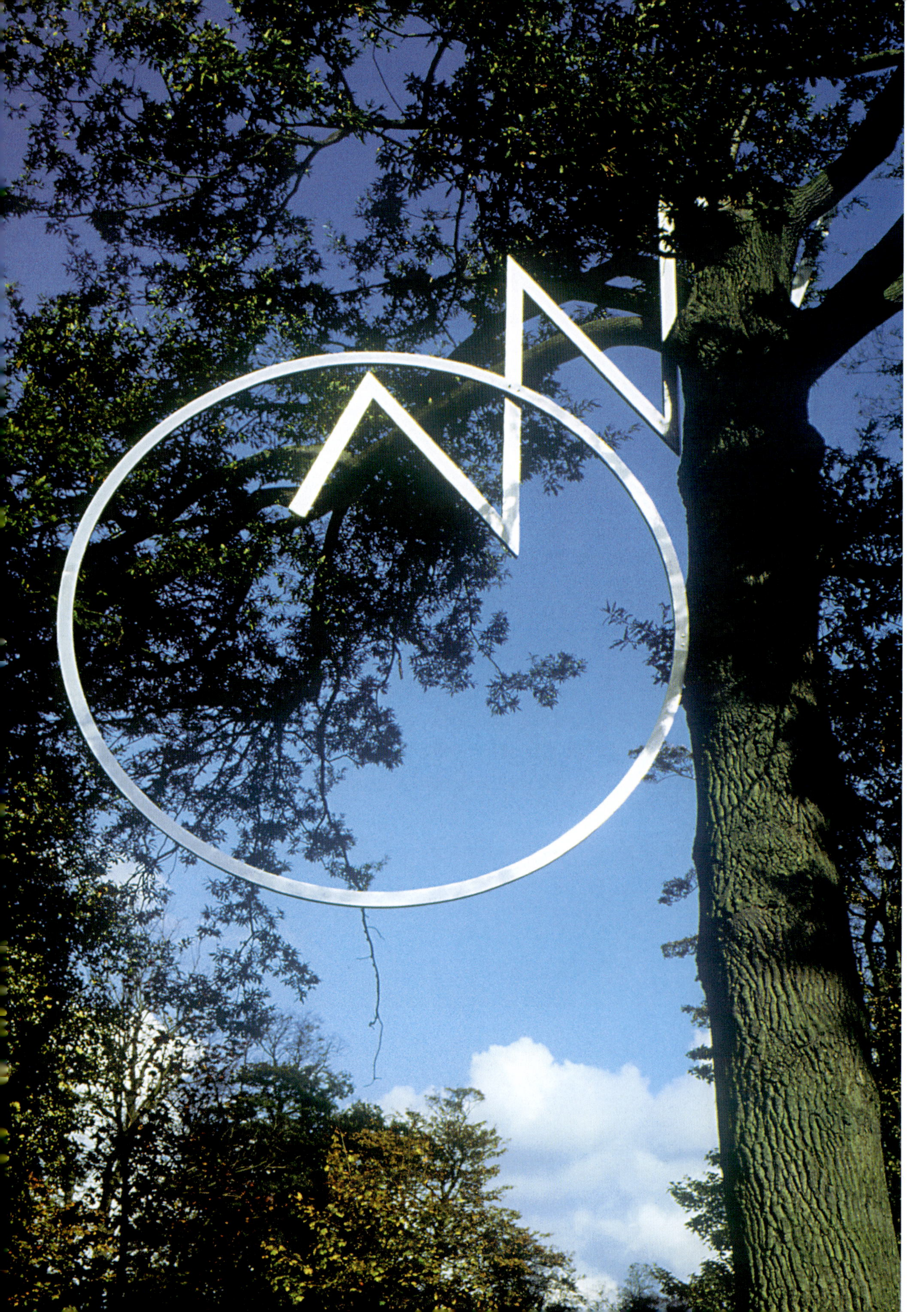

Left: **Night and Day** 1991
Aluminium
700 x 500cm
Yorkshire Sculpture Park

Below: **Swirl** 1992
Yorkshire Sculpture Park

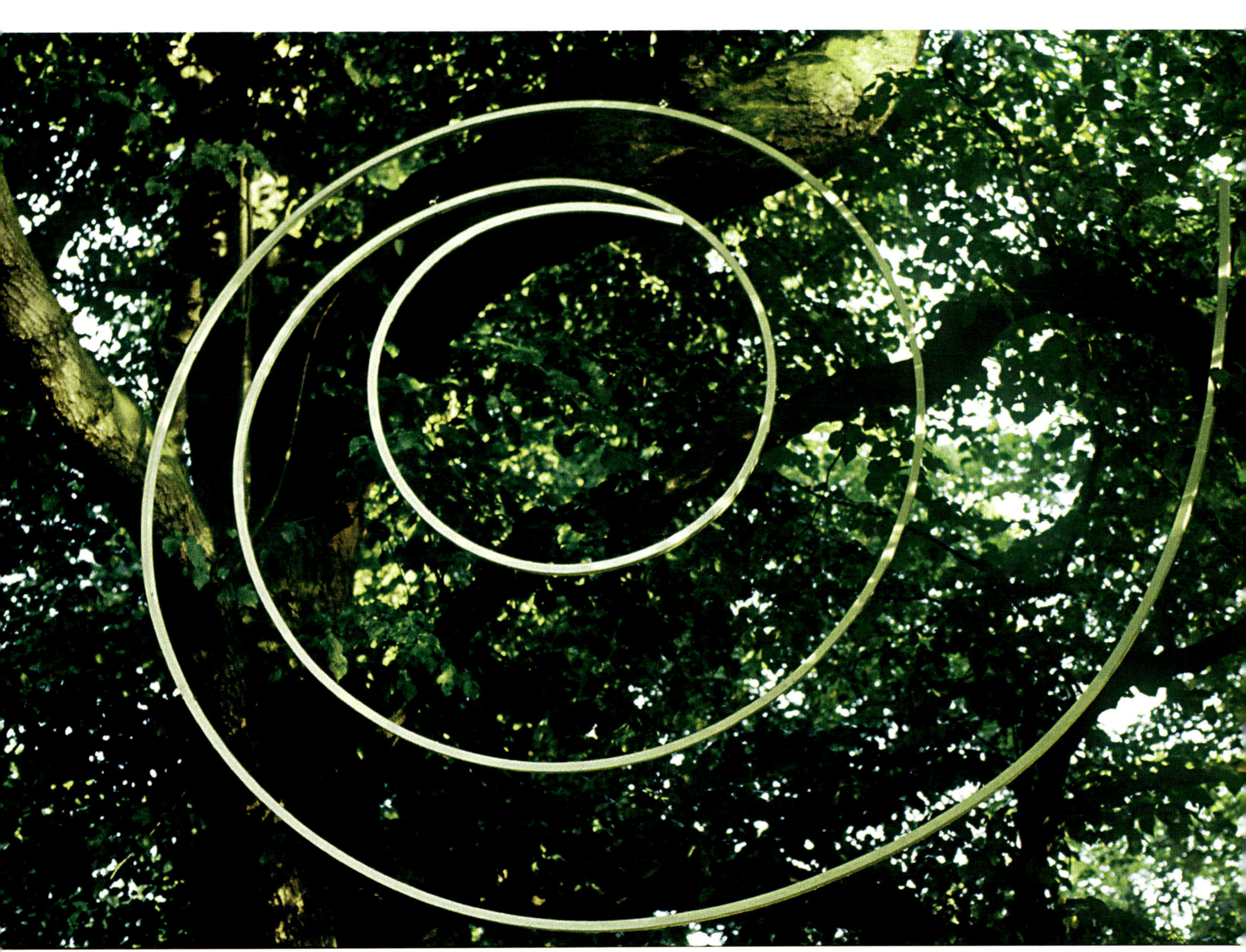

Two Swirls 1996
Aluminium and reflective surface
Approx. 500cm Ø
Honiton, Devon

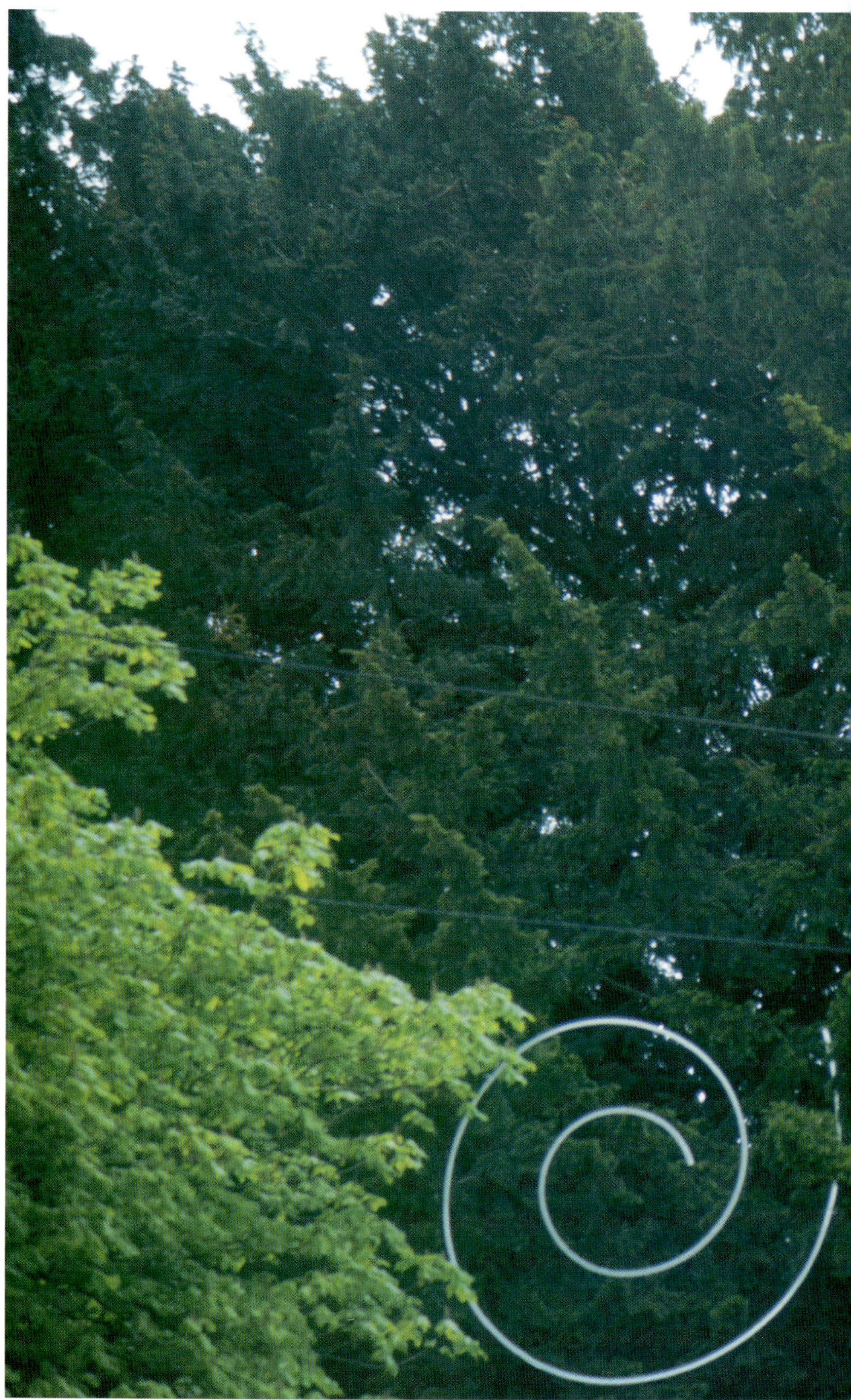

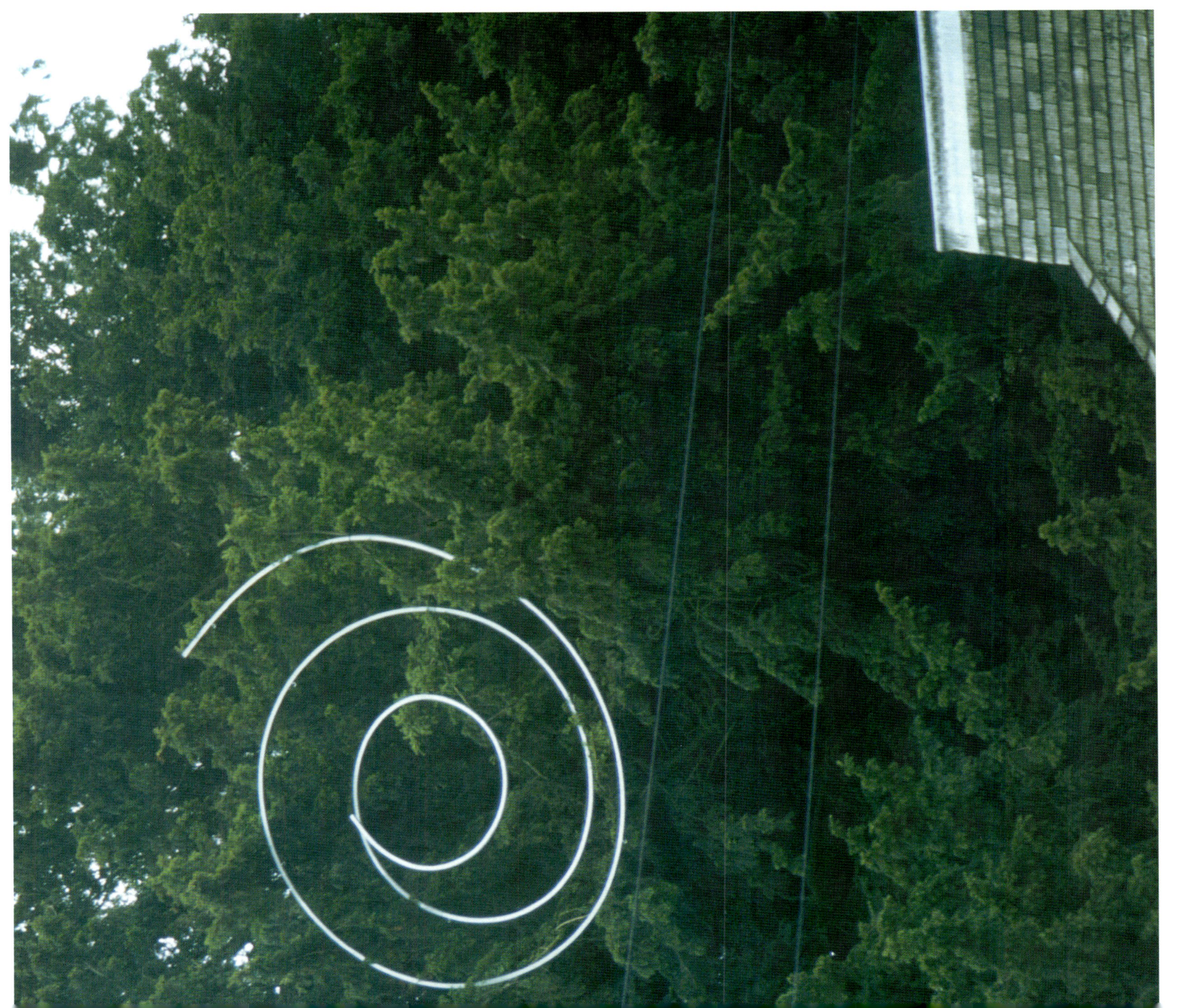

Lazy Wriggle 1992
Aluminium
20m high
Yorkshire Sculpture Park

The piece titled *Lazy Wriggle*, 1992, is also part of this sculptural family, and holds a particular interest to me as a landscape architect, because the beech tree chosen for its location had been storm damaged. Branches had been lost from one side of the trunk and the canopy was unbalanced. Such a tree might live on for many years, but could never regain its proper form. It is unlikely that Colin's sculptural addition harmed the tree in any way whatsoever, but in an aesthetic sense *Lazy Wriggle* was a kind of prosthesis, restoring an overall harmony.

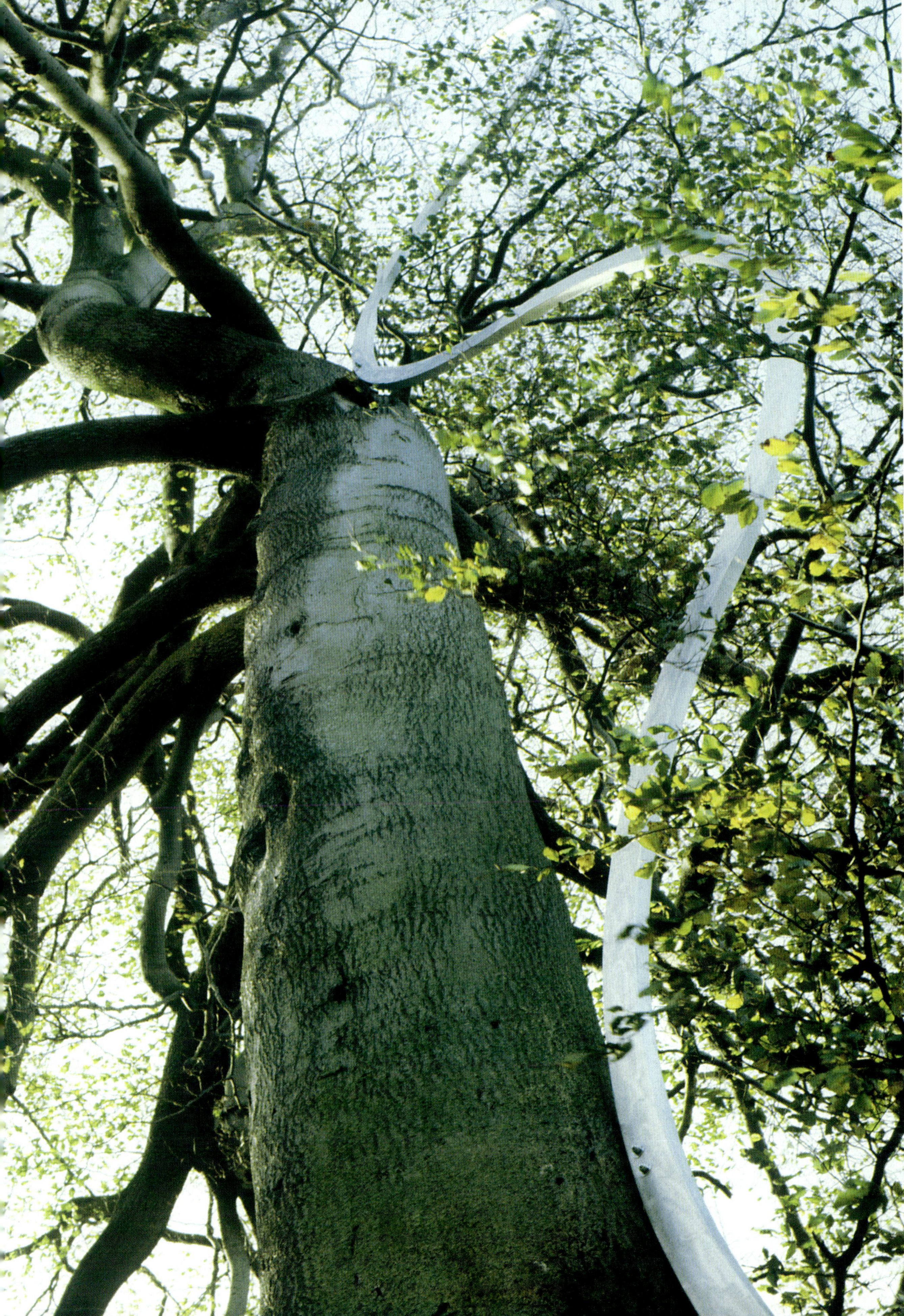

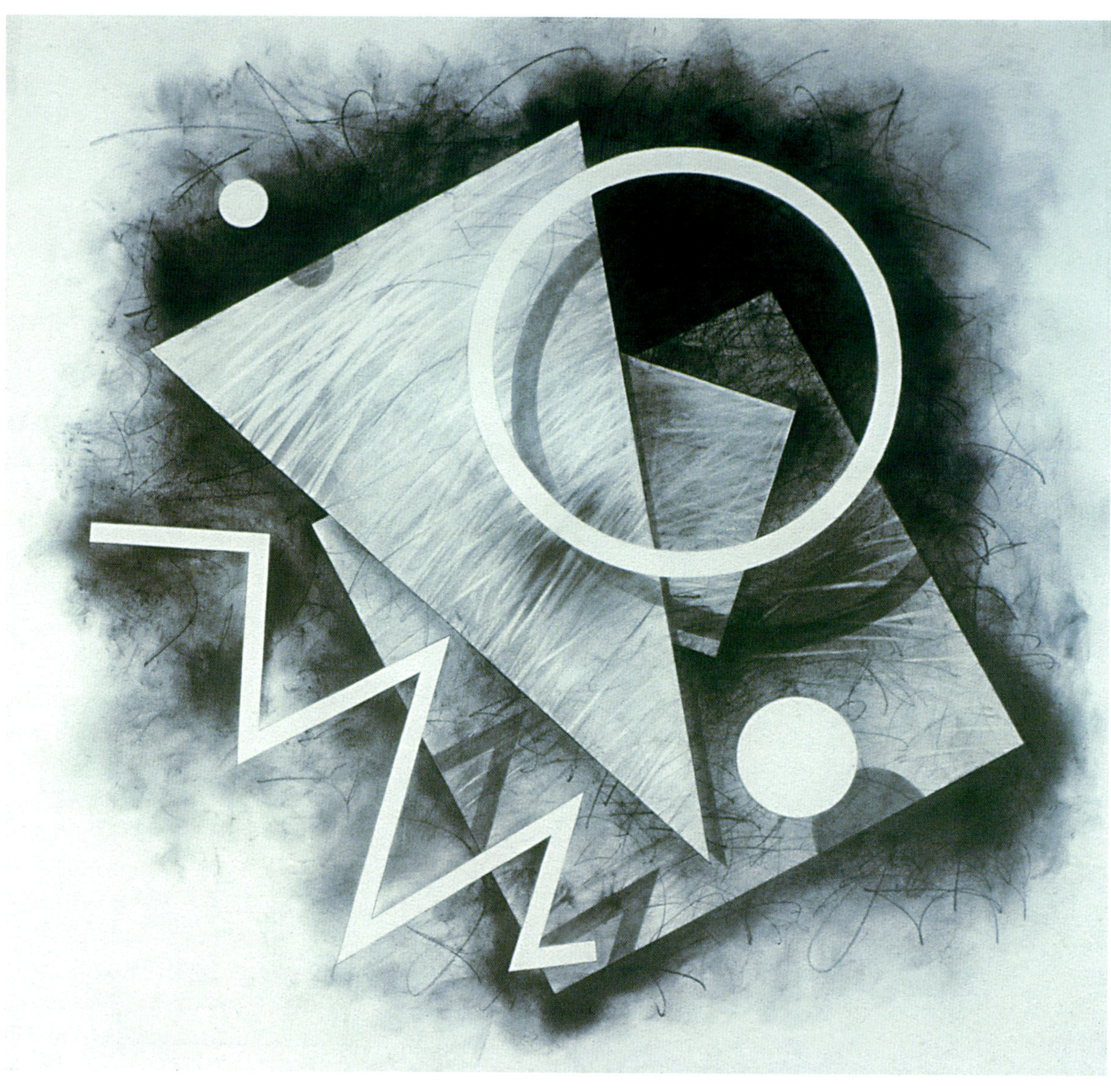

Rural and Urban

Although much of Colin's work has been developed and placed in countryside settings, and though he has chosen to live in remote Northumbrian locations, in no sense could he be described as a ruralist. The dialogue between the natural and the man-made or between the city and the countryside is rarely absent from his work. Hardly any of the British countryside is 'natural' if we mean by that 'unaltered by humankind' and even those parts which we romanticise most, such as Snowdonia, the Lake District or the Highlands, must be seen as human artifacts freighted with cultural associations. Sculptures like *Ting*, *Stonecone* or *Eye*, prompt us to confront some of our easy assumptions about the countryside, who it belongs to and what it is for. Why should a steel hoop be any more out of place than a barbed-wire fence? What are the essential differences between a drystone sheep fold and a conical pillar of sandstone? At the same time, Colin does not believe that the countryside should be littered with pieces of art and is cautious in his own practice. He recognises the values which people associate with the wilder landscapes of our coasts and hills and does not want to steal these places from them by colonising them with his art. Many of his rural pieces have been sited within recognised outdoor collections and all of his work is placed with discretion and sensitivity towards the existing qualities of place.

Born on Tyneside, Colin was originally destined for a career in industry. Apprenticed to the National Coal Board he qualified in mechanical engineering and is equally at home in the workshop and the drawing office as in the studio. His skill as a draughtsman is evident in an early work like *Cup Dreaming*, which includes a conventional plan view of a teacup and saucer, but it is greatly developed in later drawings, such as *Shell*, 1982, *Pool,* 1991, and *Starcone*, 1996, where subtleties of form and depth are explored in texture and shading. On an exchange visit to Australia in 1995 he made many drawings using the red earth of the locality, including *Four Corners* and the *Earth* sequence. Some thought that he had been unduly influenced by aboriginal traditions, but it is quite evident that these pieces use the same personal lexicon that Colin had developed in England at the time of *Pool*. Perhaps the confusion was understandable, for like aboriginal art, Colin's work is concerned with the multi-layered complexity of landscape and the human relationship to it.

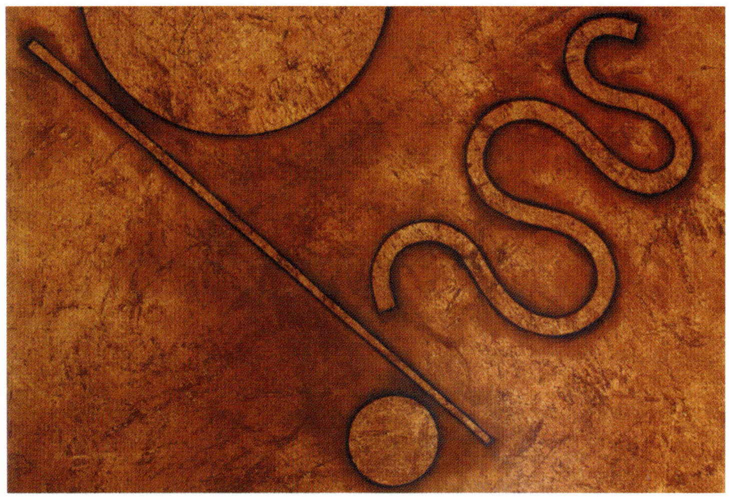

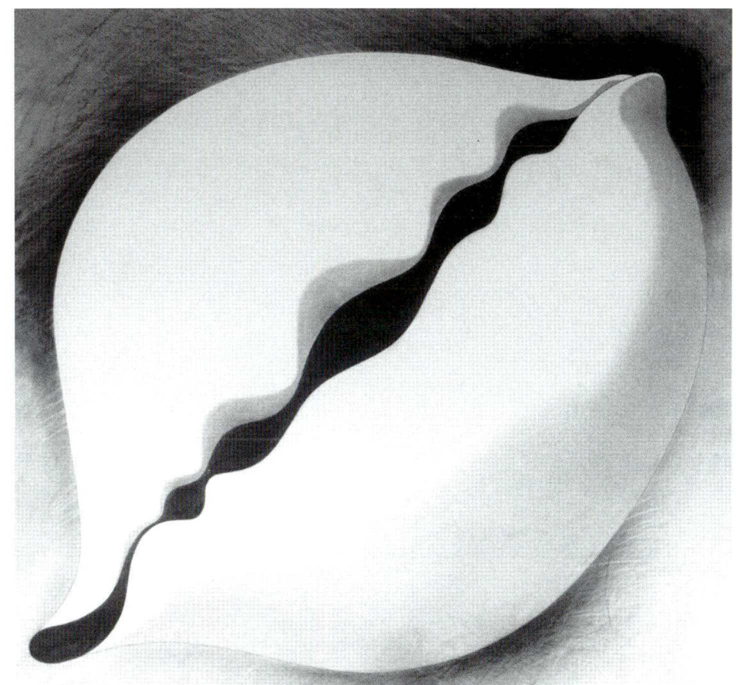

Left: **Pool 1** 1991
Graphite on paper
50 x 50cm

Top right: **Earth**

Bottom right: **Shell II**
Graphite on paper
150 x 150cm

Following page: **Four Corners** 1995
Earth and charcoal on paper
60 x 60 x 240cm

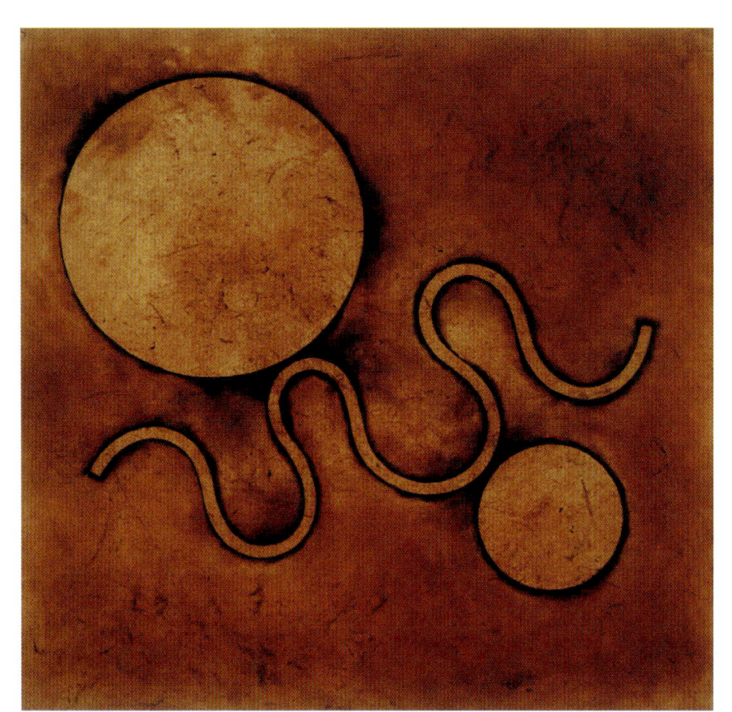
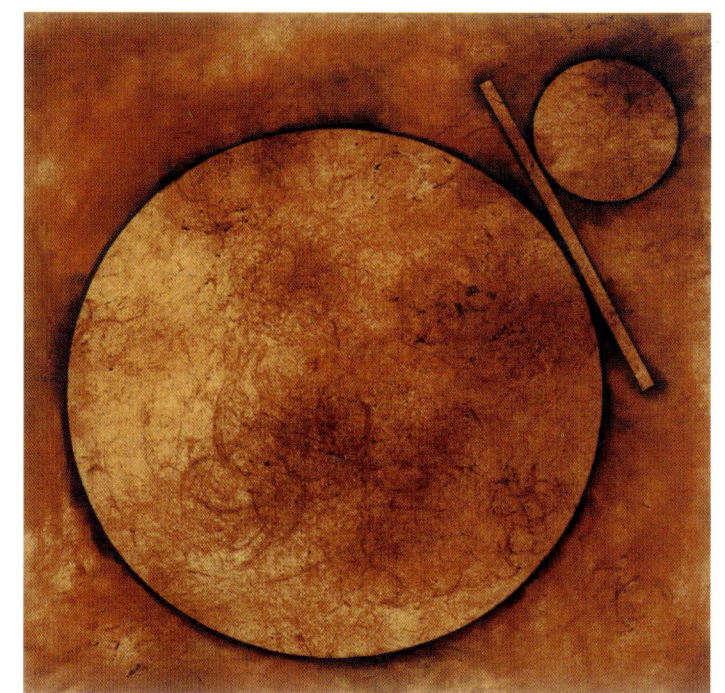

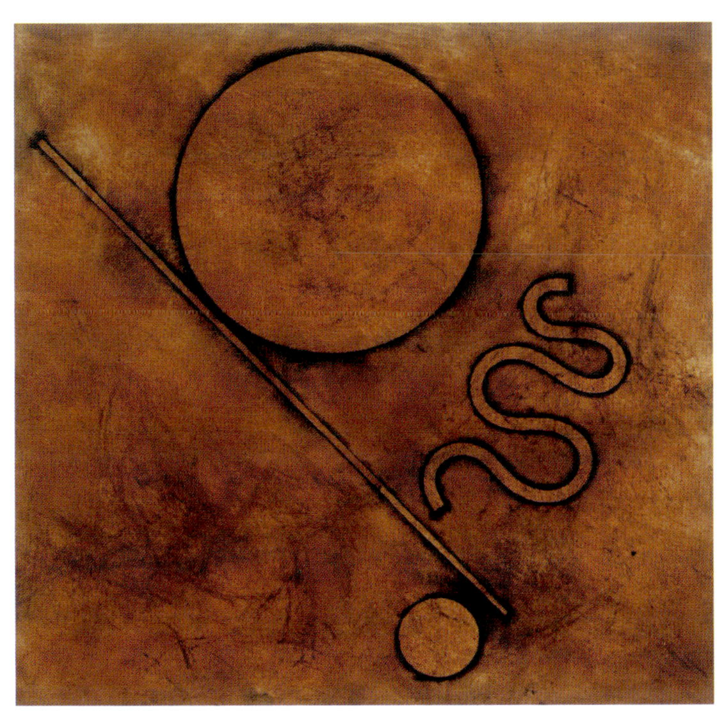 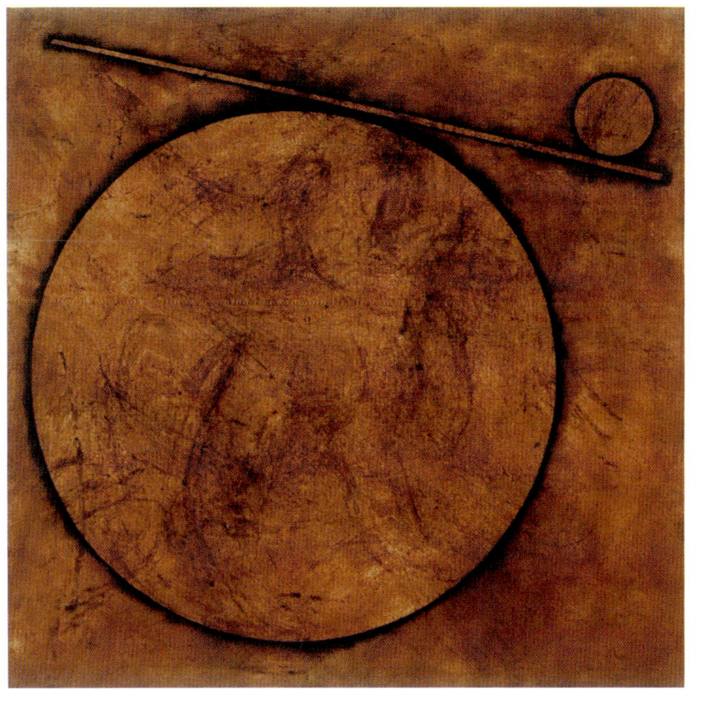

Earthcone 1995
Earth
90 x 54cm

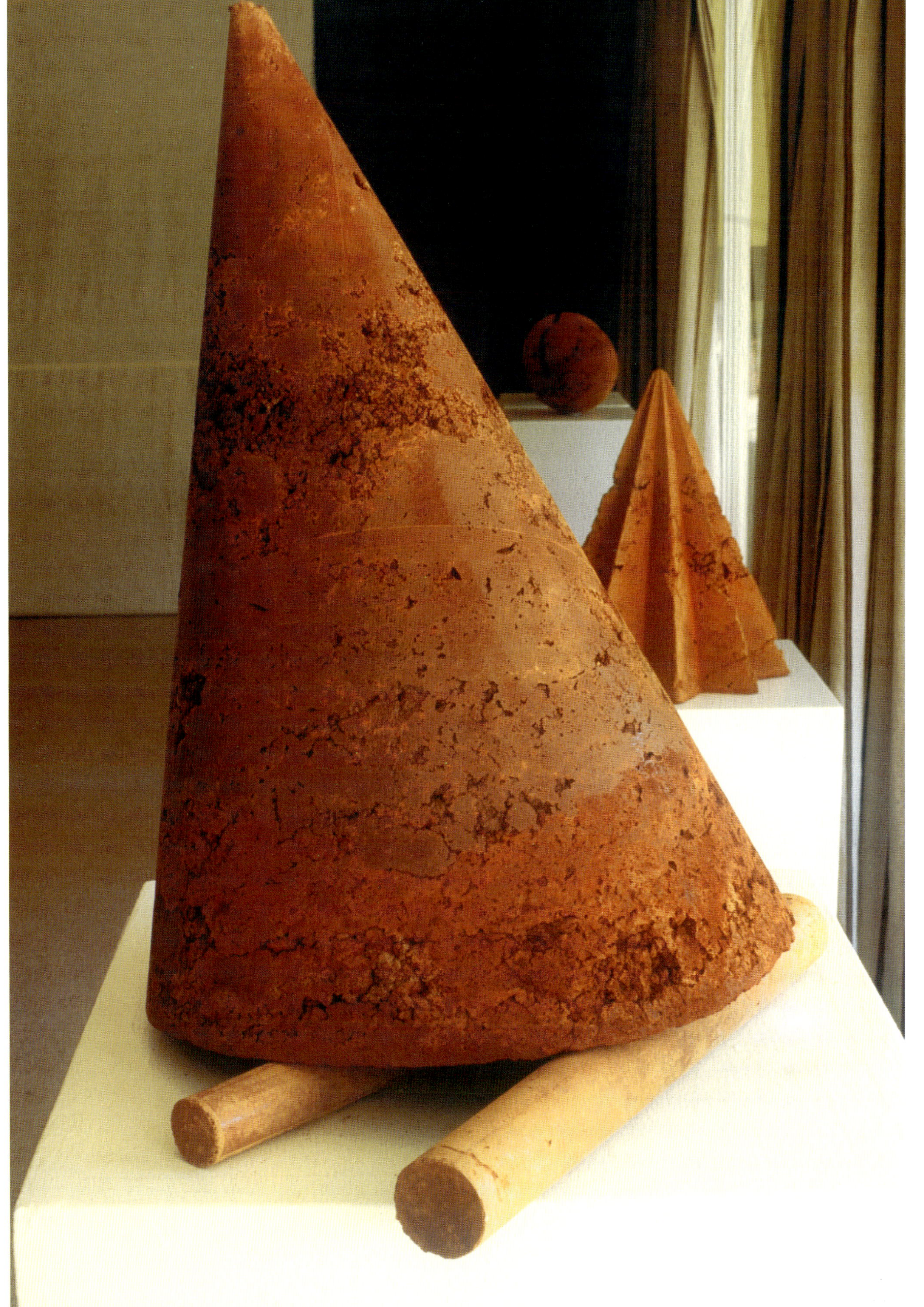

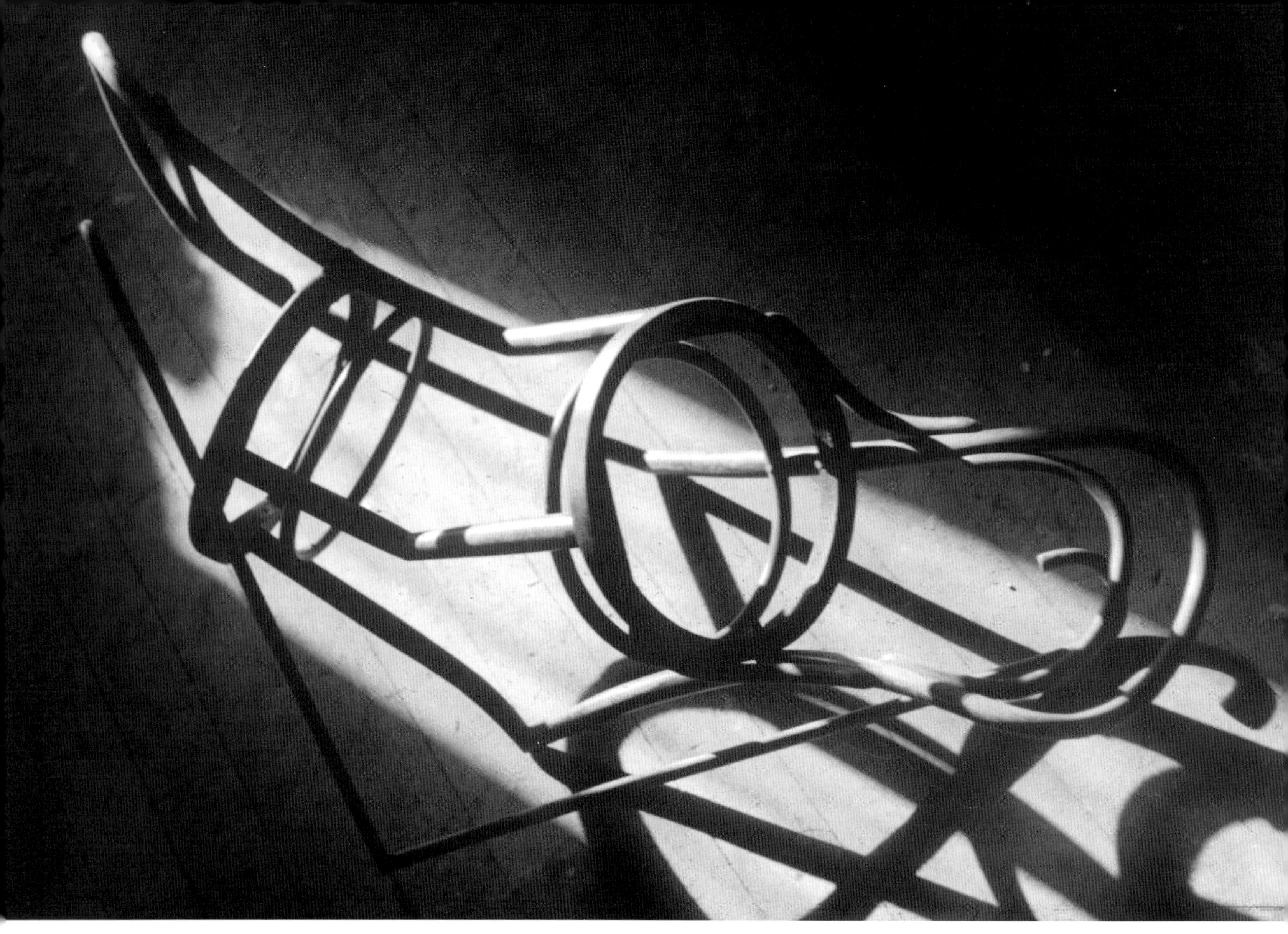

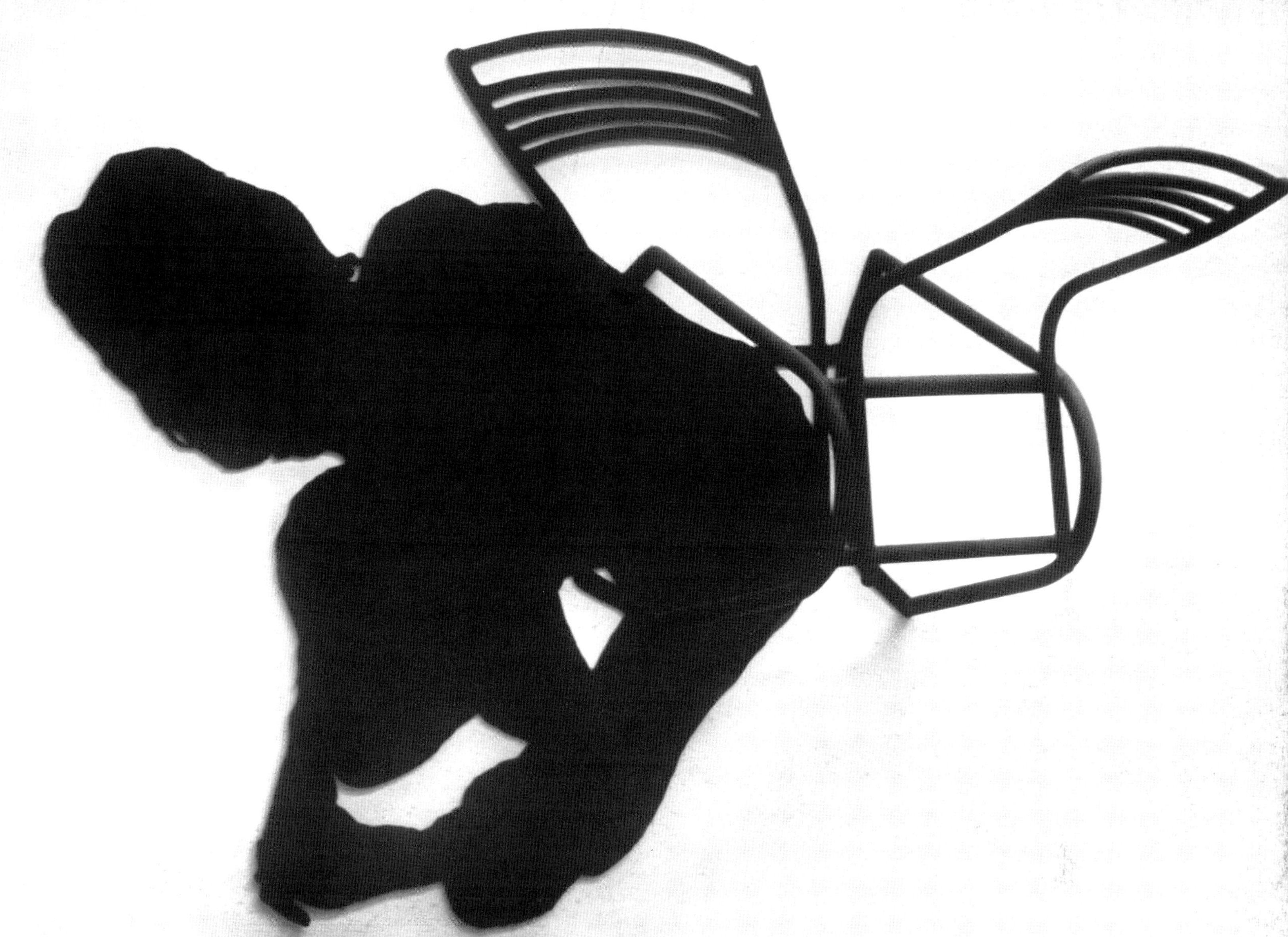

Left: **Dictionary of Lies** 1980
Beech
150 x 80 x 80cm

Right: **Thinking About A Man Thinking** 1978
Steel and formica
120 x 120cm

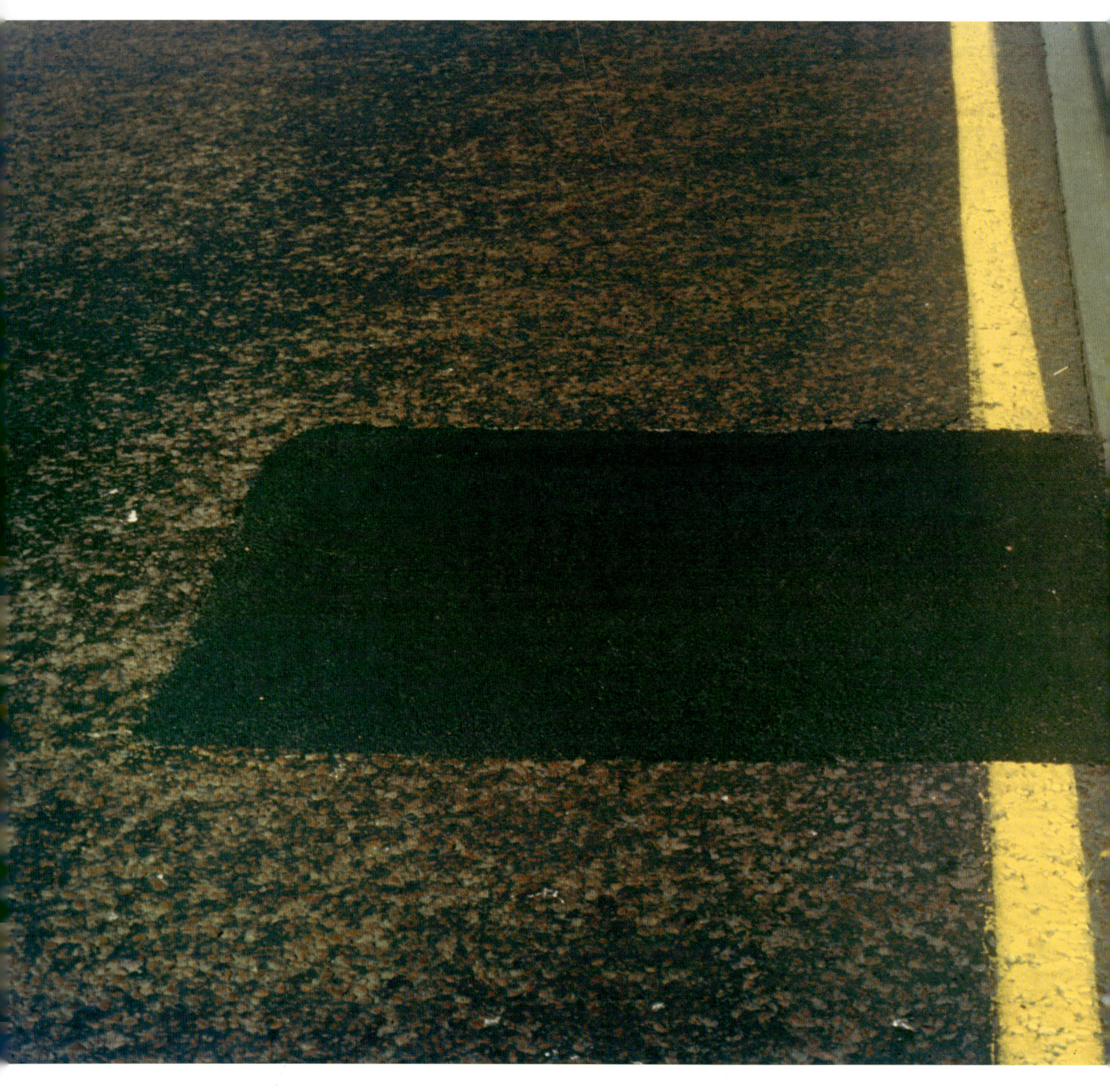

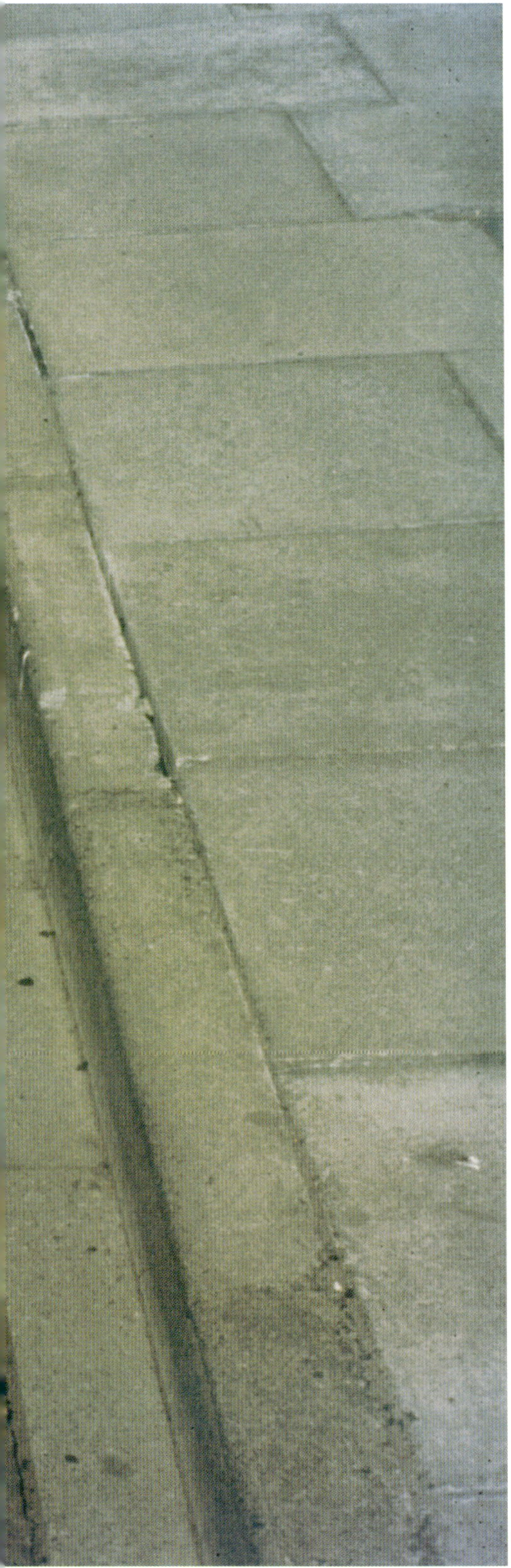

Having made the transition from engineering apprentice to artist, Colin initially avoided steel as a material because it was too familiar. He chose to work with less processed, less predictable substances like wood and stone. These more natural materials had a life about them which was to be investigated and understood. He was intrigued by the imperfect and the accidental which he saw in the world around him, like roads patched with tarmac, paving slabs crudely cut to fit around kerbs or graffiti squeezed into place. These were the antithesis of the engineered, but each marked an episode of human involvement with material and environment; each was a trace or clue and each told a story.

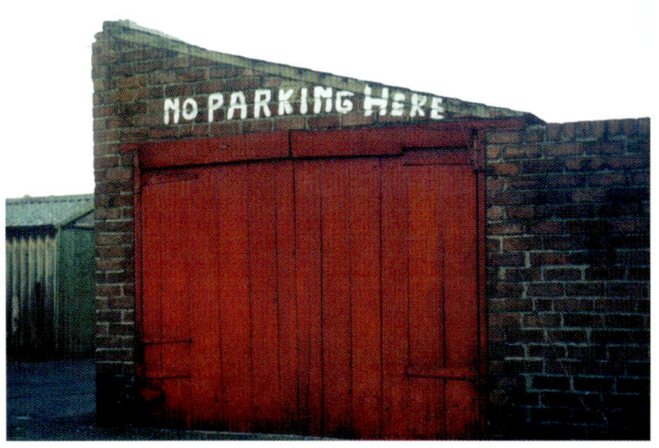

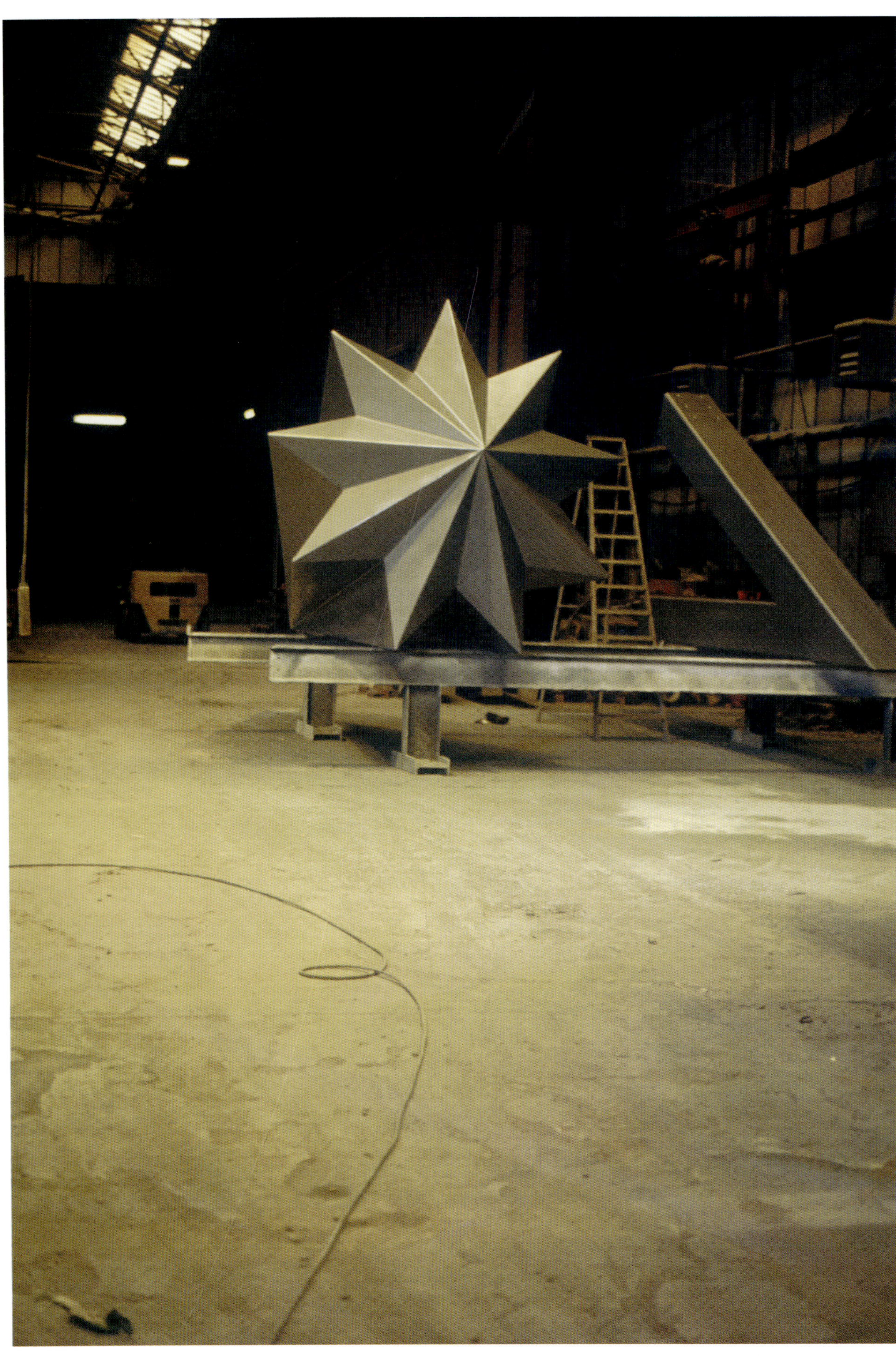

There is a parallel here with the work of the landscape architect, for although many designers share Colin's fascination for the geometrical and the perfectly made, they are usually setting themselves up for a disappointment. Vagaries of site, the stubbornness of materials, and deficiencies in craftsmanship often defeat the Platonic vision. On the other hand, it is the accumulation of small changes, accommodations and modifications that contribute to the character of a place. Landscape architects often refer to the *genius loci* or 'spirit of the place', originally a Roman notion, but one which was prominent in discussions about landscape aesthetics in eighteenth century England. There is currently a widespread interest in local distinctiveness as an antidote to the globalising uniformity of international capitalism. Colin's work sets up a dialectic between universal geometries and the nitty-gritty realities of particular objects in particular places.

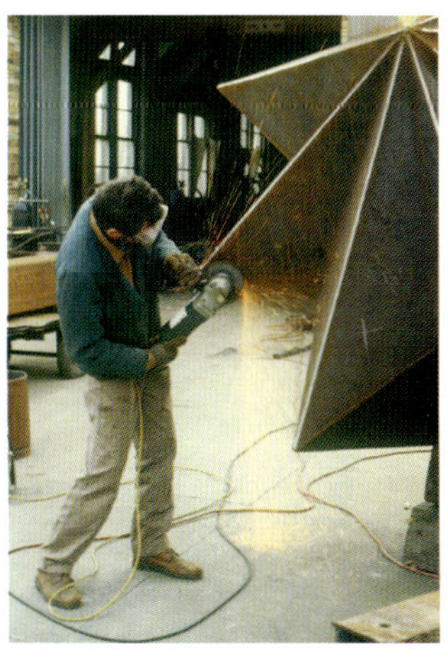

Left: **Edge to Edge** 1992
(work in progress)

Above: **Starcone 2** 1992
(work in progress)

Ting marked Colin's return to steel, and the reassertion of formal geometries. He confesses to feeling uneasy about claiming the authorship for *Ting*, because it employs a formal geometry, and such geometries have been part of Western traditions of thought since Pythagoras and Euclid and in this sense belong to us all. Later, in the *Swirl*, *Wriggle*, *Ripple* cycle, he explored the possibilities of using aluminium. In 1992 he was commissioned to produce a large piece, *Edge to Edge*, for the gateway to a new industrial park in Merthyr Tydfil, on the site of a reclaimed steelworks, which gave him the opportunity to investigate a complex new form, *Starcone*, 1992/1996. As its name suggests, this was a combination of star and cone and it is reminiscent of a drilling bit. For this commission Colin was able to draw upon his background to produce sculptures which reflected both his knowledge of industrial forms and his studies of natural objects like fruits and seeds. The other main element in *Edge to Edge* is the enormous *Coil*, 1992, which leads the mind to associations with industrial springs or electrical components. Colin also refers to these elements as "the fruits of industry" indicating their connection with other work from around this time, like *Pineball*, *Rope Ball*, and *Whirling Beans*. There is also a connection with the fanciful *Apple Pie,* 1990, a proposal for a series of giant inflatables for Gateshead Garden Festival, and with *Starball*, 1995, another sophisticated object inspired by the form of a seed, which as yet only exists in drawings and as a maquette.

Below: **Starcone I & II** 1996
Charcoal on paper
90 x 90cm (each)

Opposite: **Starcone** 1992
Galvanised steel
26 x 14cm

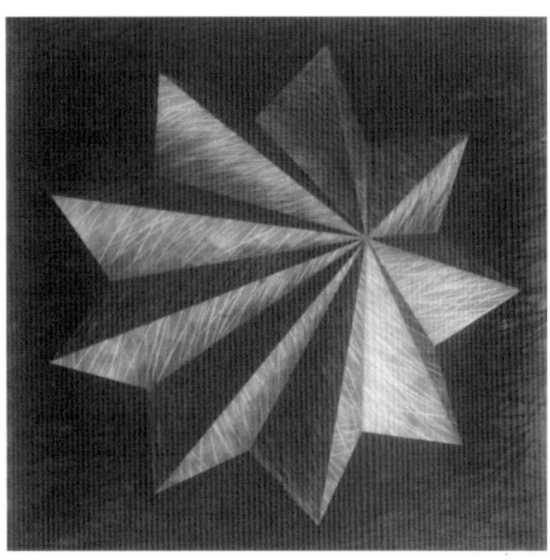
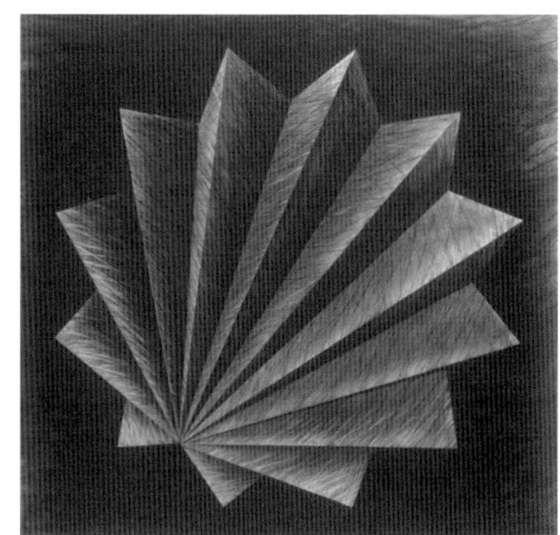

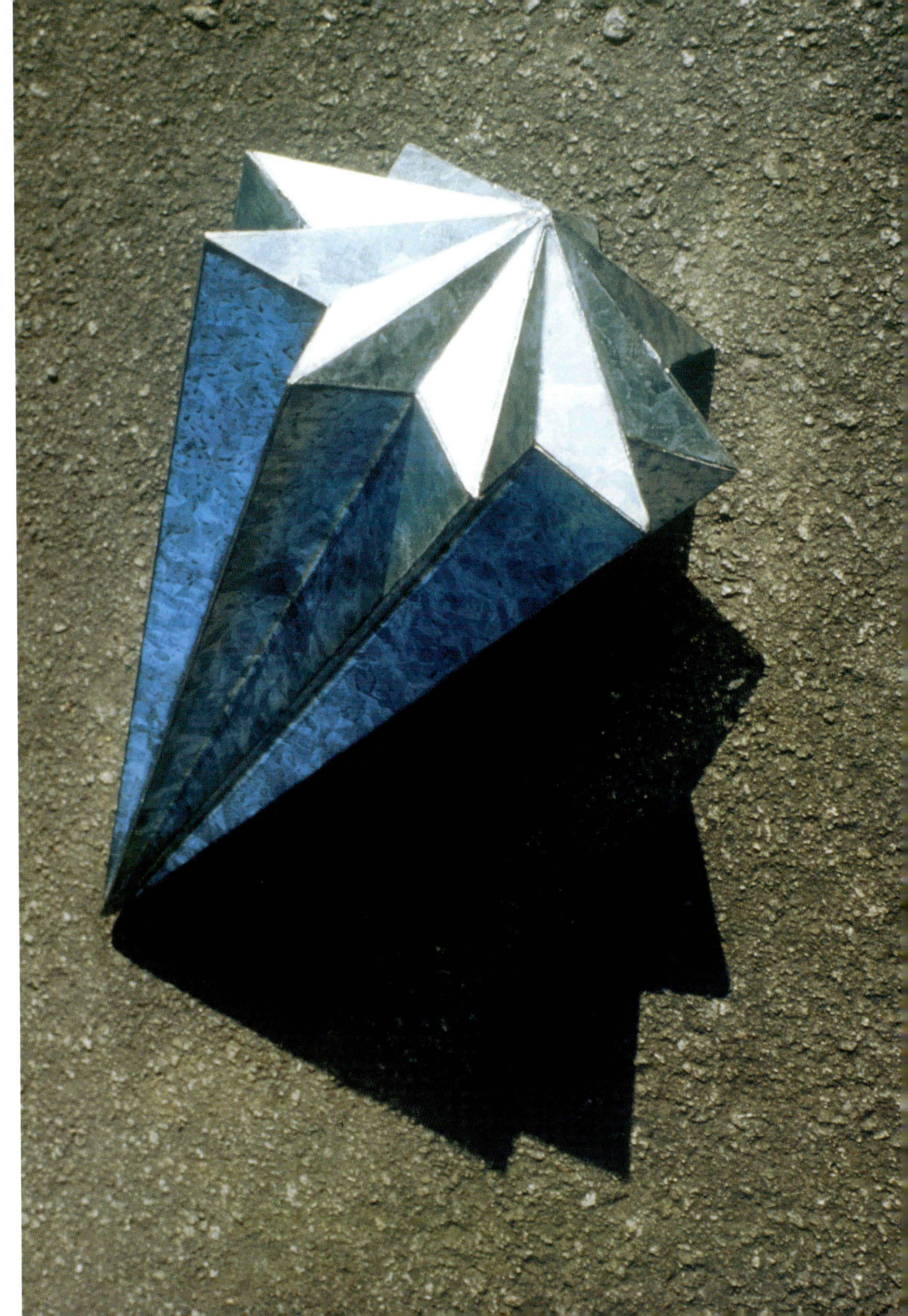

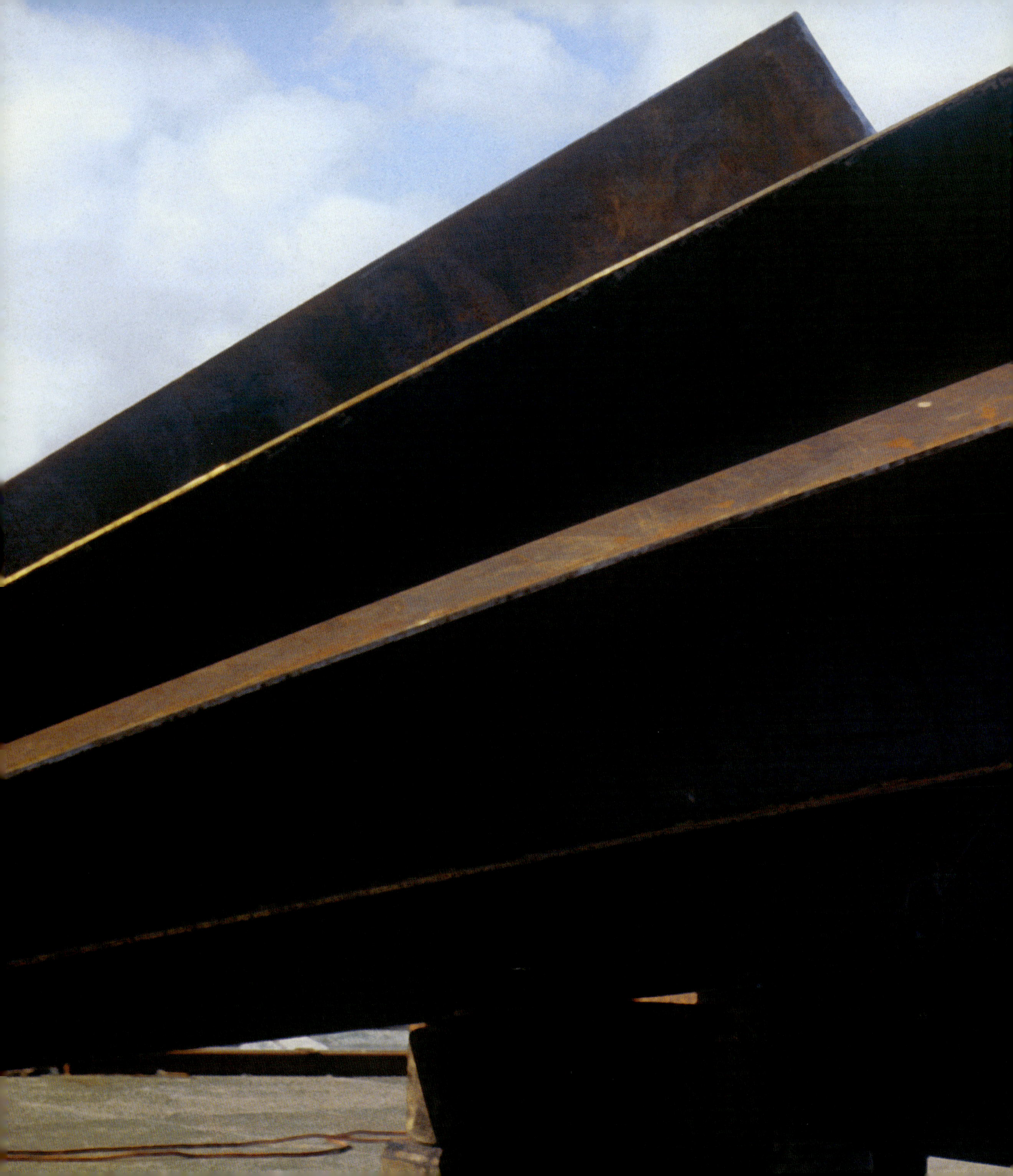

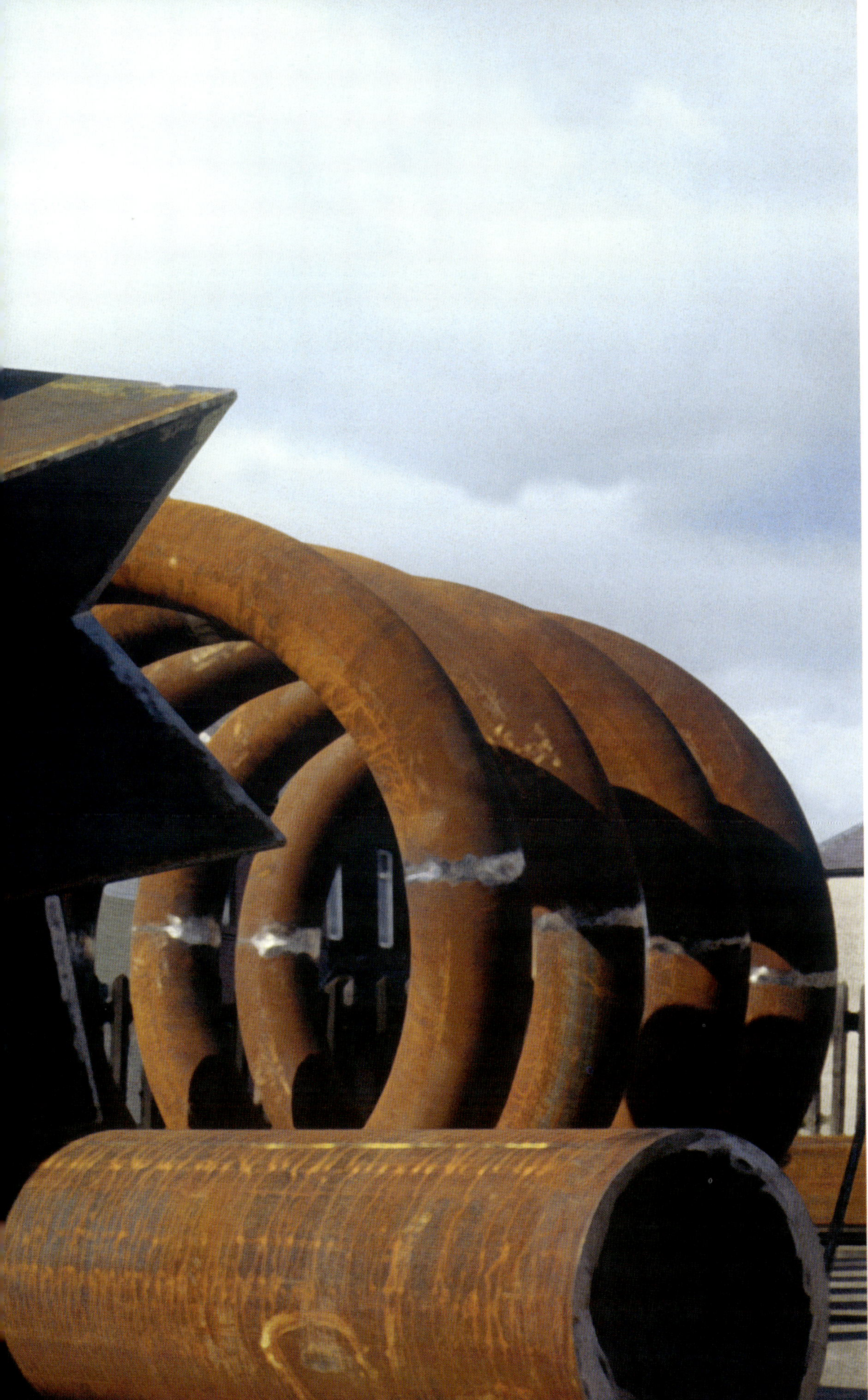

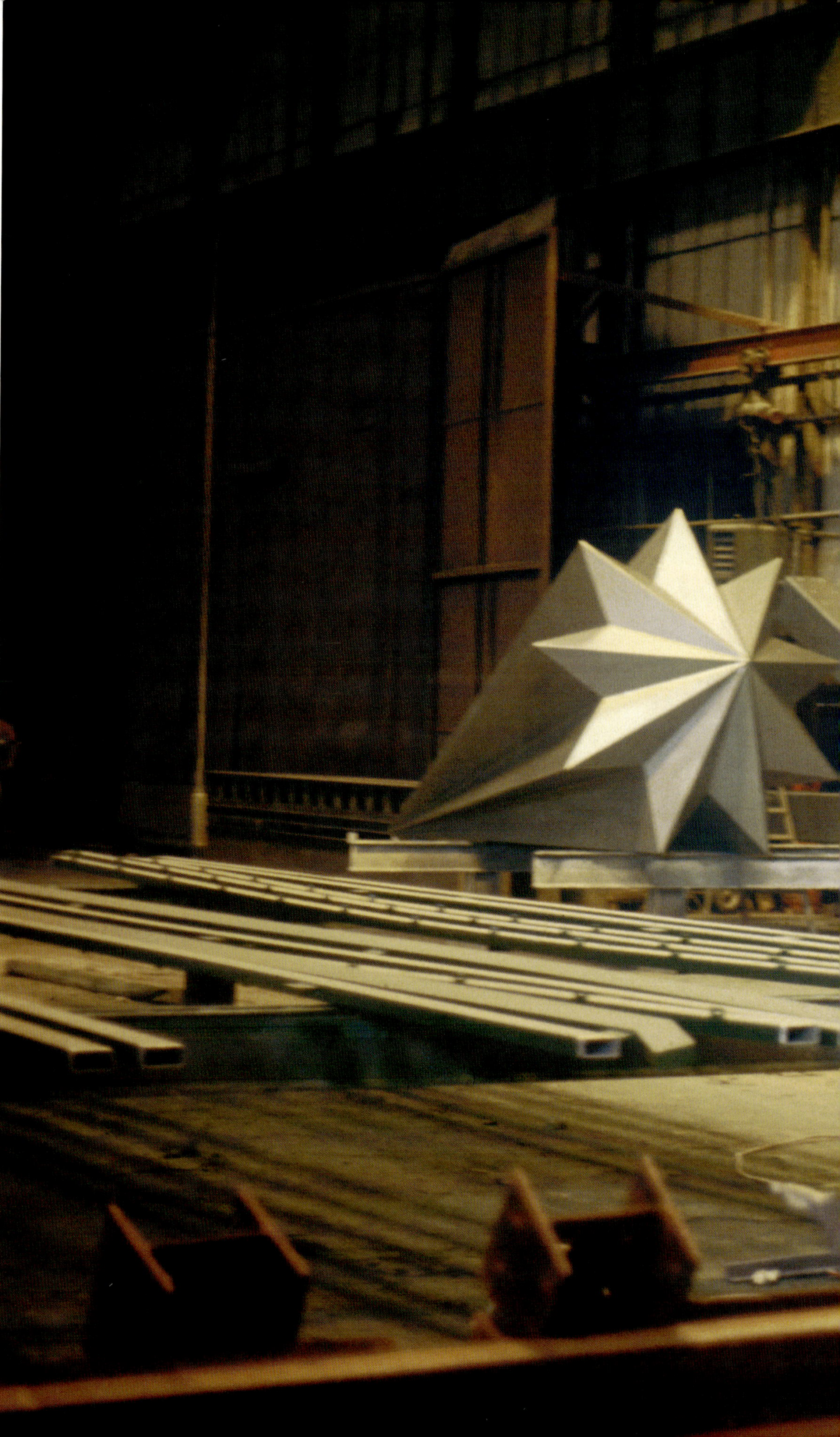

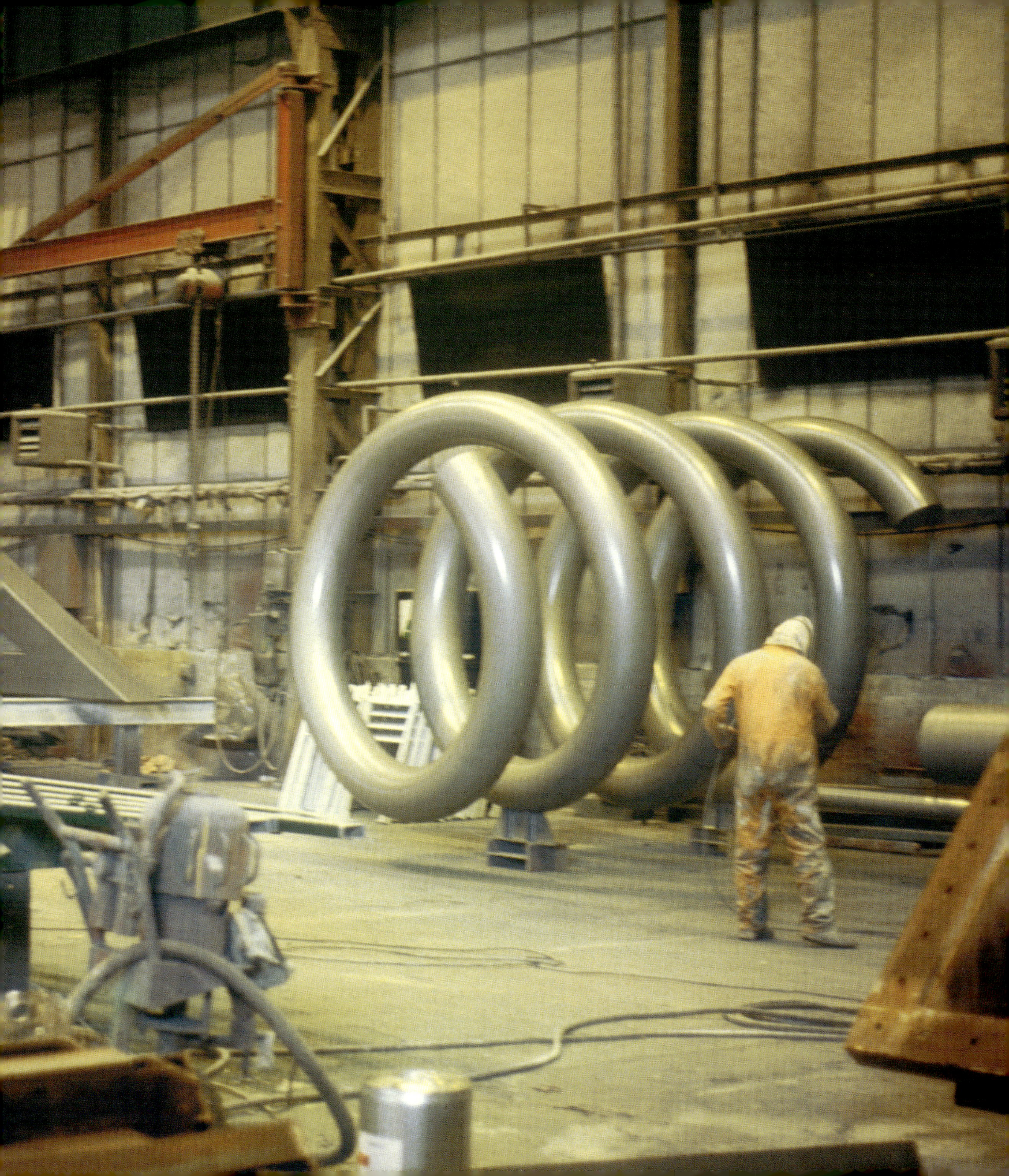

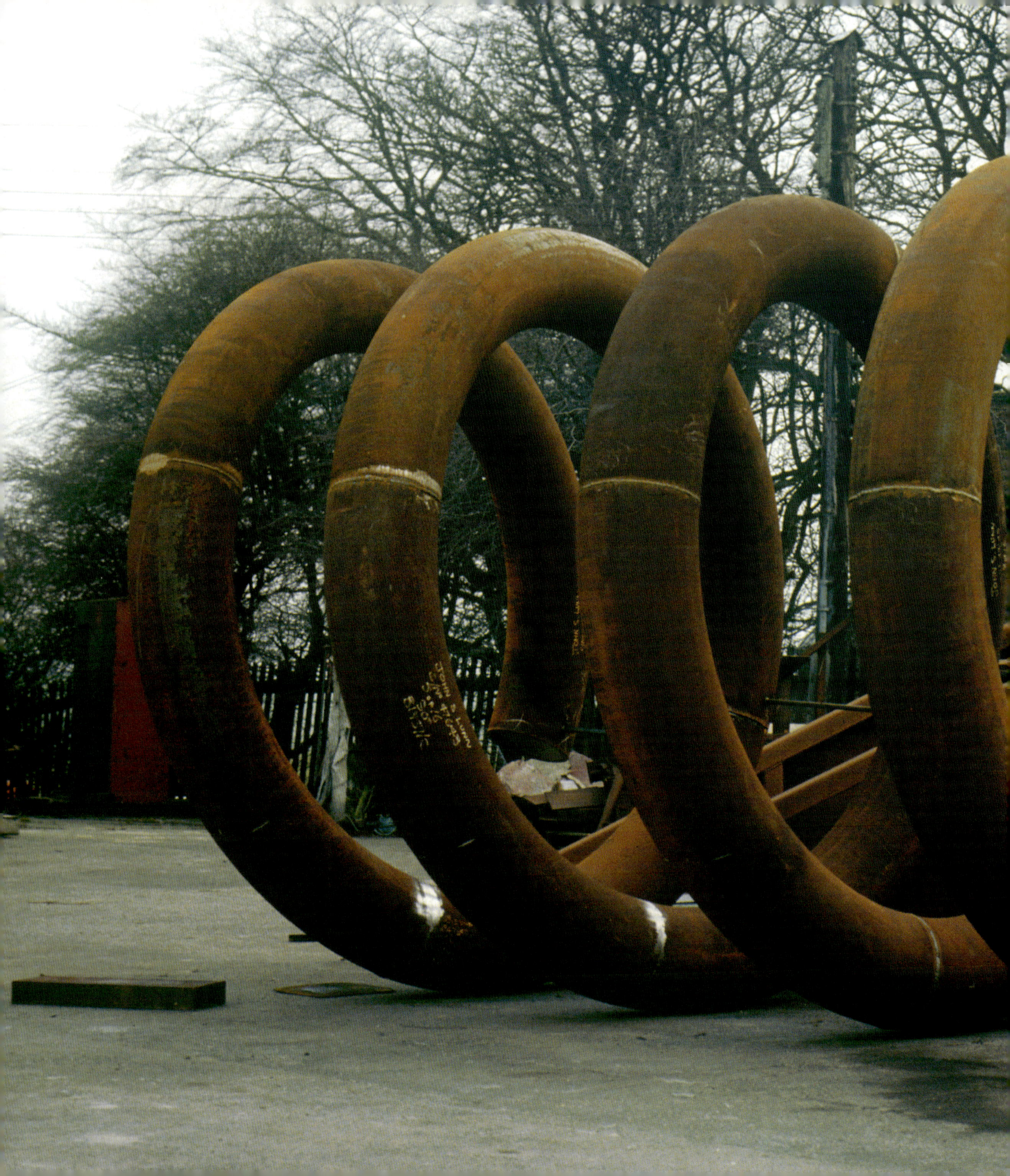

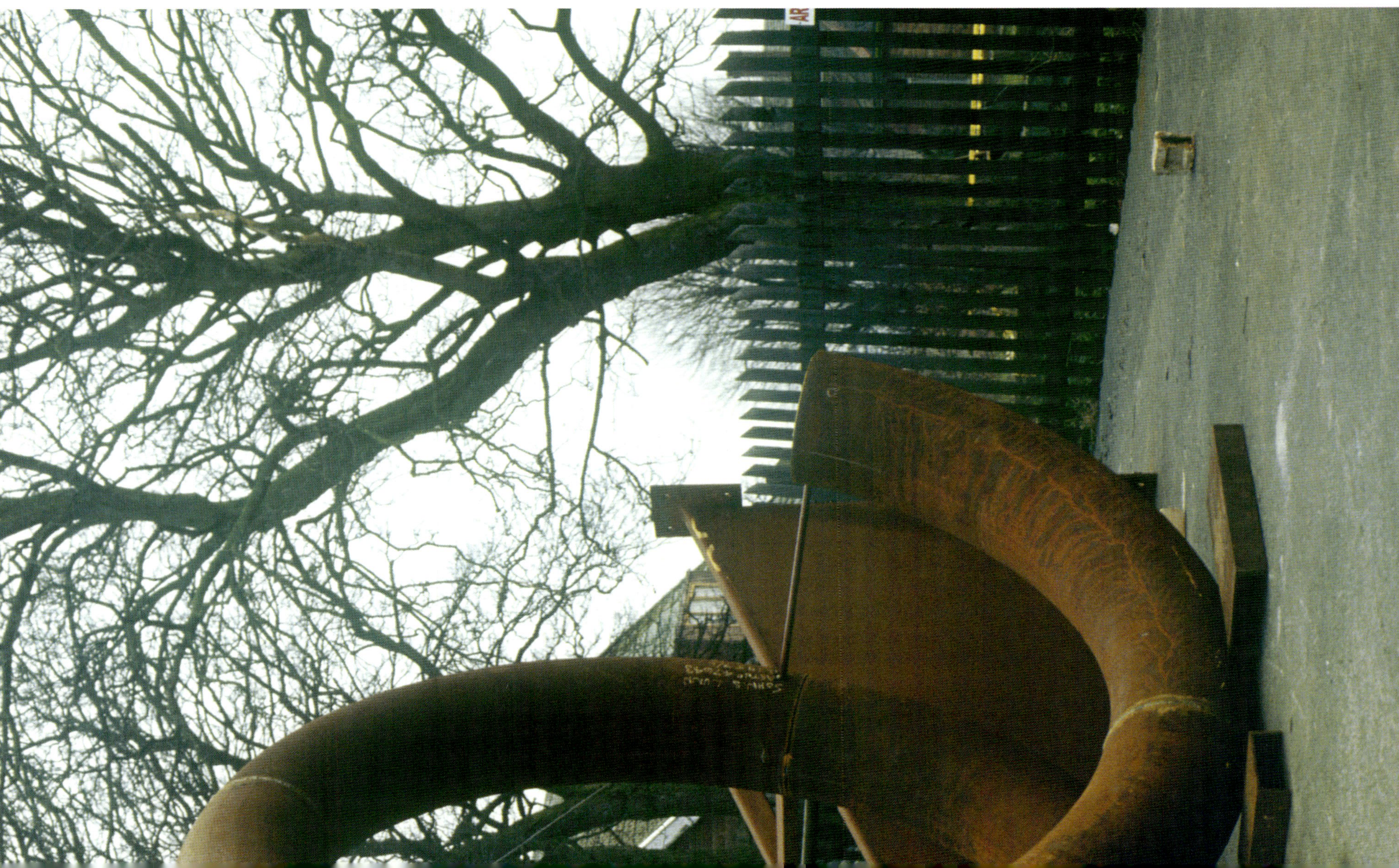

AR

Edge to Edge 5 1992
Painted steel
14m high

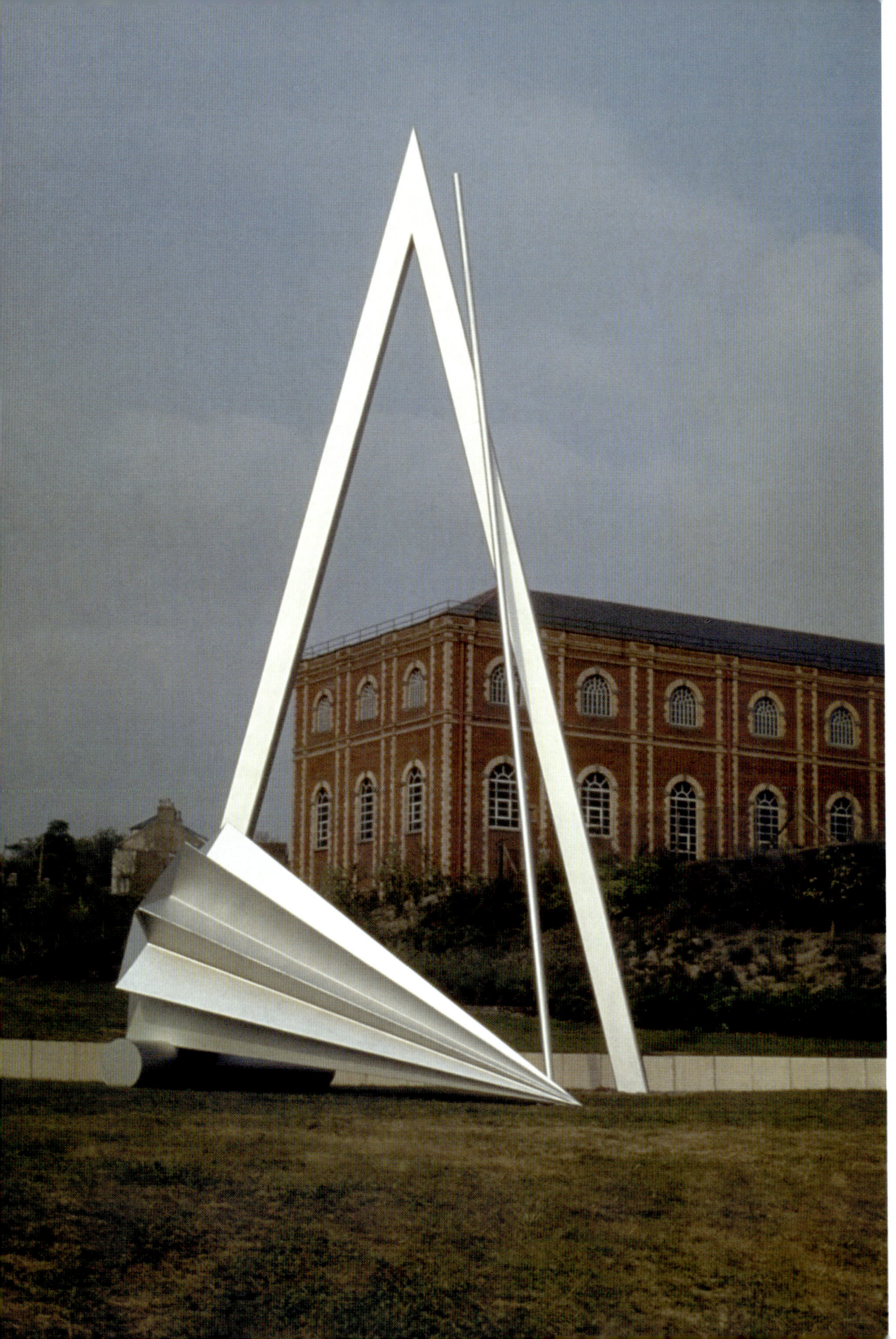

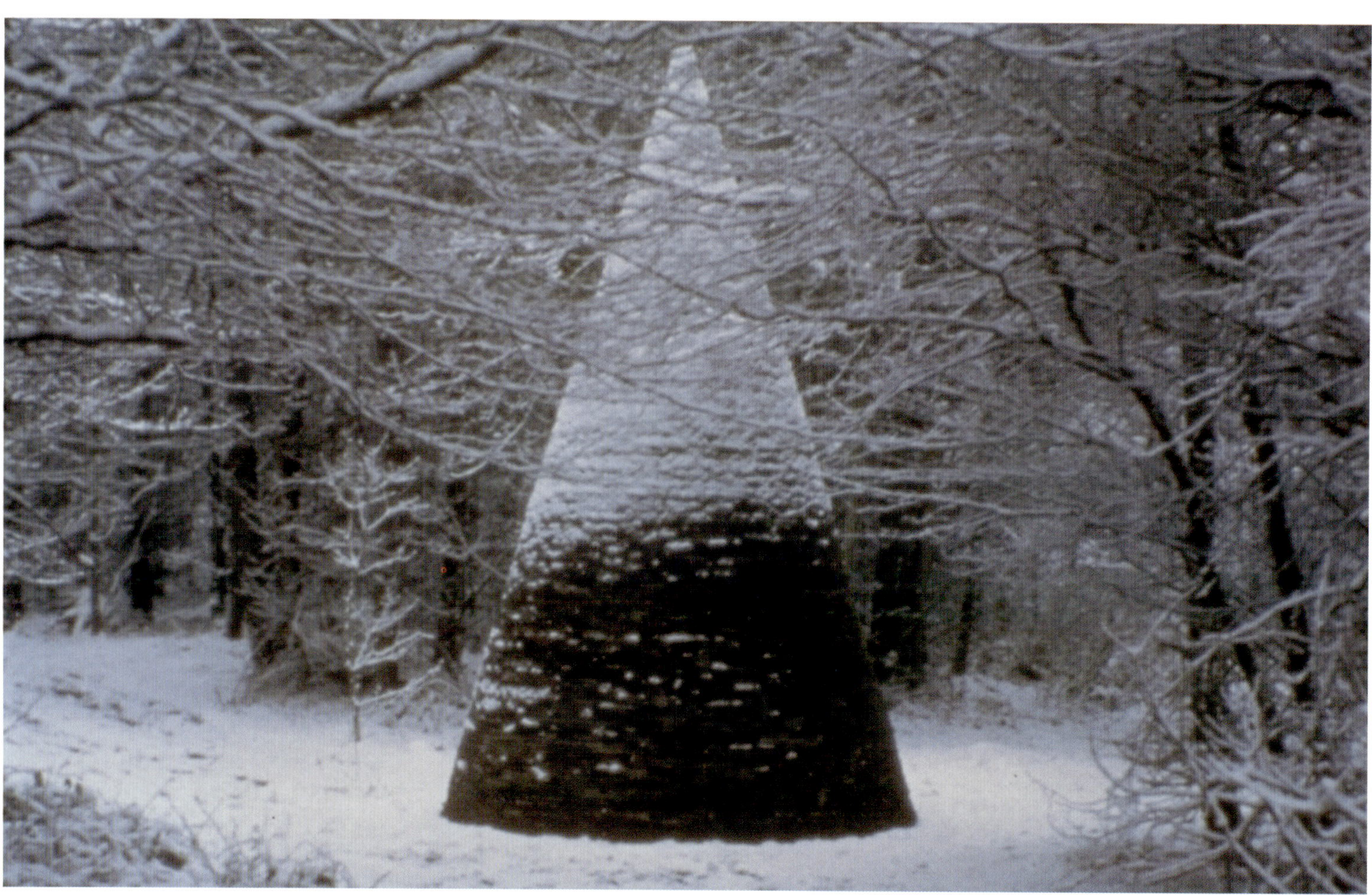

Stonecone 1995
Split sandstone
500 x 300cm Ø
Beamish, County Durham

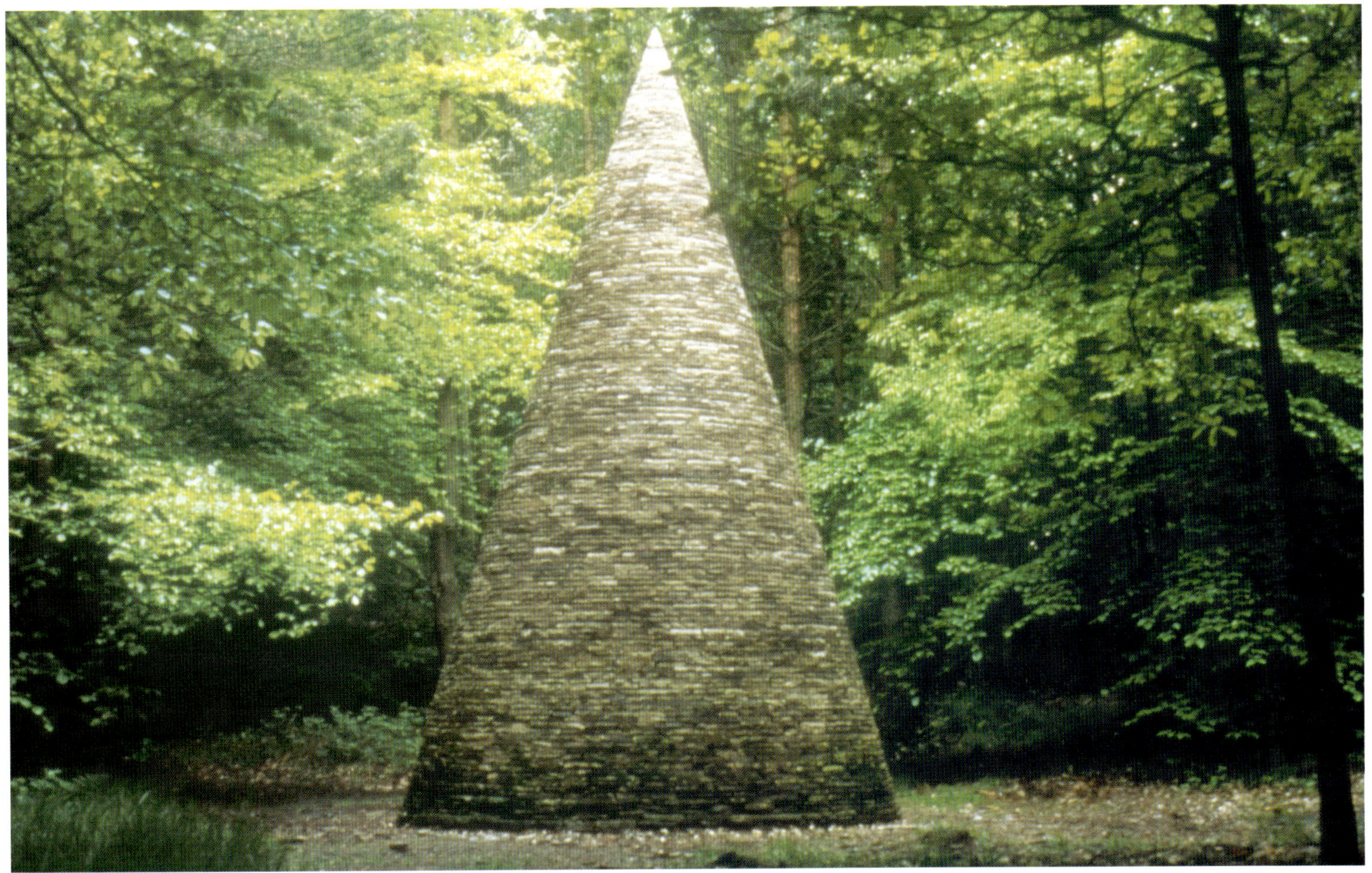

Peaks and Cones

By the mid 1990s large-scale sculptural works in the landscape were becoming a dominant aspect of Colin's practice. From 1994-1996 he was part-time sculptor-in-residence in the Great North Forest, one of 12 community forests being developed on the edge of English towns by the Countryside Agency in association with the Forestry Commission. The Great North Forest has a record of commissioning artists to work in its area. The placing of artworks into the woodland is seen as a way of stimulating people to ask questions: "Why is this thing here?", "What does it mean?", "Why is it in this place?", which will lead on to deeper questions about their lives, their locality and their connections with the environment. Colin's original idea was to build a series of cones which would march across the landscape, but there were so many problems with land

ownership that only one was built. This is *Stonecone*, which stands in a woodland at Eden Hill close to the Beamish Open Air Museum. Here his wish to locate the piece in a secluded location was respected, so that the visitor comes upon it unawares, which adds to the mystery of the object.

Colin built the piece from split sandstone. On learning that local rock-climbers were waiting to climb it, his mischievous response was to make a cavity near the top and fill it with honey so that the bees which had troubled him during construction might make it their home. One of the most successful and satisfying aspects of the cone is the way in which its character is transformed by the seasons. In summer it has a welcomingly warm appearance against the light and feathery foliage of the glade; in winter it wears a white cap of snow which stands out against the blackness of the surrounding woods.

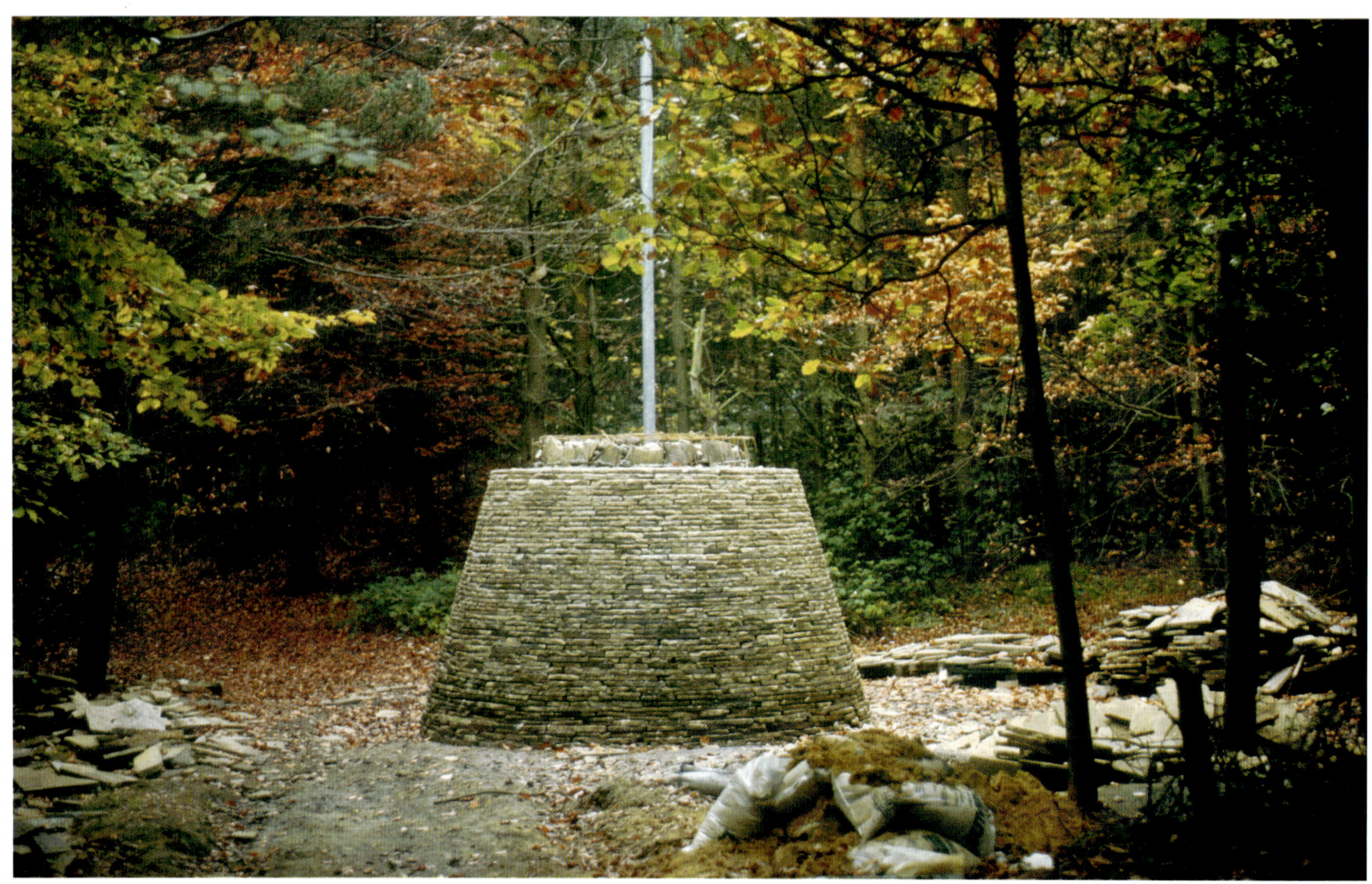

Stonecone 1995 (in progress)

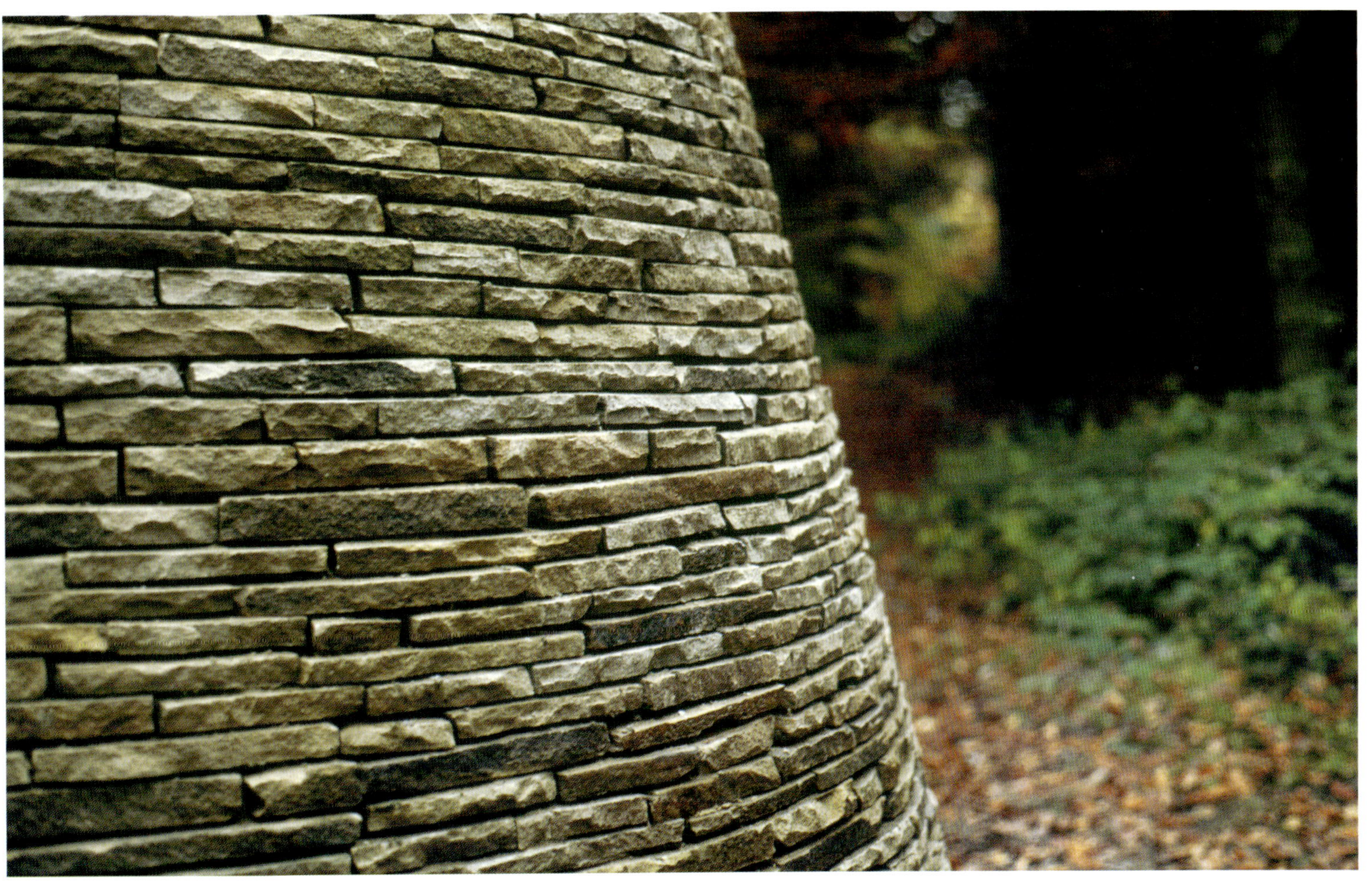

Peaks 1998
Split quarry tiles, resin and gold
700cm high
Royal Victoria Infirmary. Newcastle Upon Tyne

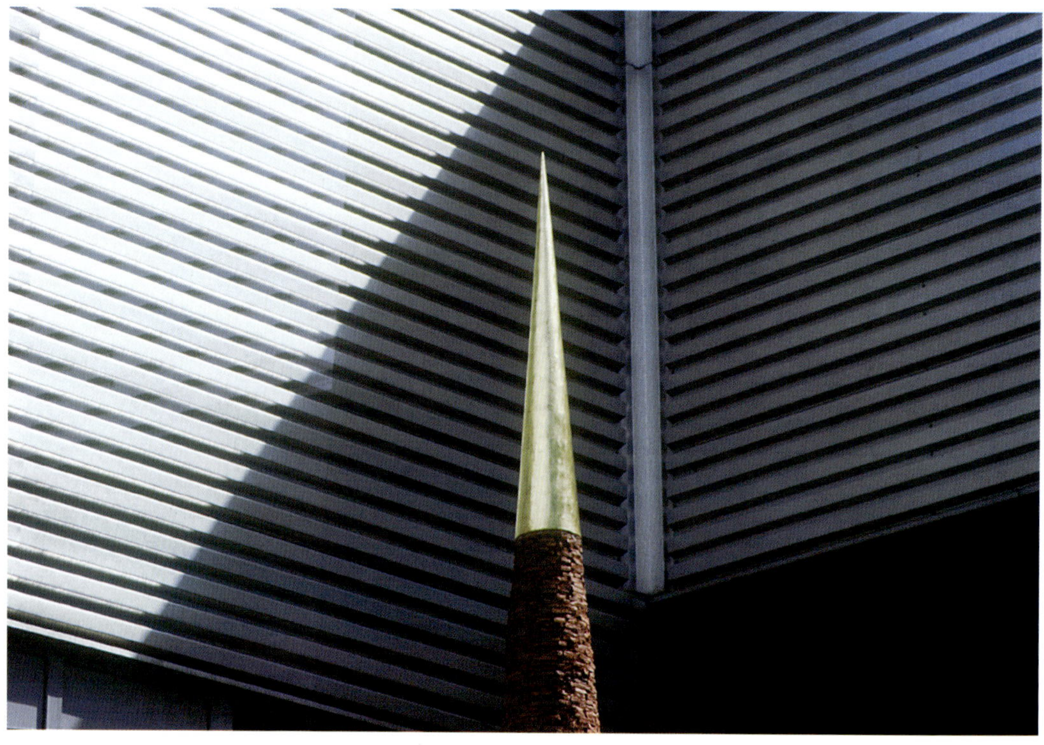

Commissions for further conical sculptures followed. The
piece known as *Peaks*, 1998, was made for a courtyard in
the Ophthalmology Department of Newcastle's Royal
Victoria Infirmary, and consists of three slender cones built
from split quarry tiles, the tallest being seven metres high.
Because the tips of the cones were too thin to be made in
this material, and because the primary audience for this
piece would have limited vision, he decided to cap them
with gold finials, which would glint in the sun against the
enclosed view of the sky. The surface texture of the cones
would also be pleasant and interesting to someone who
could not enjoy the visual aspects of the sculpture. The later
sculpture *Eye*, is akin to both *Stonecone* and *Peaks* although
it is situated next to a remote Scottish loch. The name of
the sculpture refers to a small hole through it for sighting
across the loch. Originally the work was conceived in two
parts; there was to have been a complementary piece
consisting of a split sphere with a triangular slot, which
would have been placed on the opposite side of the loch,
setting up an optical relationship between the two works.

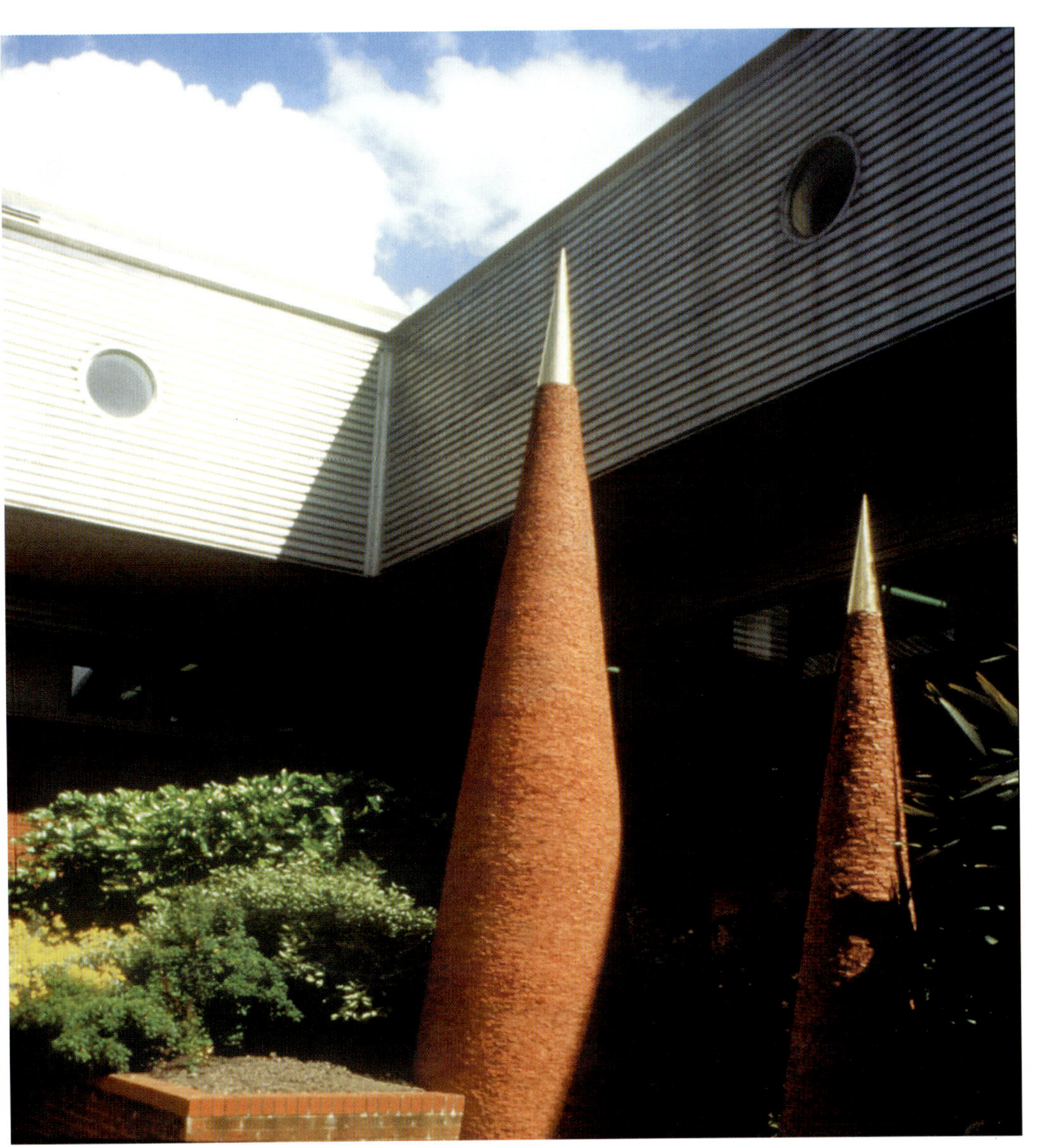

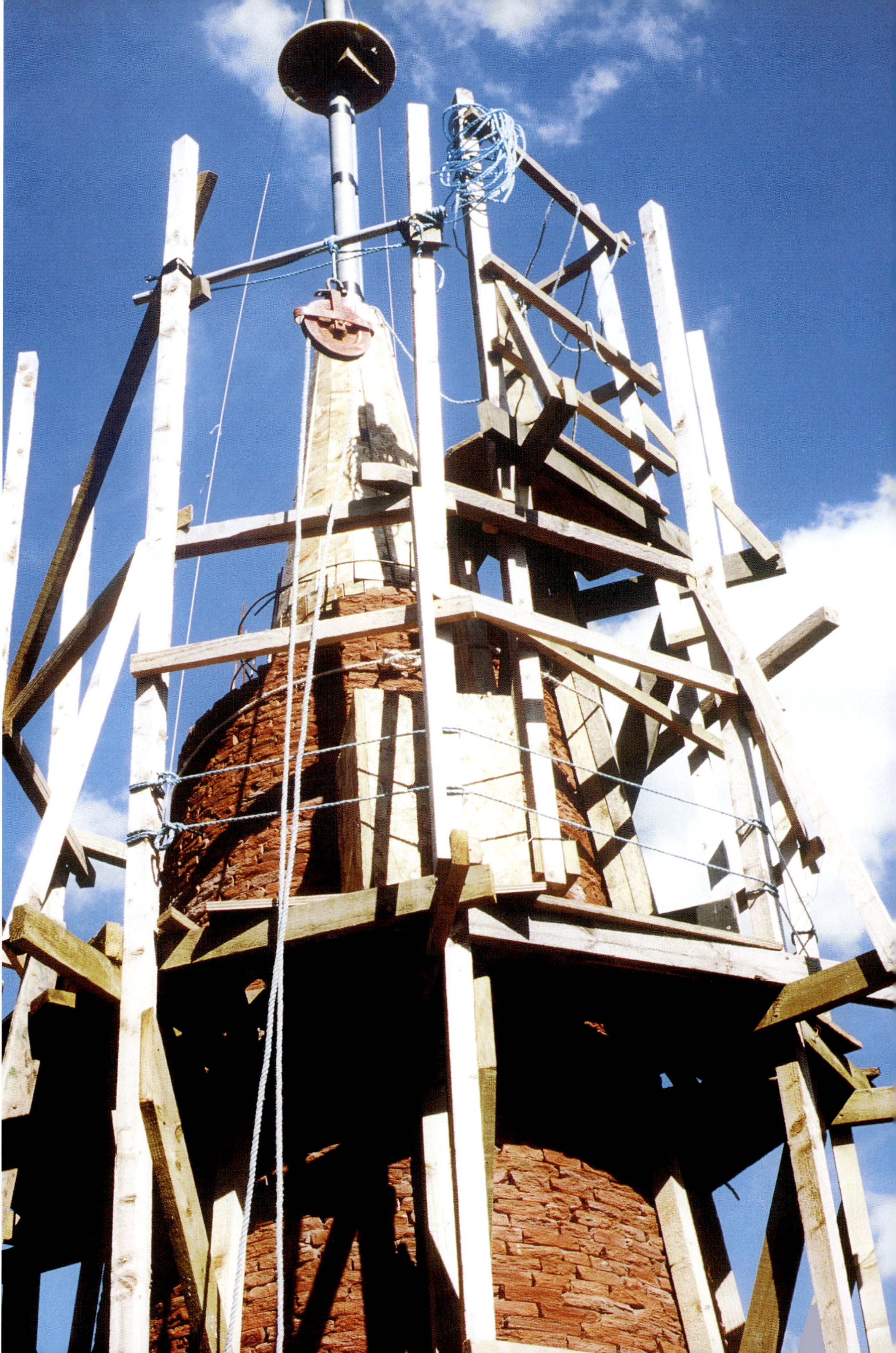

154 **River** 1996
Galvanised steel
500 x 120cm Ø

Swirls and Eddies

Colin has the capacity to find the everyday world extraordinary and intriguing, an attitude he shares with scientists and metaphysicians. When he became interested in the water cycle in the late 1980s, he asked unorthodox questions like: "How far has a raindrop travelled before it hits you on the head?'" or "How much of a cloud does it take to make a glass of water?". For over a decade these musings on water have bubbled through Colin's work like an underground stream, but when they have surfaced, it has often been in a very abstract manner. *Cloud,* 1987, for example, relates water in the air to water in its terrestrial forms, but it is anything but fluffy. *Two Rivers*, 1990, uses hard-edged shapes to represent volumes of water, but includes two sinuous elements resembling meandering rivers. The gallery piece, *River,* 1996, flows like a slinky serpentine from ceiling to floor, while the inverted cone of *Peaks and Waves*, 1996, looks like the bob of a plumbline tracing a wave pattern on the gallery floor.

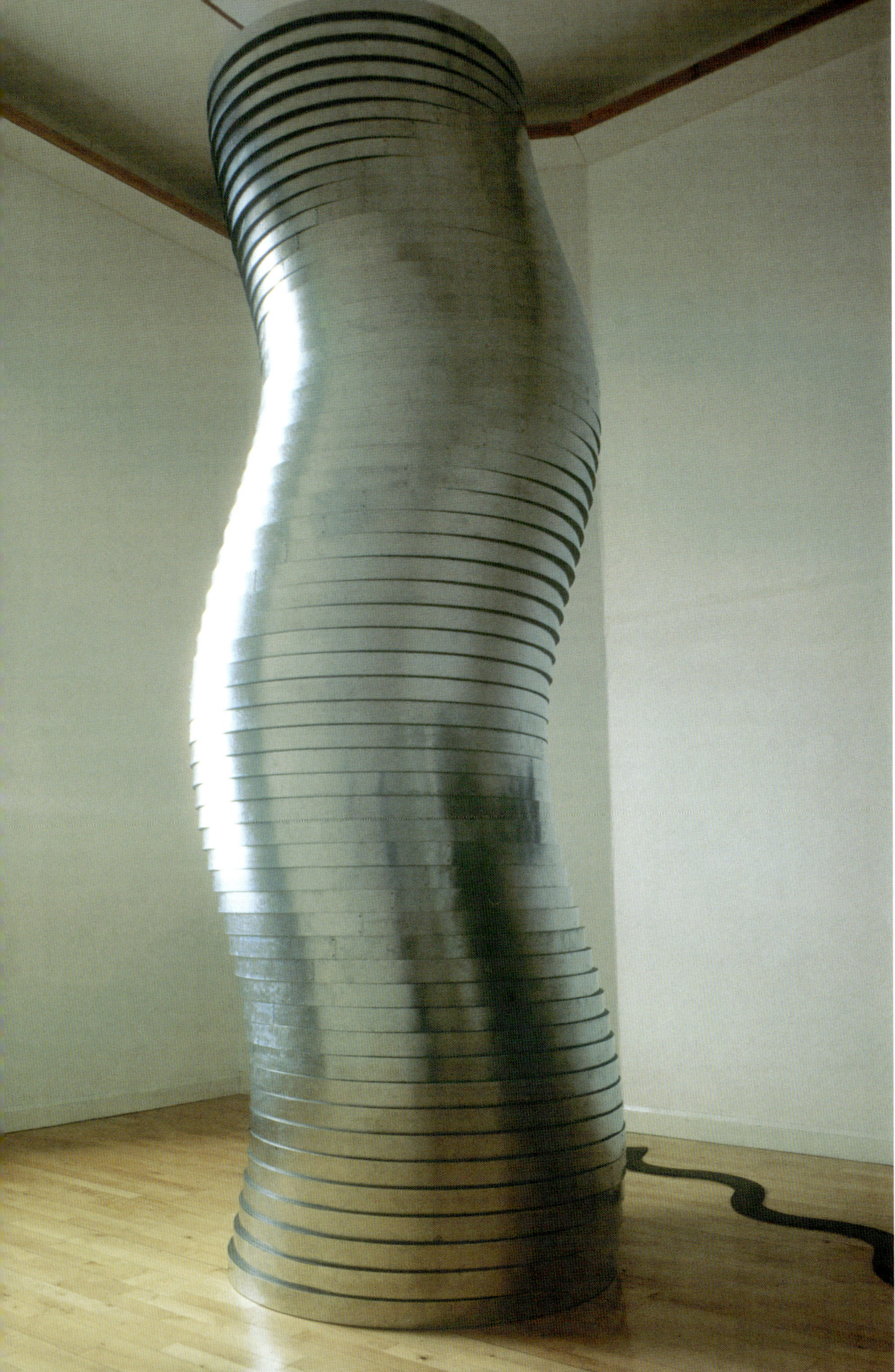

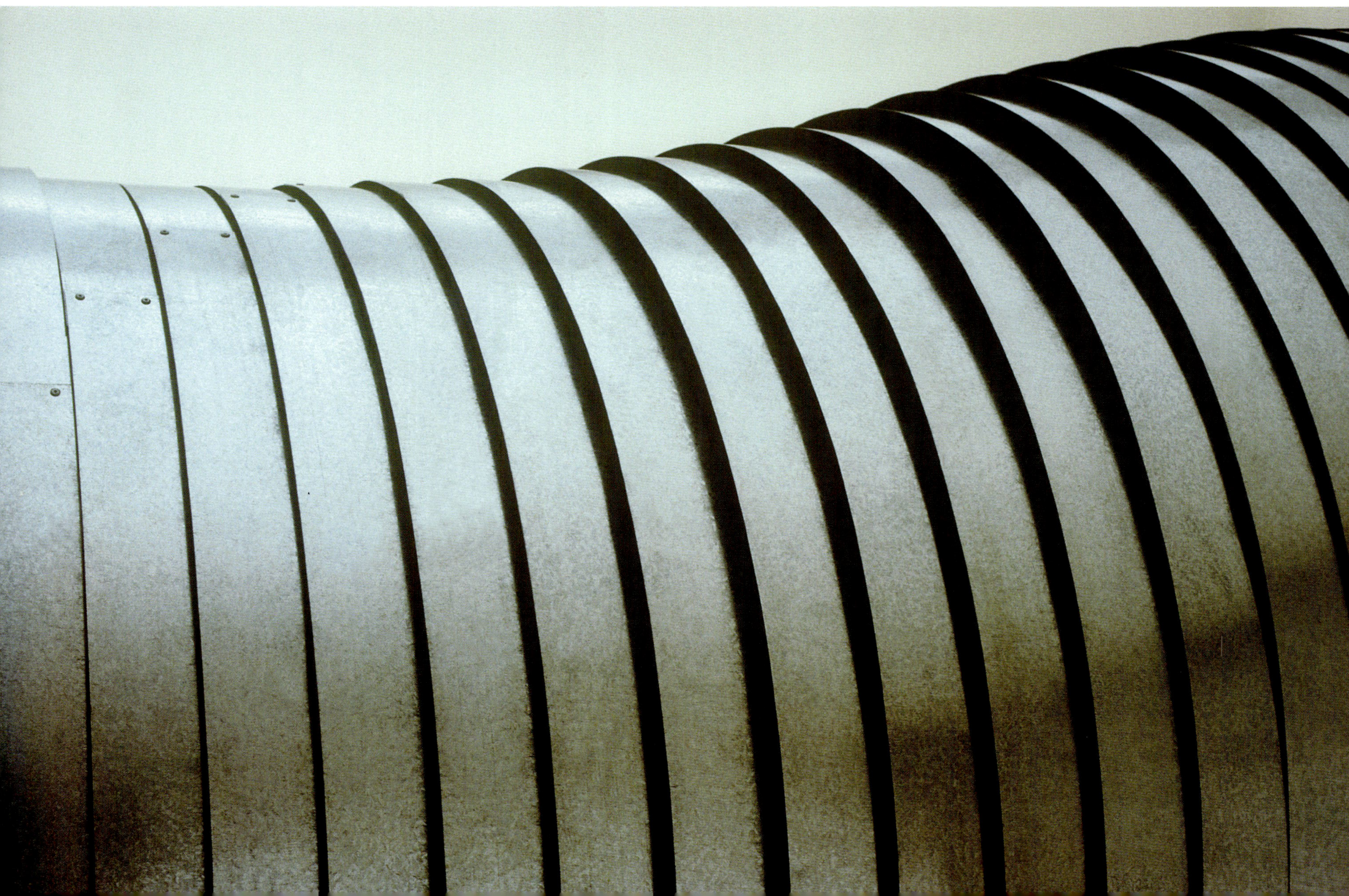

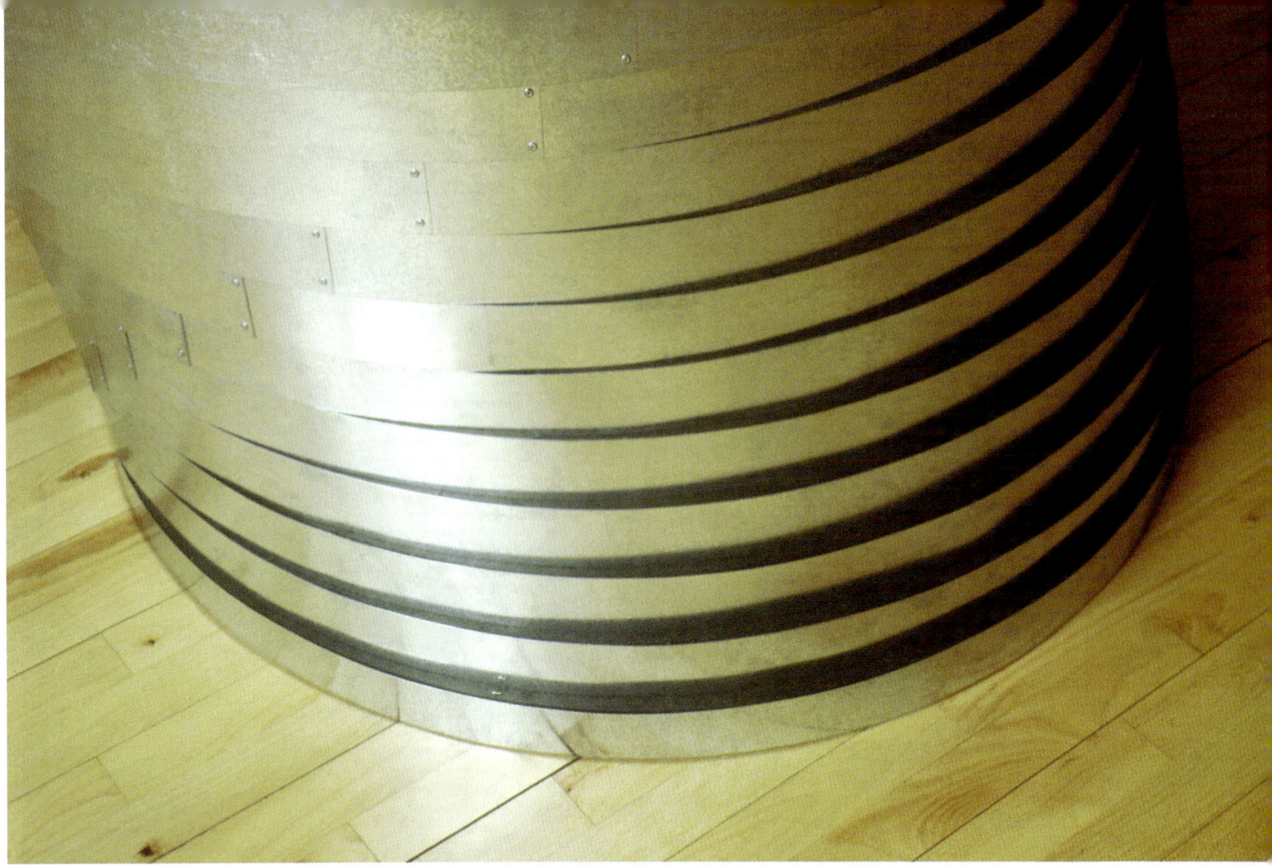

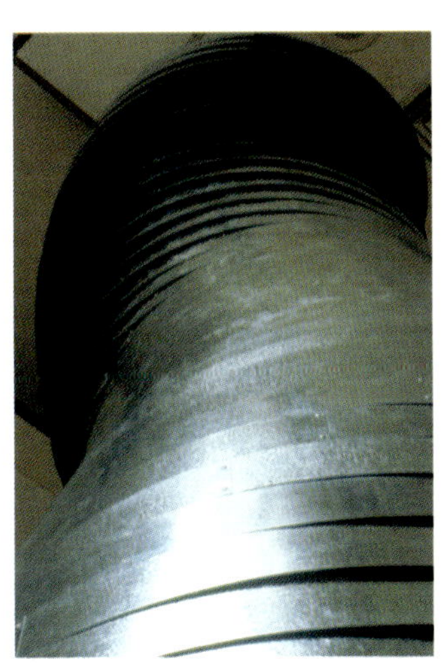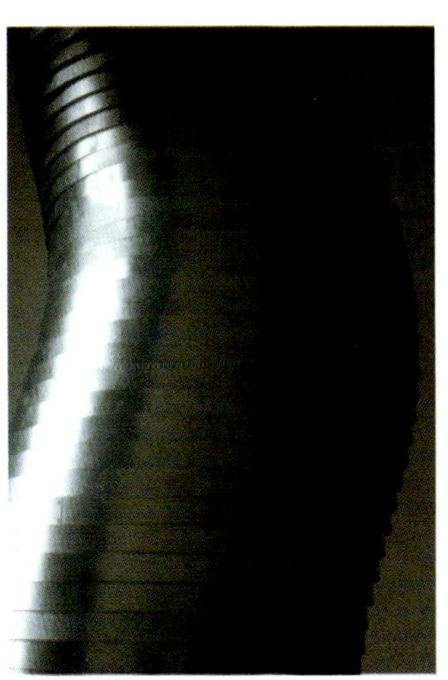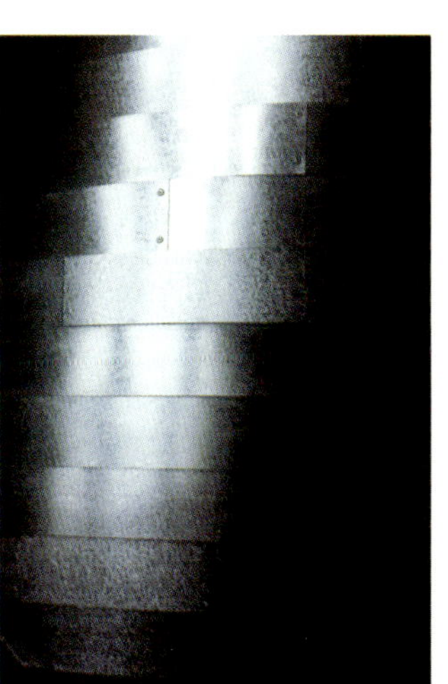

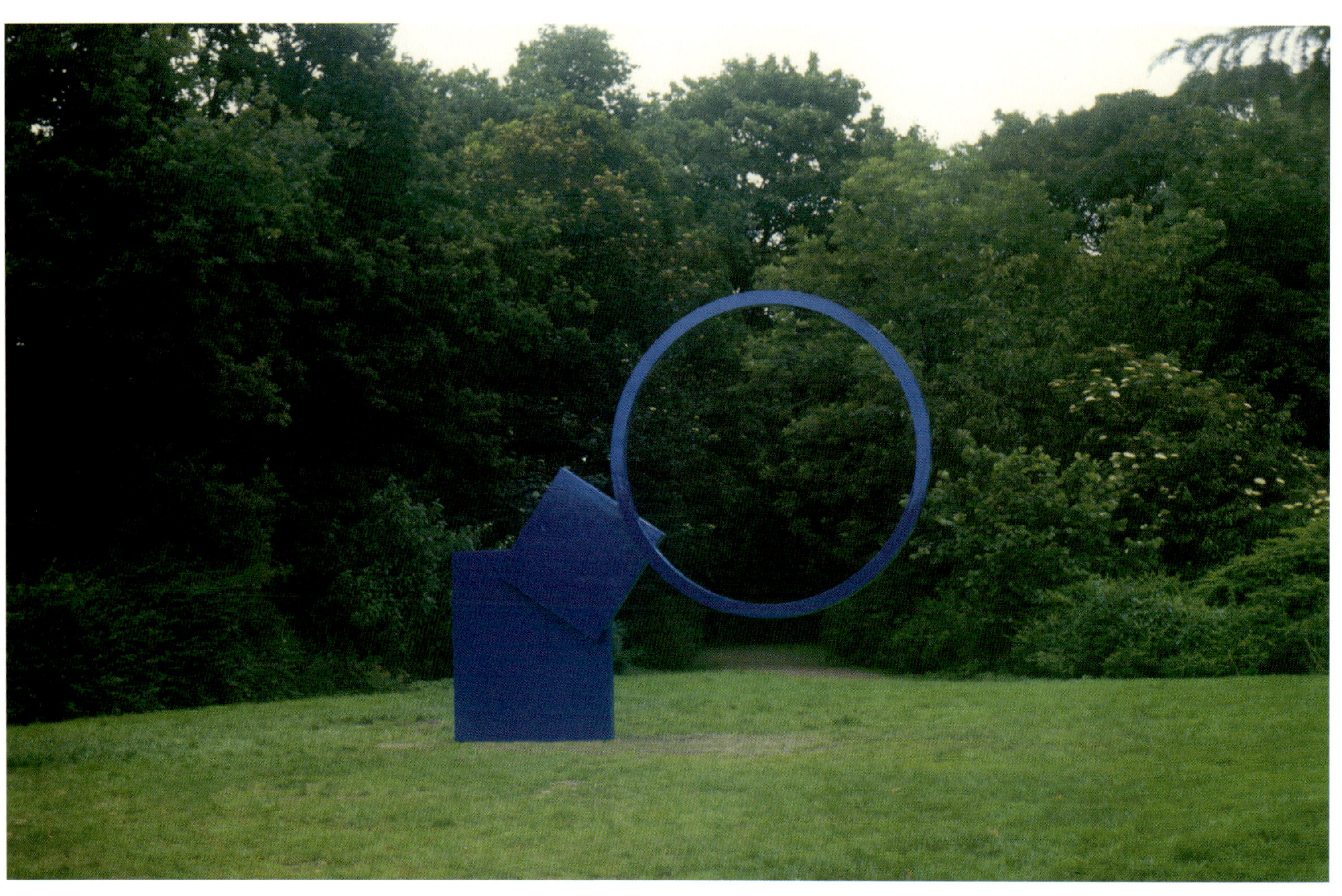

Cloud 1987
Painted steel
400 x 400cm
Krefeld, West Germany

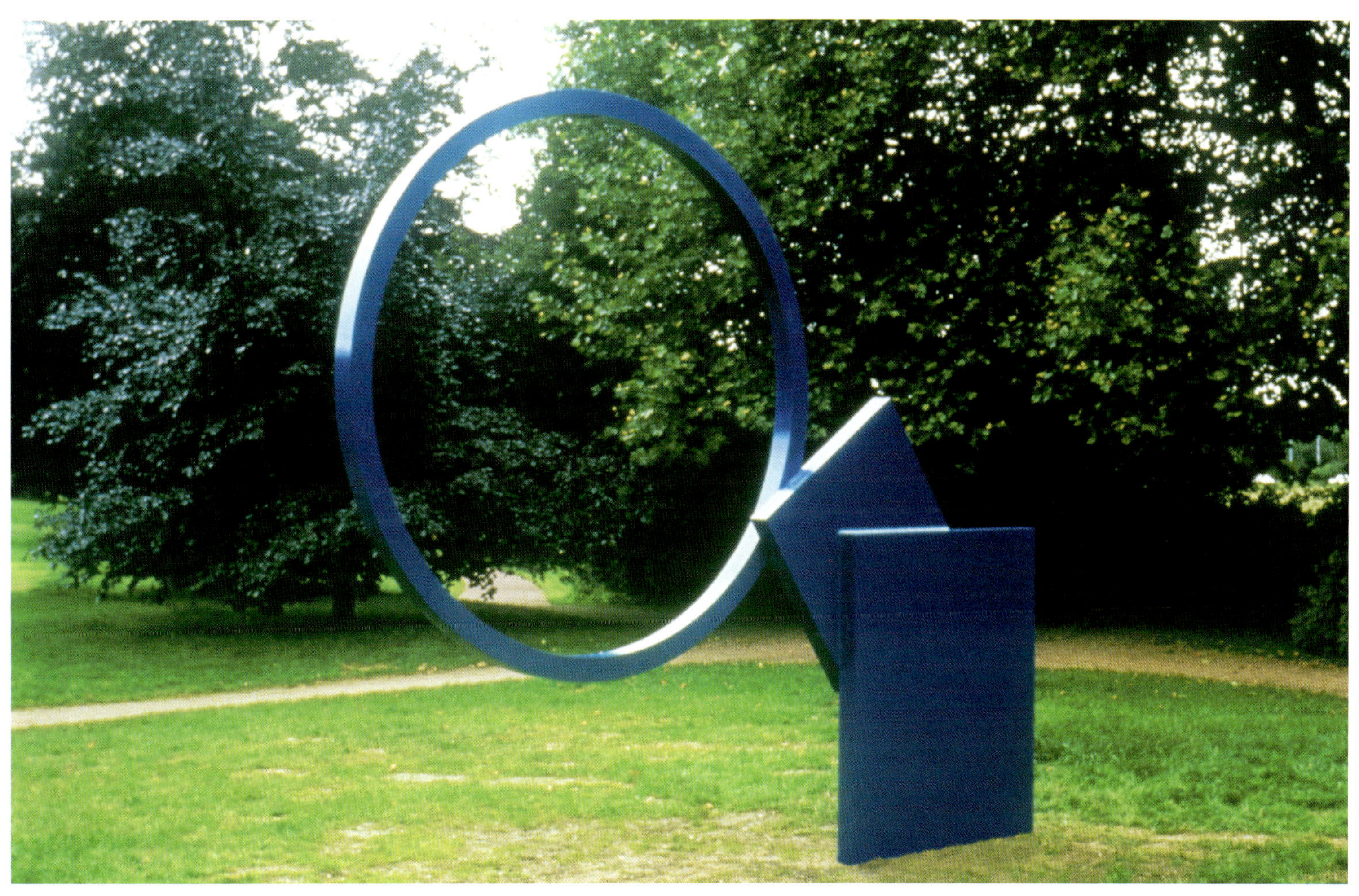

Below: **Peaks and Waves** 1996
Galvanised steel

Right: **Beam** 2001
Stainless steel
600cm high
Wakefield

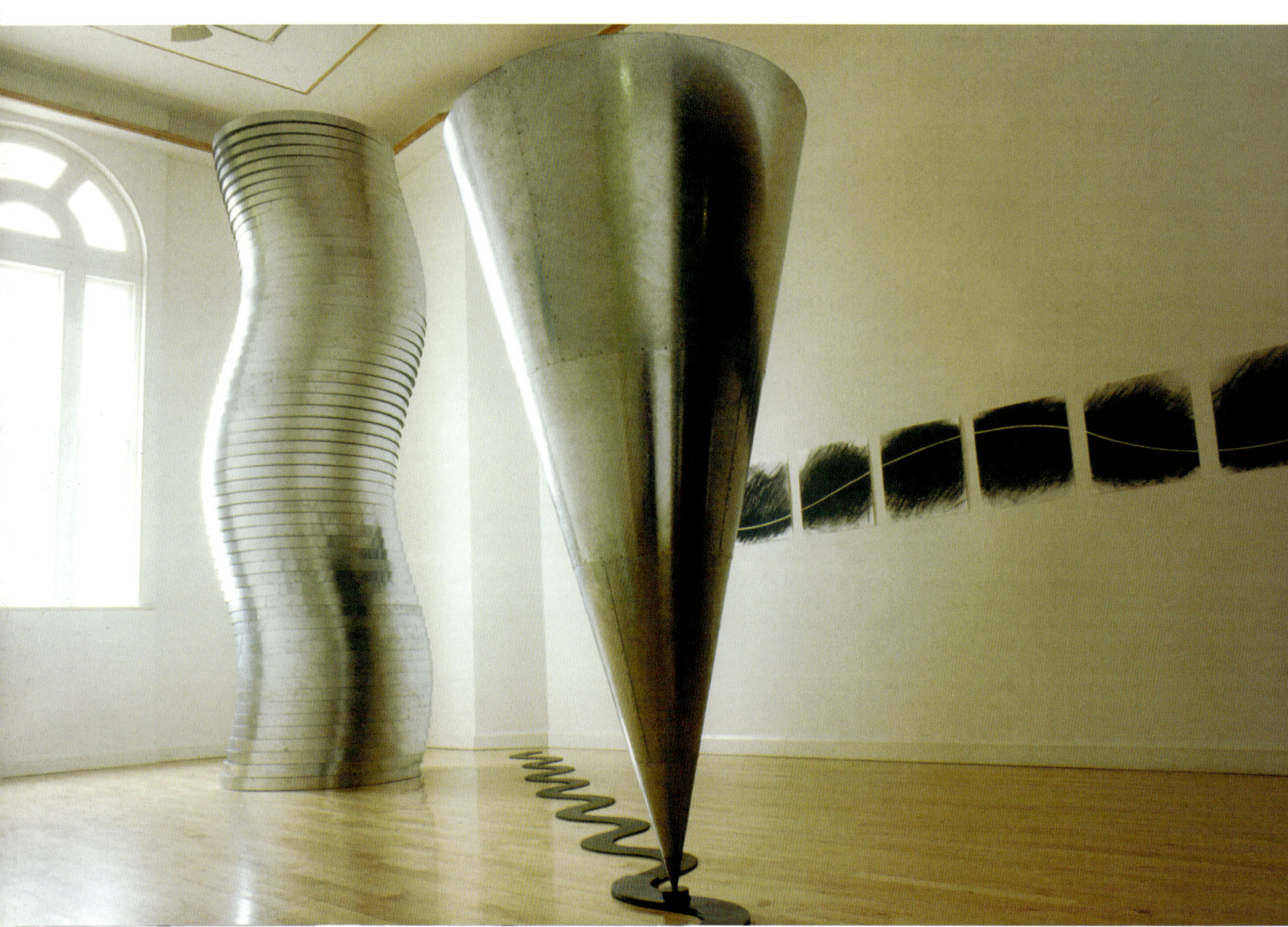

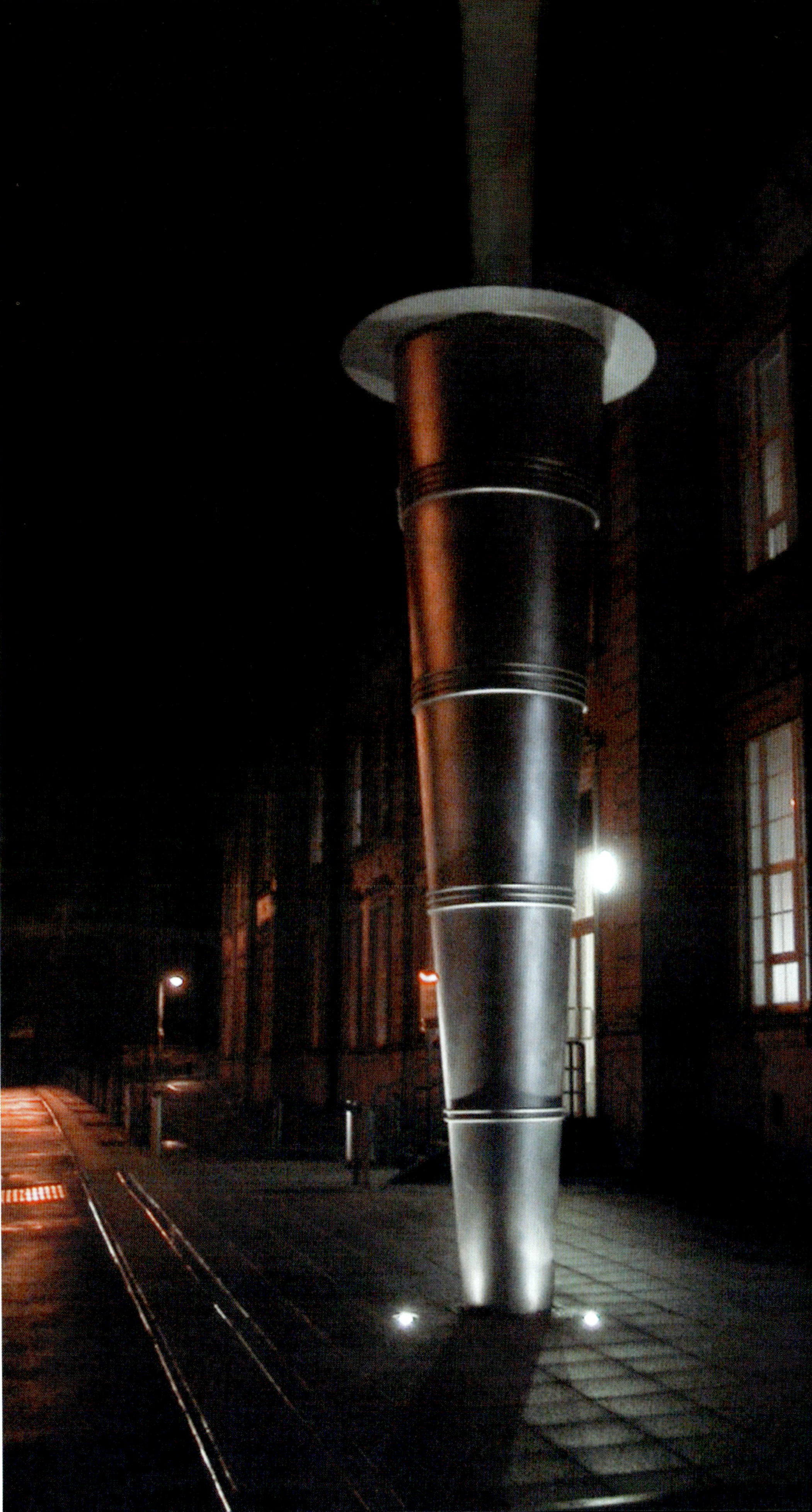

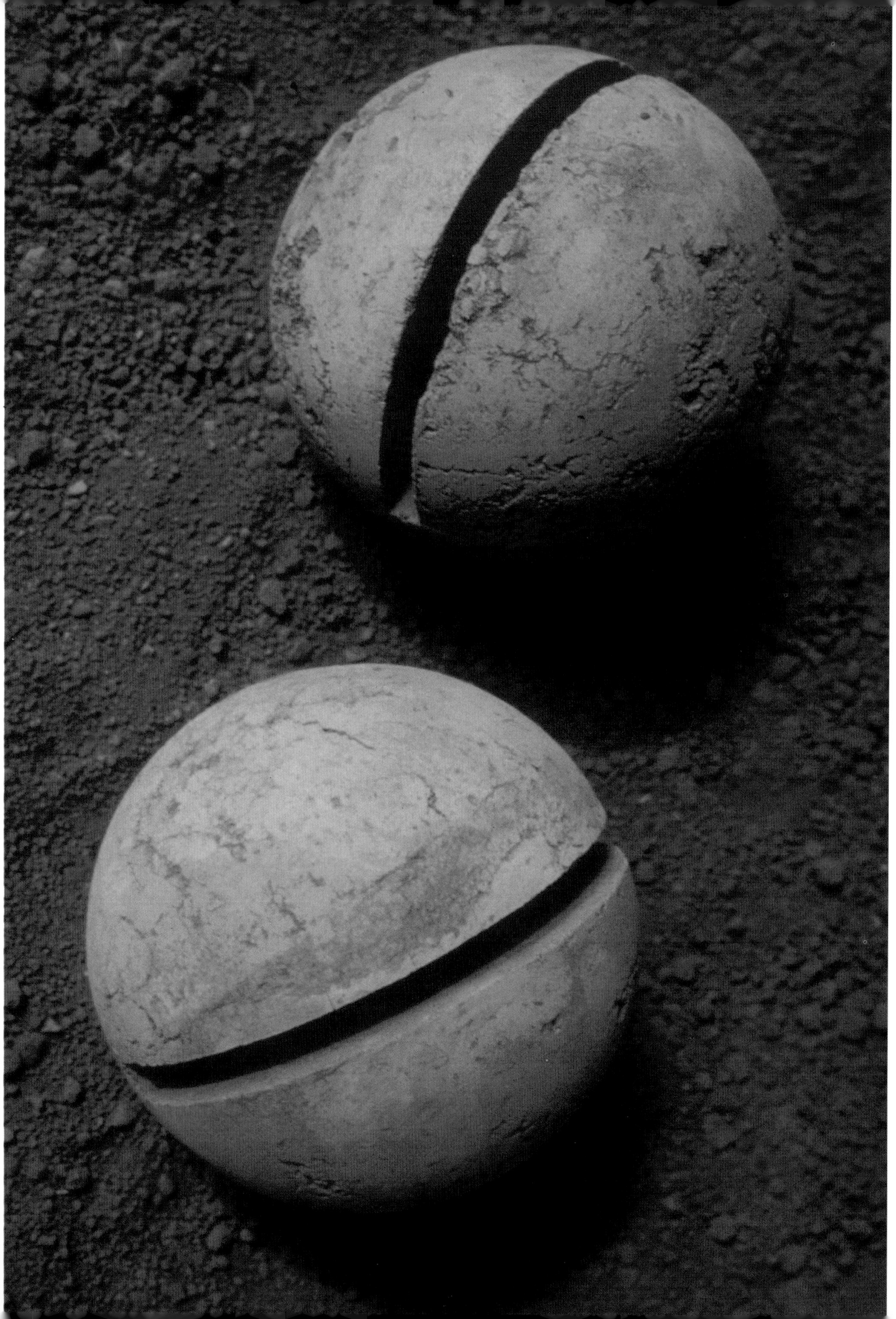

Split Spheres 1995
Earth
20cm Ø
Queensland, Australia

Analogies can be glib and misleading, but I would venture that there are criss-crossing currents in Colin's work – astronomy, language, landscape, domestic life, geometry, water – which are constantly recombining to produce new insights. Ideas float on the surface, sink for a while, then resurface with new vigour. The flow is not all in one direction; there are swirls and eddies. The spherical form which appeared in *Shelf*, reappears as a steel ball in *Window*, 1986, and *Rolling Moon*, but also as *Pineball, Rope Ball, Whirling Beans, Split Spheres*, 1995, and, in modified form, as *Starball*. Its most recent manifestation is in *Meteor*, 1998, a piece commissioned for the Jodrell Bank arboretum. In this piece the spherical theme converges with the interest in astronomy demonstrated in *Rolling Moon*, *Two Moons* and *Moon*.

The Jodrell Bank commission was an exciting one, but Colin
soon realised that he should not try to compete with the
overpowering form of the radio-telescope which is about 85
metres high. Instead he chose to make an object which
would seem to have fallen from space. *Meteor*, drew upon an
idea which Colin had proposed for the Great North Forest,
which was to have been a large upright discus-shaped object
that would seem to have been thrown into the landscape
and rolled, ploughing a furrow behind it. The Jodrell Bank
commission presented an the opportunity to develop this
idea, replacing the discus form with a sphere plunging into
the ground. It was sited beneath a gap in the tree canopy,
suggesting that it had sliced its way through. There is also
an echo of a photograph which Colin took much earlier in
his career which shows a tyre embedded in a field, and
although the hollow around the tyre has been made by
children playing, both objects have a feeling of timelessness
and certainly *Meteor* is about as permanent as an artwork
can be. Cast from white granite dust mixed with cement, it
is entirely solid and weighs 20 tons.

Meteor 1998
Polished white granite composite
250cm Ø
Jodrell Bank, Cheshire

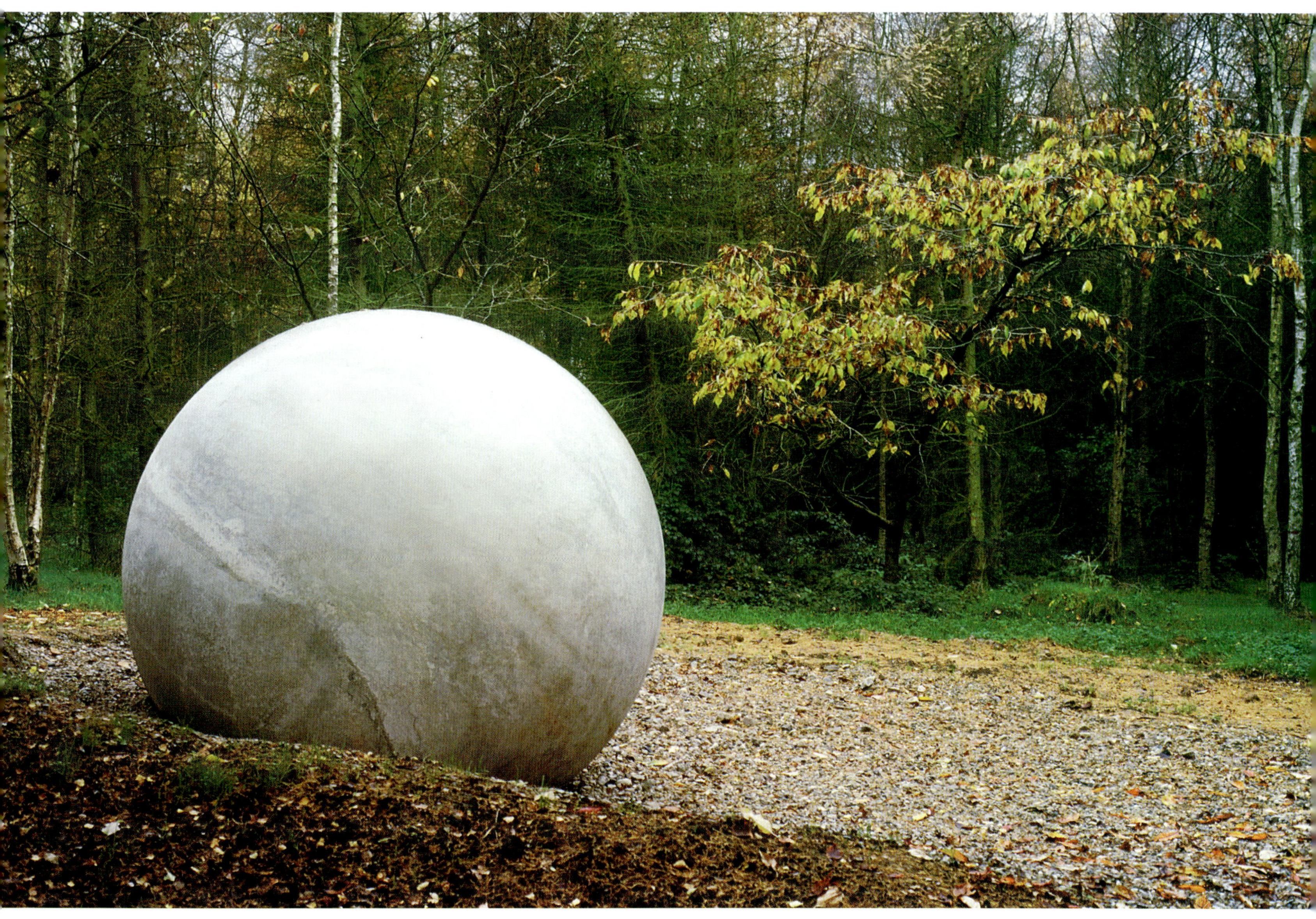

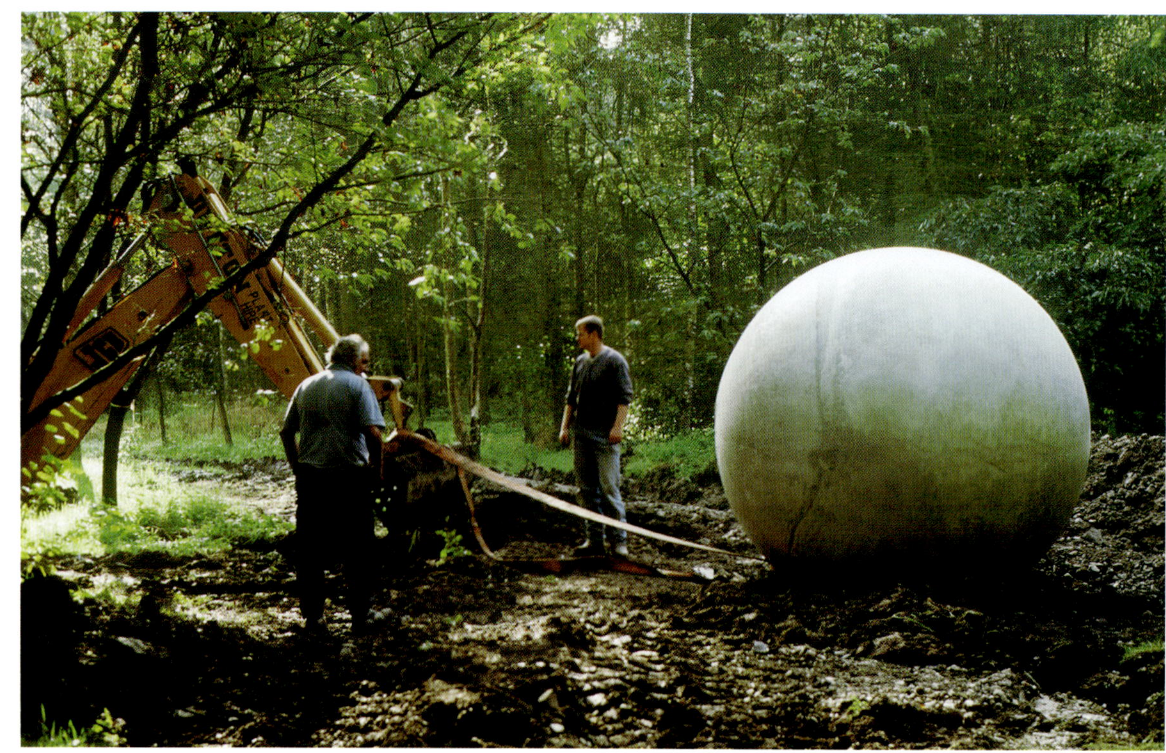

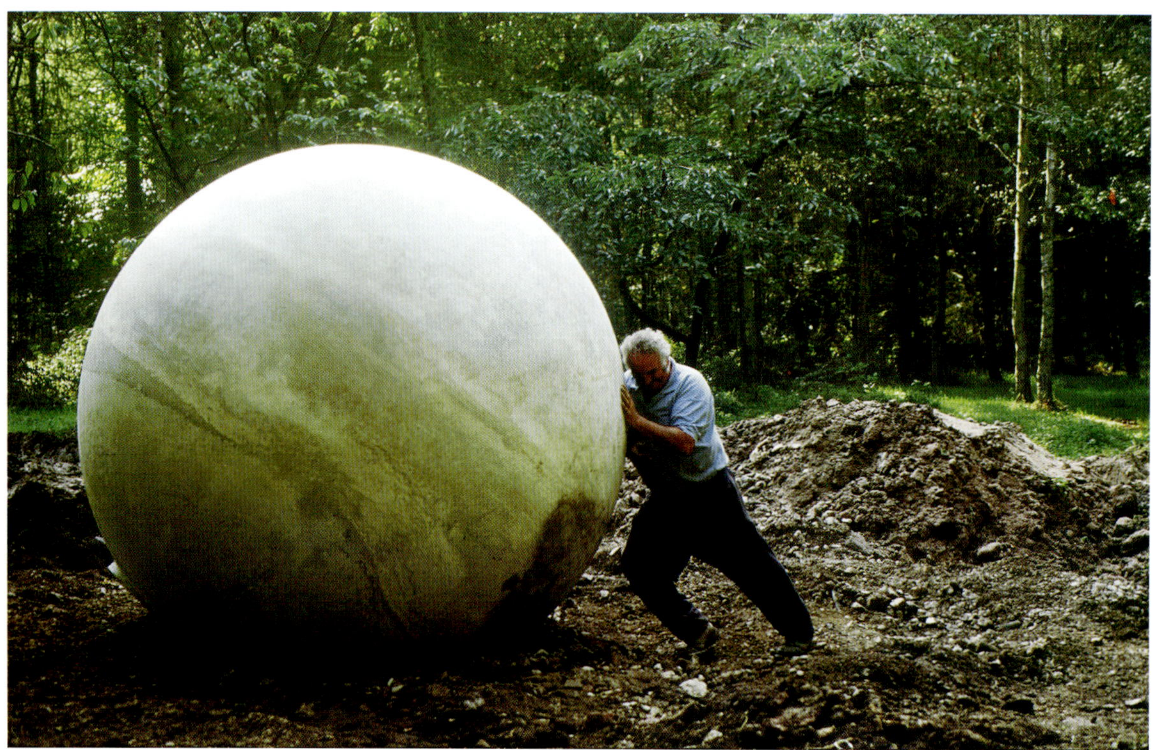

Muscularity and Poise

Making large scale sculpture, particularly in remote or inaccessible places, is a physically demanding activity. Someone like myself, who has always worked through drawings and written instructions, finds the thought of the personal labour involved in some of these pieces completely daunting. For *Stonecone*, for example, the 20 tons of sandstone had to be carried up to the site, and construction took a whole year. If you have any qualms about stepladders, imagine the difficulties involved in securing giant rope balls high in the branches of trees. The simplicity and serenity that characterises much of Colin's work utterly belies the effort that goes into their creation.

One might imagine that a sculptor with such an interest in precise forms would find it difficult to delegate any part of the production process, but Colin's engineering background has taught him that the fabrication of large steel structures is a co-operative activity. Not only would it be impossible for him to make a piece of the dimensions of *Rolling Moon* or *Edge to Edge* single-handedly, he also likes the idea that room can be made within his works for the contribution of others, so he will often document the stages in the manufacture and installation of such pieces photographically.

Right: **Disc (Ship)** 2001

Opposite: **Meteor** 1998

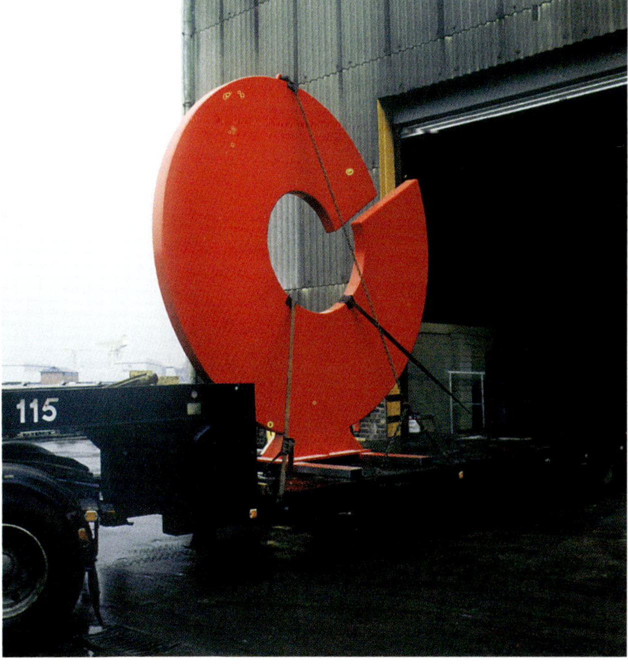

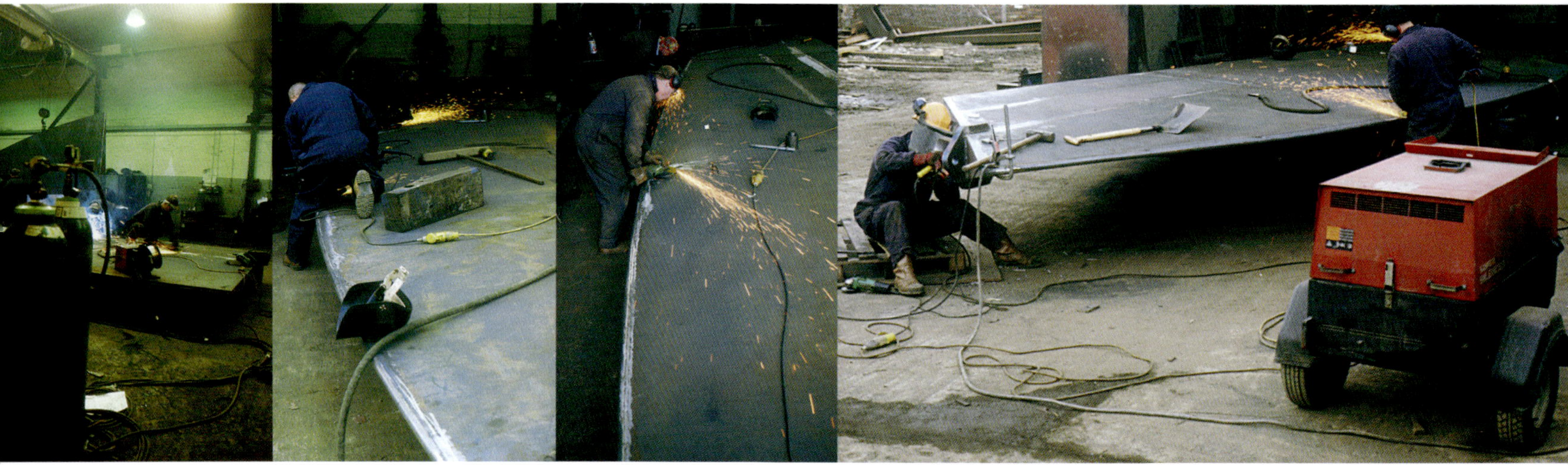

Some of the processes involved in making a large steel sculpture are the same as those used in shipbuilding: casting, cutting, bending, welding and grinding. Colin's most recent major commission is for a work in which this relationship becomes explicit. In 2001 he was asked to produce a sculpture for an urban space in Jarrow, a town which received unwanted fame in the 1930s when its redundant shipyard workers marched on Westminster, but which should be celebrated for the century of shipbuilding that preceded it. It was here that the world's first steam-powered collier, the *John Bowles*, was launched in 1852. Colin has made two pieces for a shopping centre based upon the idea of a vessel. He recognised that a sculptor could not build a ship, but he could produce something of sufficient size to represent that industry. His proposal was for full-size bow and stern pieces to be put in place with a keel-line cut into the ground between them. Because of the relationship of these to the buildings on the site, it would not be possible to see one from the other without turning a corner, an experience that would involve initial astonishment followed swiftly by comprehension.

Bow (Ship) 2001
Jarrow

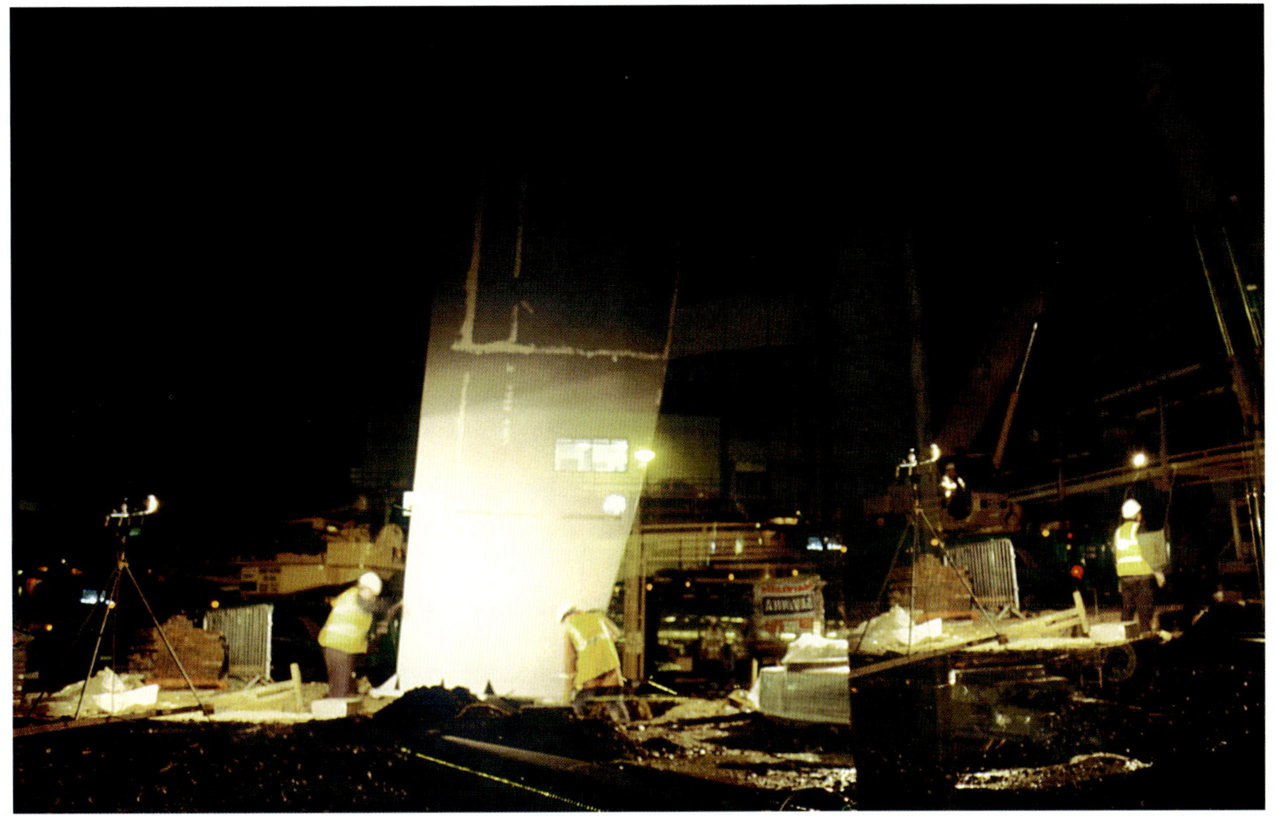

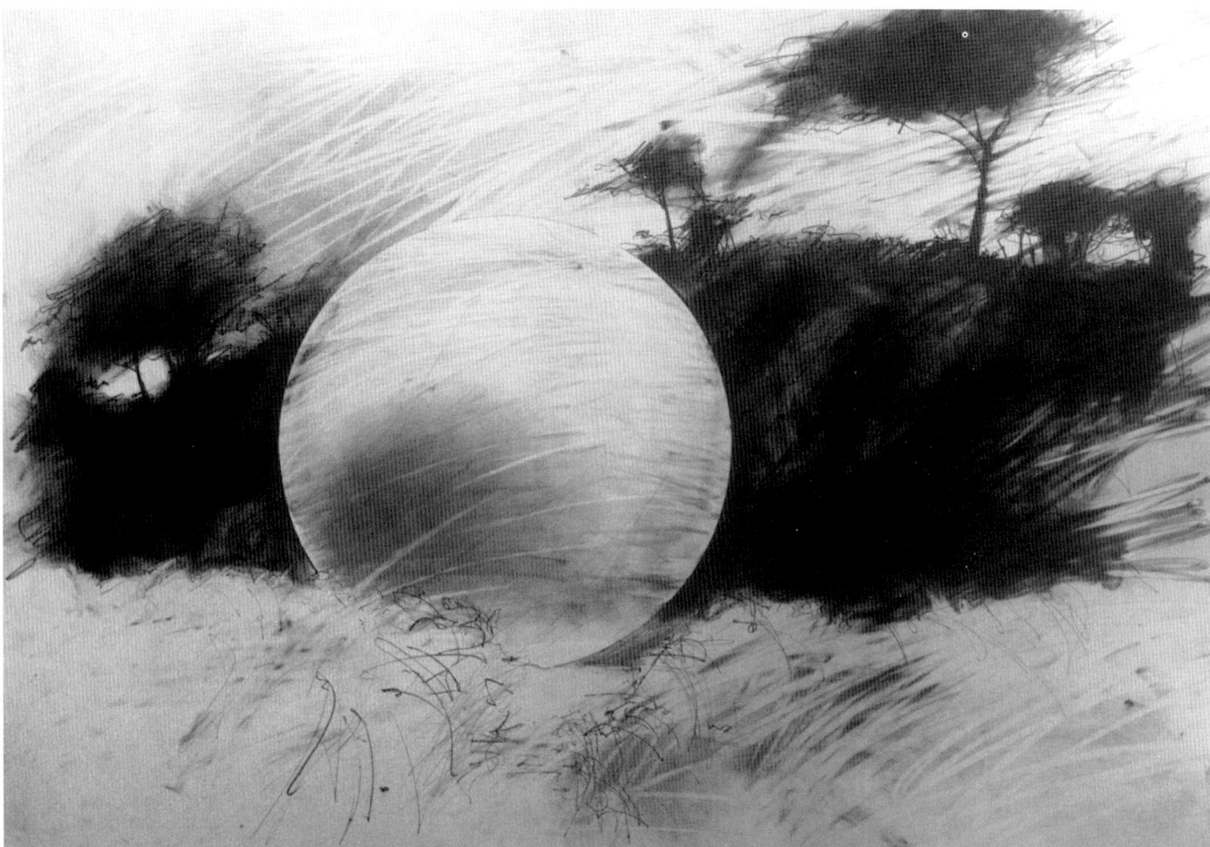

Left: **Disc** 1996
Graphite on paper
60 x 84cm

Right: **Disc (Ship)** 2001
Painted steel
400cm Ø
Jarrow

The artist who is commissioned to make work for public places is often faced with issues, such as Health and Safety or the risk of vandalism, which are less likely to impinge upon those who exhibit in galleries. A degree of compromise with various public authorities is sometimes required. *Bow,* 2001, for example, stands 12 metres high and is made from steel 2 centimetres thick. The original proposal for the stern piece resembled a screw propeller, but it was rejected because it had sharp edges which were judged to be potentially dangerous. Colin's response was to remove the offending edges by making the work more abstract. *Disc,* 2001, is a representation of the motion of such a propeller.

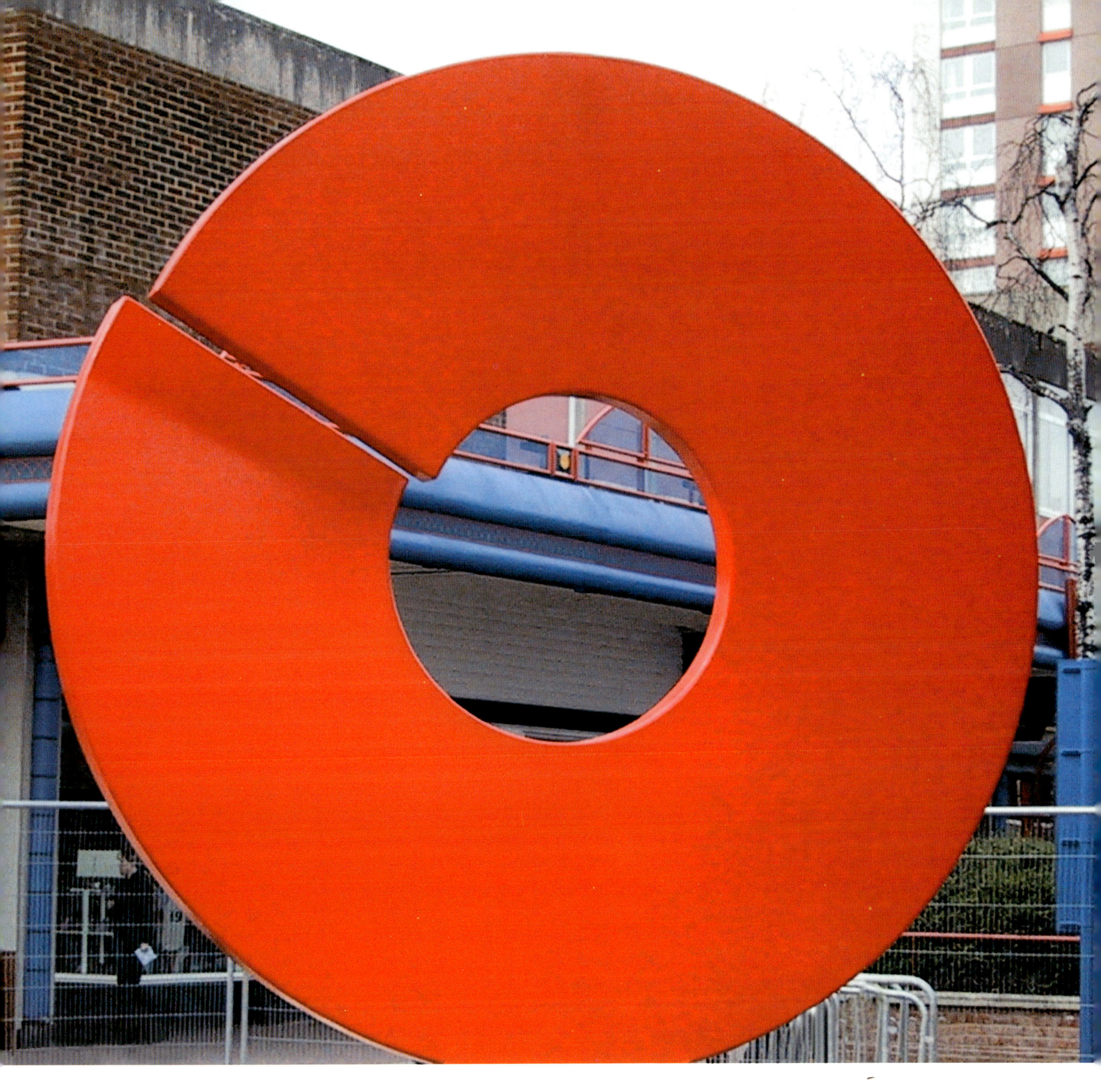

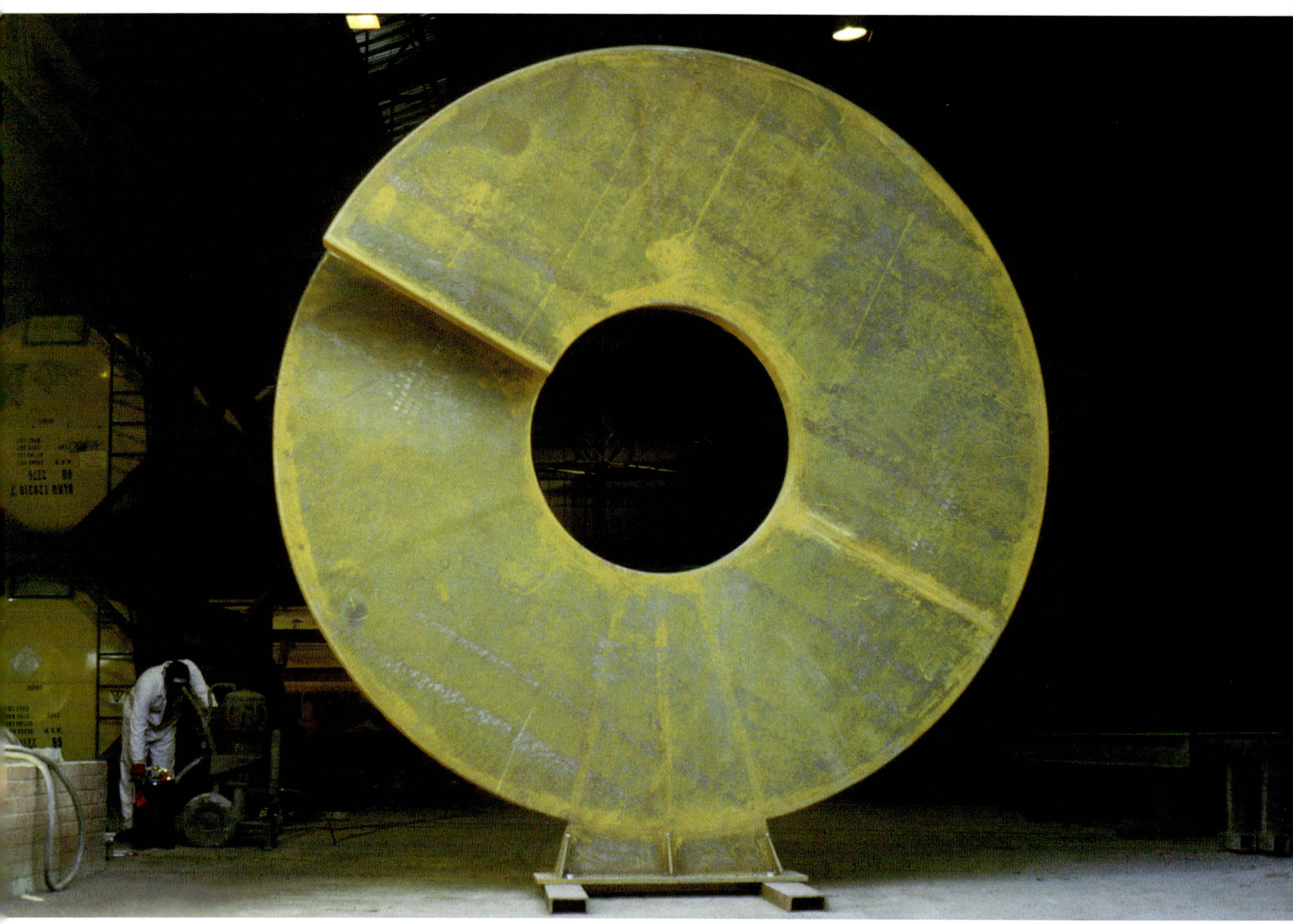

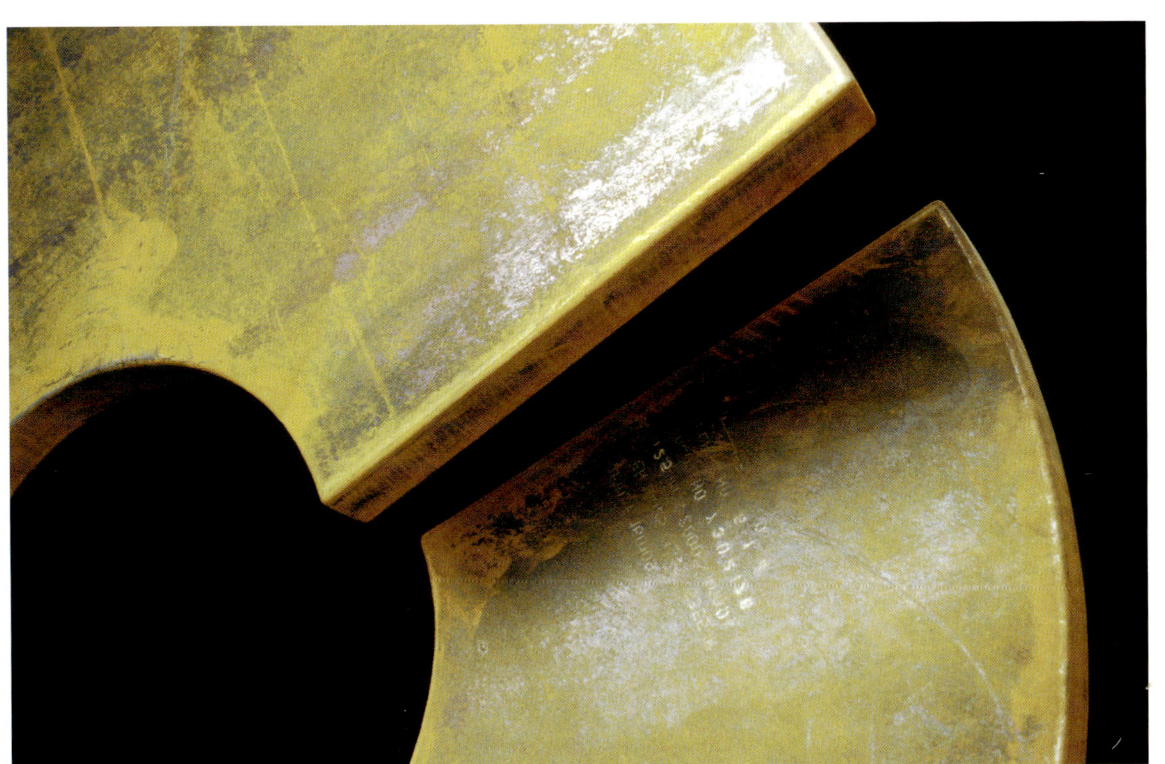

There is a muscularity in Colin's larger public works which should never be confused with machismo. Part of this is derived from the materials used and the engineering skills employed and it relates, usually in an indirect way, to the traditional industries of Tyneside. Boats were made of timber, ships of steel, and bridges of stone and iron. Even the coiled hawser used in *Whirling Beans*, has its nautical connections. Although Colin has produced small works for intimate places, some of his pieces are very large, as they need to be to hold their own at the scale of the landscapes concerned. Dimensions which can seem large in a studio suddenly dwindle when an object is taken out of doors. *Rolling Moon*, for example, was originally sited at Glasgow Garden Festival, where only its size and simplicity saved it from being swamped by its kitsch surroundings; it was later re-sited on the Gateshead riverside where it must keep company with Tyneside's famous bridges. Equally important is the clarity of the language in which Colin's work speaks. There is never anything fussy or superfluous. It is perhaps this quality above all which has contributed to his continuing popularity amongst architects, urban designers and landscape architects. He is recognised as an artist who understands the complex relationship between landscape and built form, and one of his greatest satisfactions is to see a work absorbed into the fabric of a place. If the Cumbrian cows relieve an itch by scratching themselves on *Ting*, or the kids of Tyneside lean their bicycles against *Bow*, he sees these as marks of acceptance. Colin believes that art should never have to apologise for its existence. "The acid test for any piece of art in a public place", he says, "is whether anyone would notice if it was taken away."

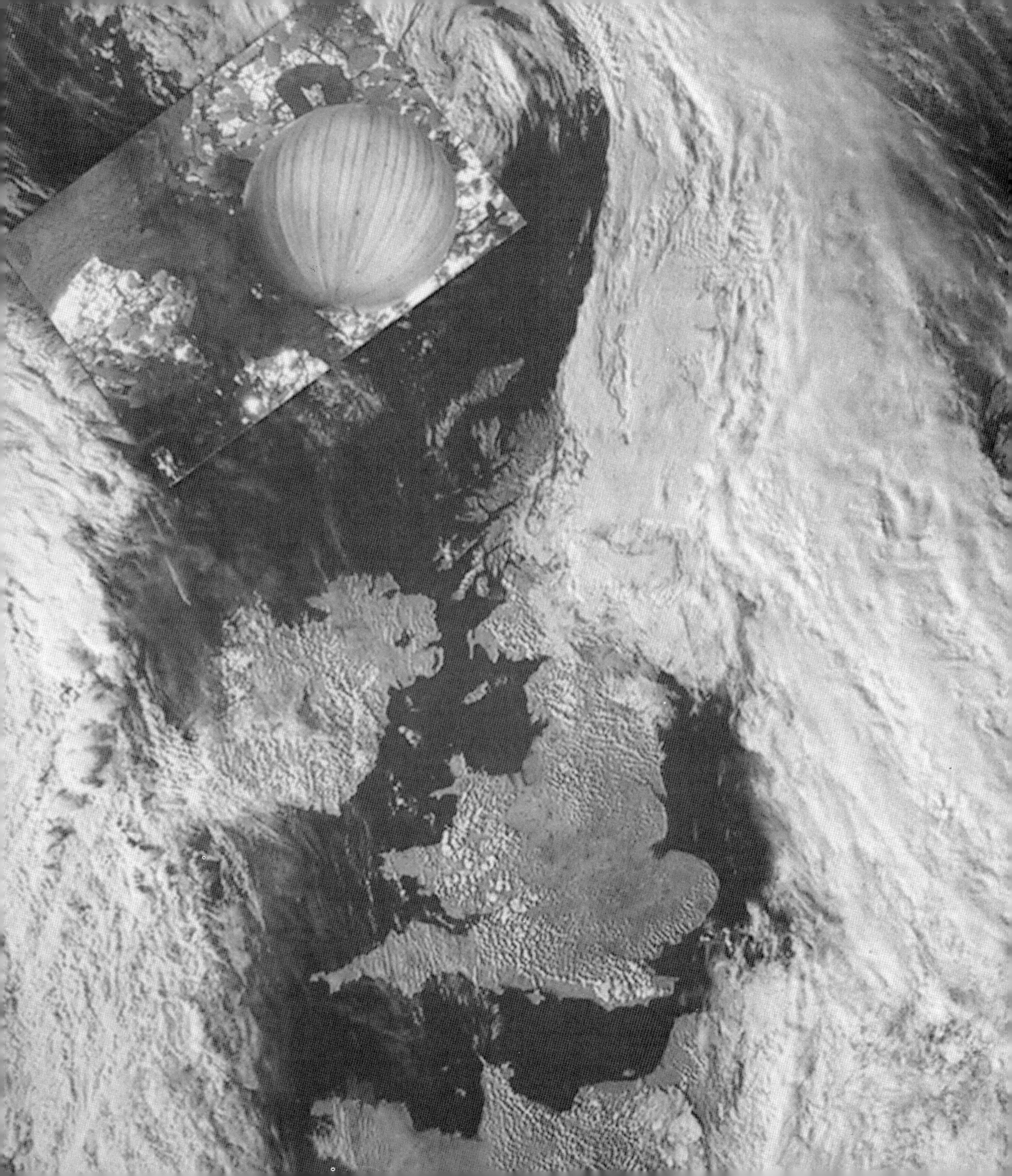

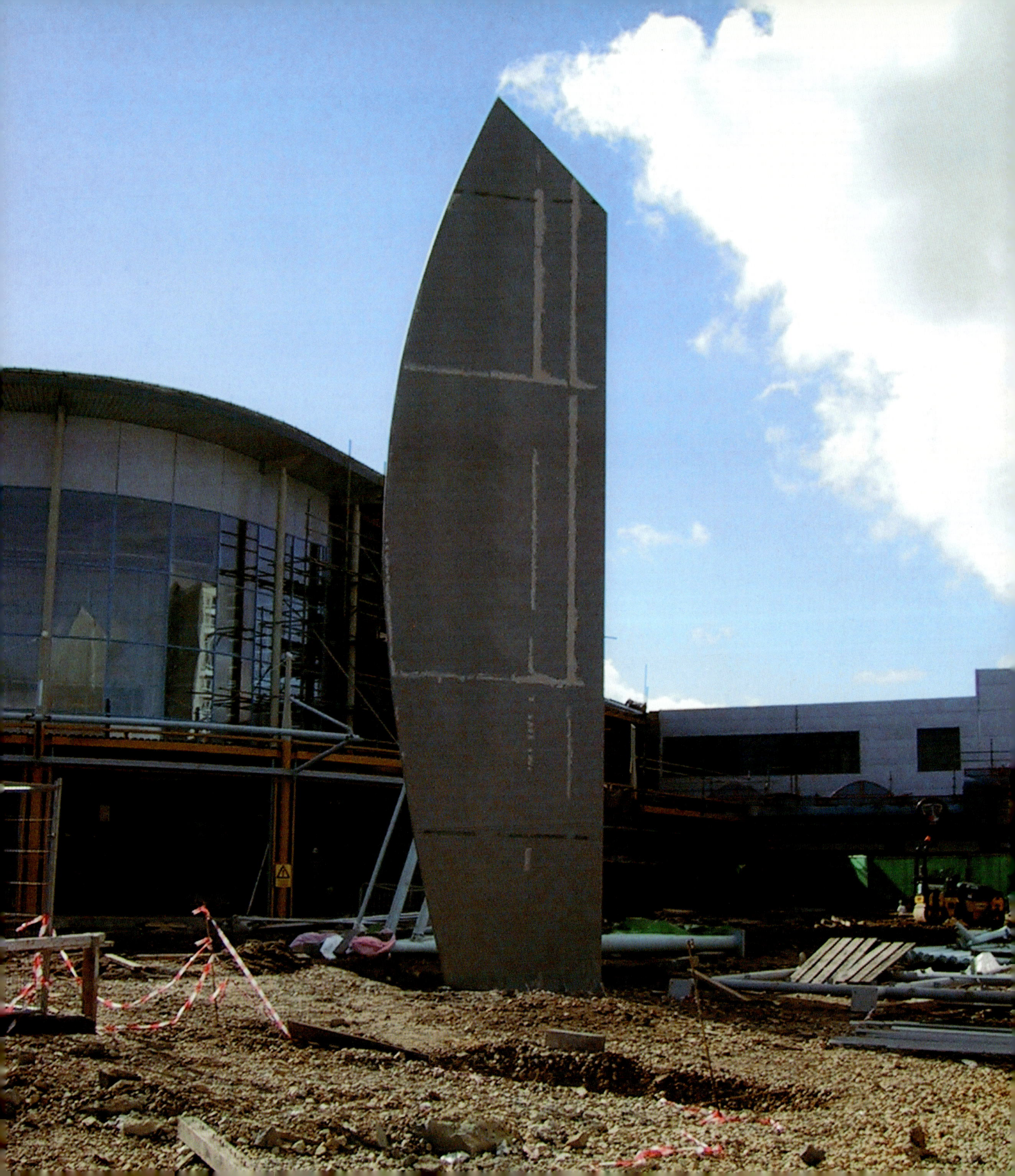

Left: **Bow (Ship)** 2001
Painted steel
12m high
Jarrow

Below: **Gates** 1998
Powder coated steel
300 x 400cm
Arts & Crafts Centre, Knaresborough, Yorkshire

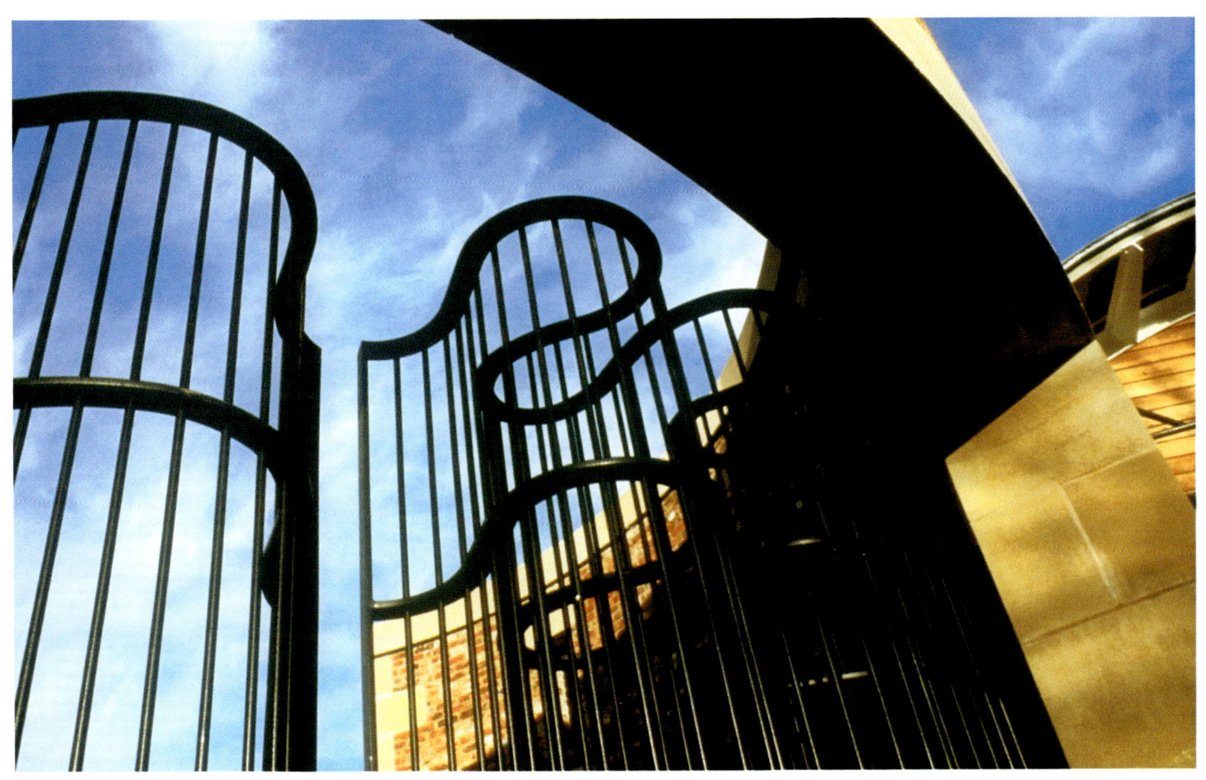

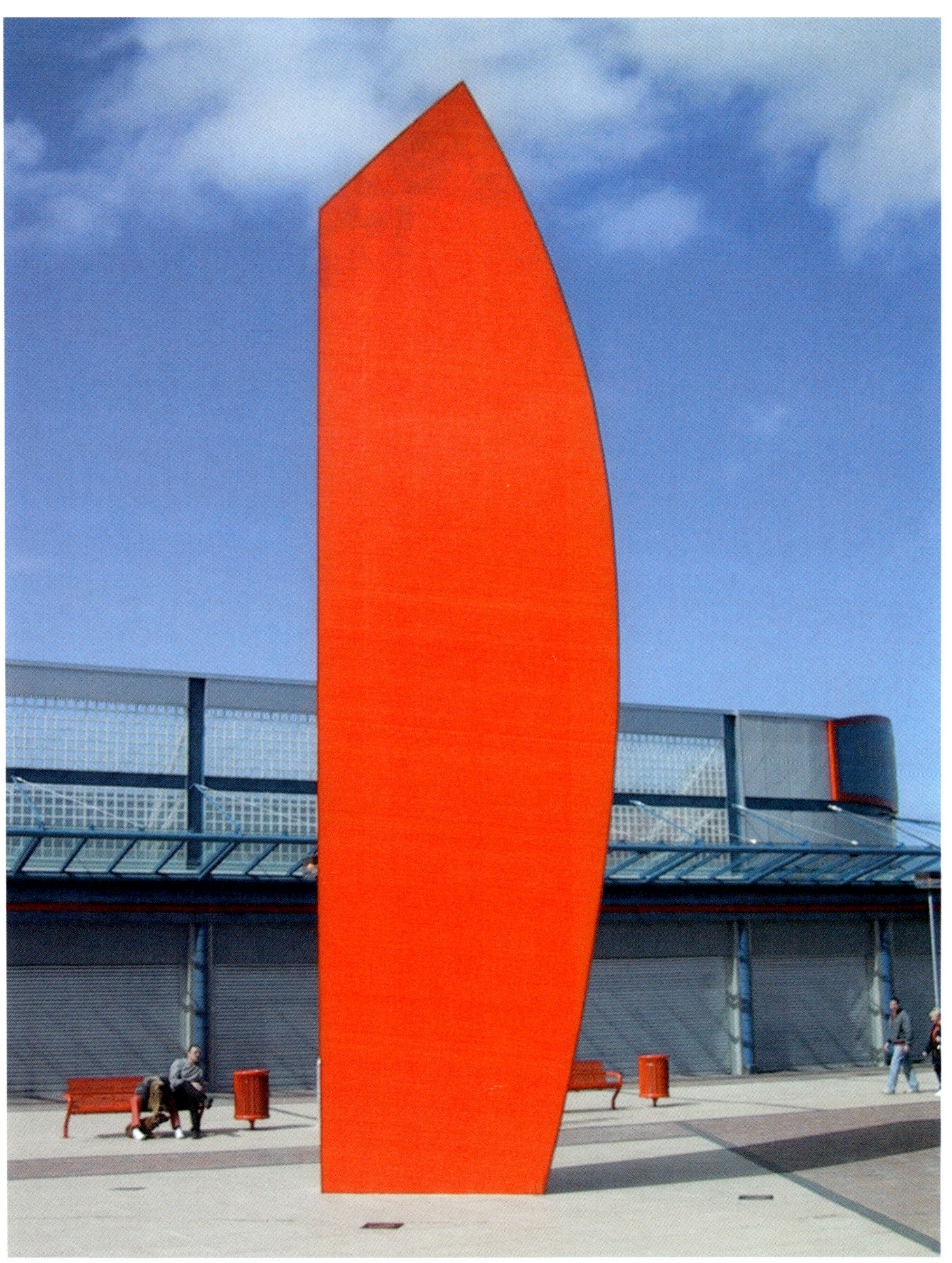

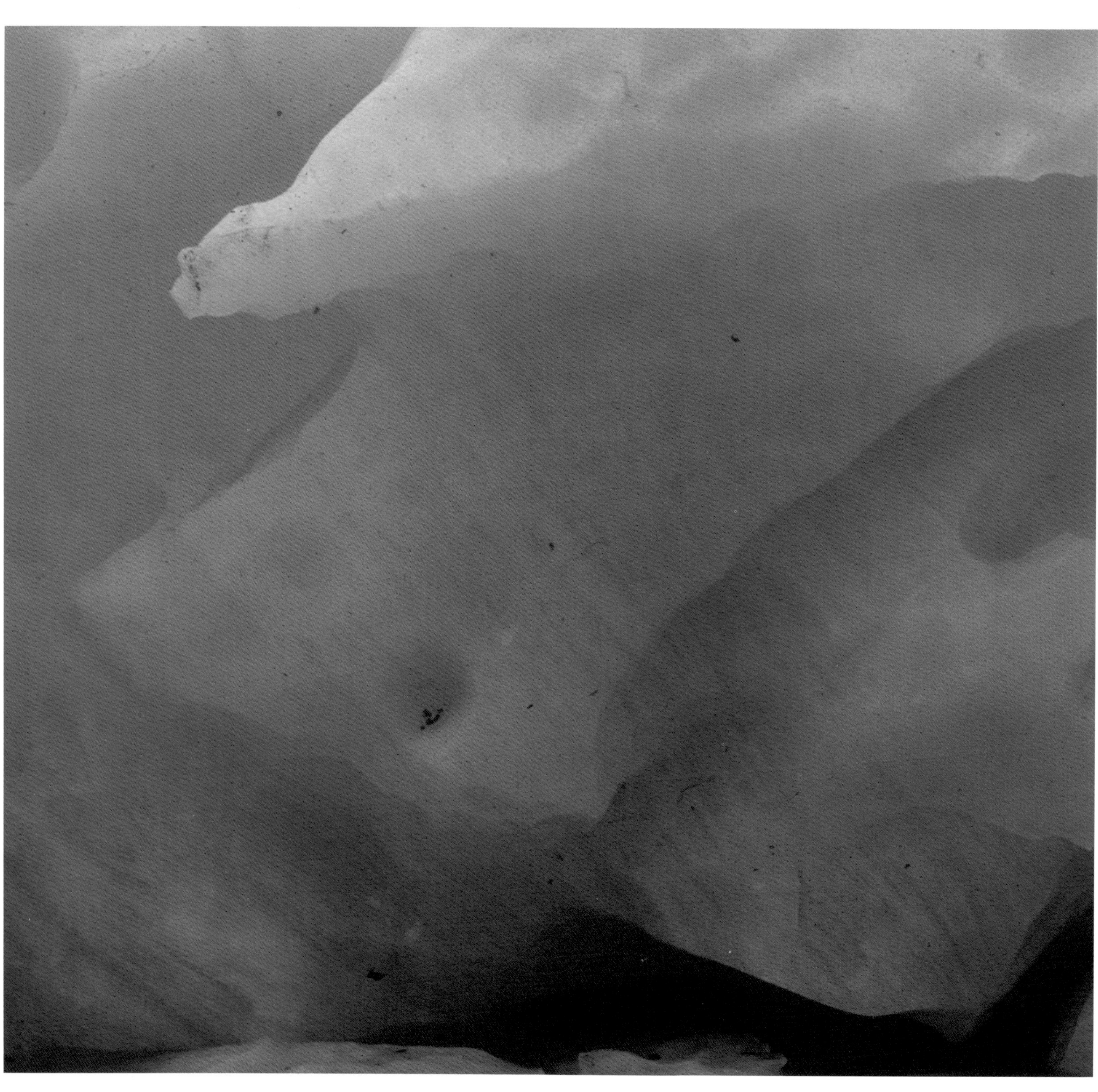

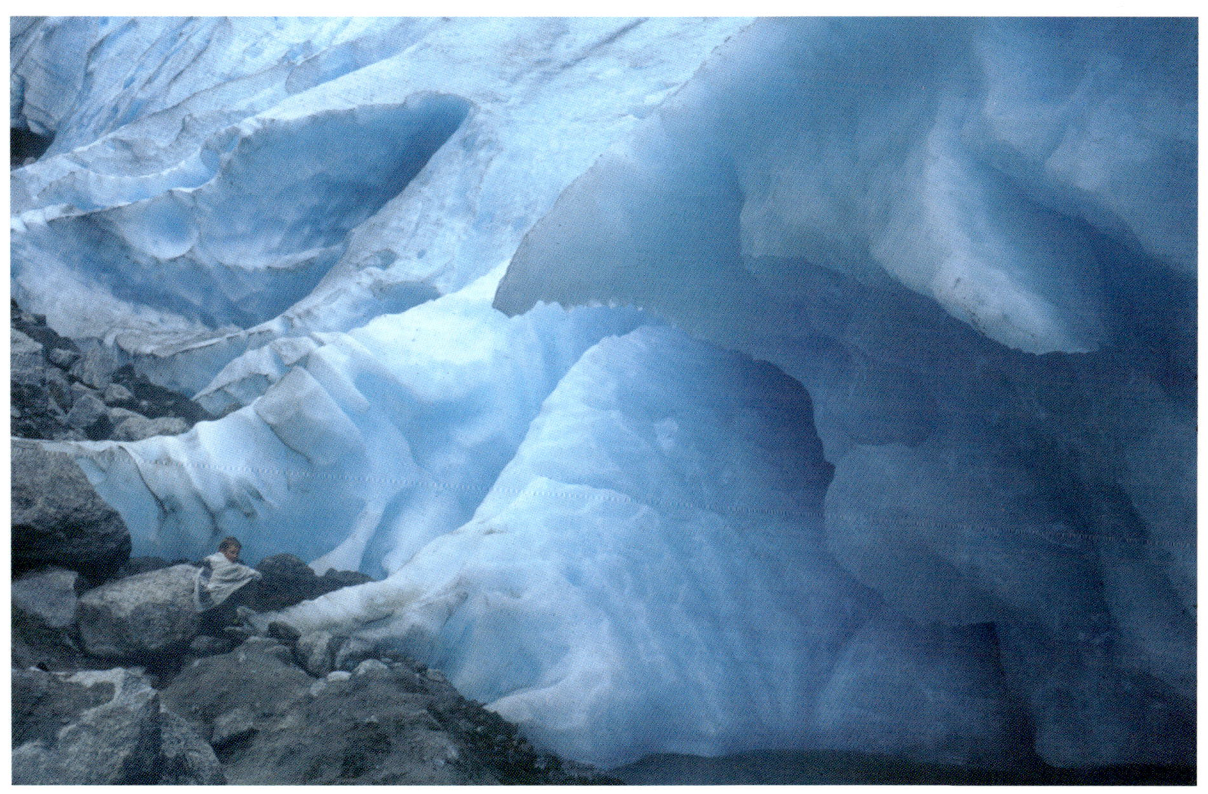

Roundy 2002
Mining Memorial
Cast concrete
350 x 200 x 200cm
Ushaw Moor, Co Durham

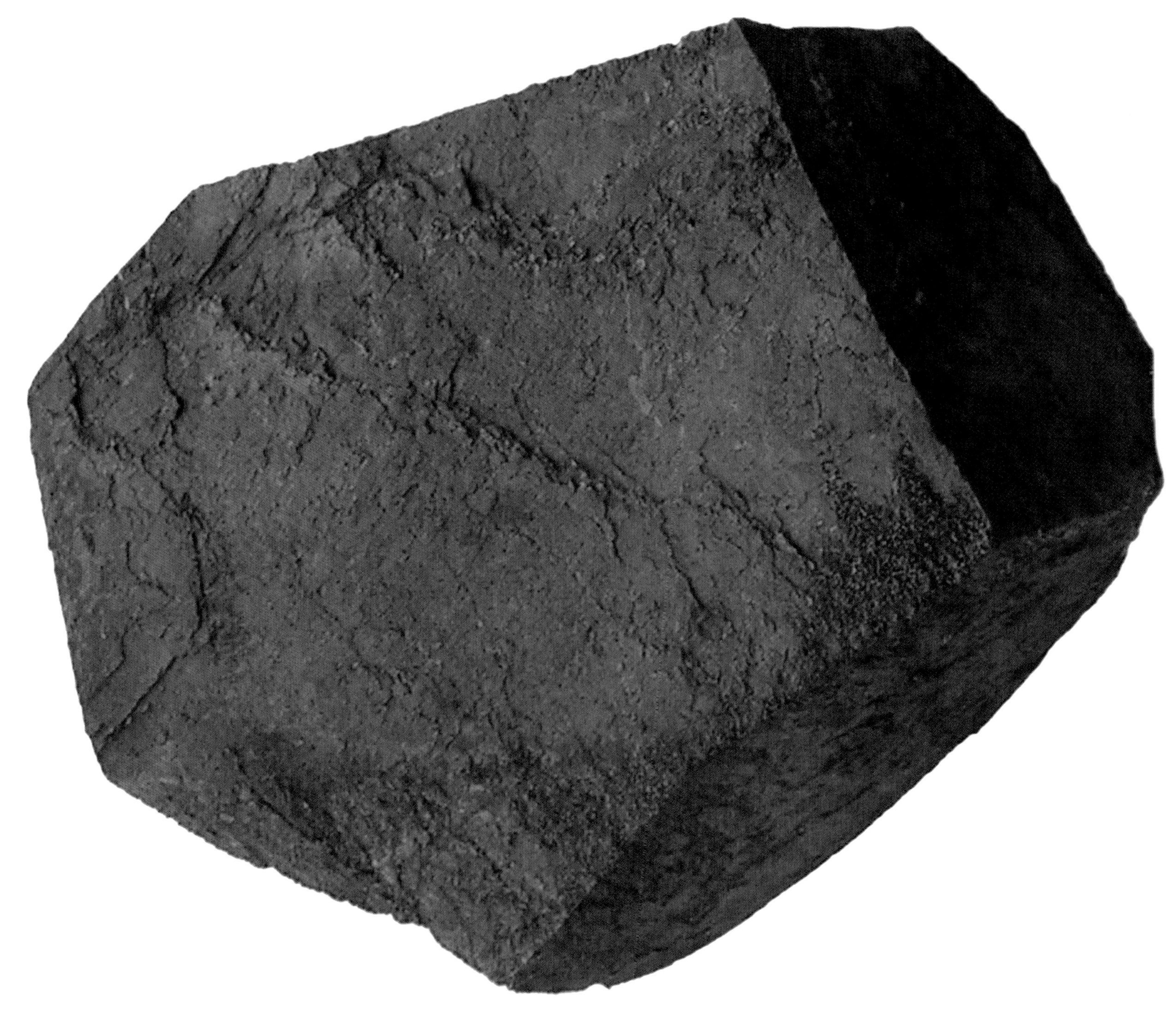

Colin Rose

Biography

1950   Born Newcastle Upon Tyne.

1973-1976   Newcastle Upon Tyne Polytechnic.
BA Hons.

1977-1979   University of Newcastle Upon Tyne. MFA.

1977-1989   Visiting and Part-time Lecturer in Fine Art
at Newcastle Polytechnic,
Sunderland Polytechnic and Newcastle University.

1987-1999   Part-time Lecturer, School of Architecture,
Newcastle University.

1991-1995   Part-time Lecturer, Fine Art, Newcastle College.

1993-   Senior Lecturer, Fine art,
University of Sunderland.

1996   Visiting Lecturer, Fine Art,
Bretton Hall College, Wakefield.

1998-2002   Visiting Lecturer, Landscape Design,
Newcastle University.

1999-2002   Visiting Lecturer, School of Architecture,
Newcastle University.

Lives and works in Northumberland.

Solo exhibitions and commissions

2001   Commission: Sound Reduction Barriers
M1 & M62 Motorways, West Yorkshire

Roundy Mining Memorial: Sculpture Commission;
Ushaw Moor, Co Durham

Ship: Sculpture Commission; Jarrow Town Centre

Ship: Drawings & Sculpture; Viking Gallery, Jarrow

Beacon: Sculpture Commission;
Resource Centre, Wakefield

2000   Villes et Valises: Strasbourg, France

Discs: Design Commission: Wakefield College.

1999   Design for Sculpture: Seacroft Green, Leeds.

Eye: Sculpture Commission; Galloway Forest, Dumfries.

1998   Meteor: Sculpture Commission;
Jodrell Bank, Macclesfield.

Commission, Gates Design,
Henshaw Arts & Crafts Centre, Knaresborough.

Sculpture Commission; Galloway Forest, Dumfries.

Commission, Seating Design, Tyne and Wear Metro.

Sculpture Commission: Royal Victoria Hospital,
Newcastle Upon Tyne.

1997   Broken Wave: Isis Gallery, Melrmerby, Cumbria.

Voices in Stone: (Collaboration with writer
Joan Poulson), Durham Art Gallery and
Norton Priory Museum, Cheshire.

1996   Earthworks: The Powerhouse, Casula, NSW Australia.

Peaks and Waves: Customs House, South Shields.

Floating Rocks: Watergate, Gateshead.

Commission, Garden Design for Gateshead,
Chelsea Flower Show.

1995   Commission, Street Furniture, Gateshead Town Centre.

Earthworks: Lewers Gallery, Penrith, NSW Australia.

Whirling Beans: Sculpture Commission, Kielder Forest,
Northumberland.

Sculpture Commission, Astra Pharmaceuticals Ltd.

1994   Stonecone: Beamish, County Durham.

1993   Kilkenny Castle, Kilkenny, Ireland.

1992-1993   Edge to Edge: Sculpture Commission,
Merthyr Tydfil, Wales.

1992   Night and Day: Tree and Ground Sculptures,
Yorkshire Sculpture Park.

1990   Commission, Design for International
Engineering Award.

1989   Rolling Moon: Banks of the River Tyne, Gateshead.

Commission, British Alcan, Lynemouth UK Ltd.

1988   Sculpture Commission, Glasgow Garden Festival.

1986   Window: Sculpture Commission,
Rawling Road, Gateshead.

1981 & 1985   Sculpture in Grizedale Forest, Cumbria.

1982   Drawings & Sculpture: Wallsend Art Gallery,
Tyne & Wear.

1979   Hatton Gallery, Newcastle Upon Tyne.

1978   Selected Work: Calouste Gulbenkian Gallery, Newcastle.

Drawings and Sculpture: Wallsend Arts Centre,
Tyne and Wear.

Group exhibitions

2002 Agenda: The Gallery, Newcastle Upon Tyne Arts Centre.

World Contemporary Print: Art House,
Newcastle Upon Tyne.

Journey of Stones: Bonhoga Gallery, Shetland,
Scotland & European Tour.

2001 Design Exhibition, Design Centre, Barnsley.

Journey of Stones: Galerie de Beerenburght, Holland.

1999 Newcastle Group. Tree of Life: International Centre
of Life, Newcastle.

Links & Connections: Reg Vardy Gallery, Sunderland.

1998 Sculpture in the Garden 1: Wylam, Northumberland.

Links & Connections: L Gallery, Moscow.

Newcastle Group: City Art Gallery, Newcastle,
NSW, Australia; & Tour.

Greenham Common Project, Royal Society
of British Sculptors, London.

The Third Area: Newcastle Group,
The Gallery, Gateshead.

1997 Sculpture Trail: Lewes, Sussex.

Northern Print: Sandgate House, Newcastle Upon Tyne.

Cityscape: Newcastle Upon Tyne.

North East Artists: Sloane Square, London.

1996 Artlanta: (Selected Artists from North East England)
Hatton Gallery, Newcastle Upon Tyne and King Plow,
Atlanta, USA.

Great North Forest: Durham Art Gallery.

Sightlines: Honiton, Devon.

Exchange of Views: Washington Arts Centre,
County Durham.

Northern Rock Art: Durham Art Gallery.

Public Art: Sunderland University.

Four Seasons: The Gallery, Gateshead.

Watermarks: Northern Print Studio Exhibition,
Customs House, South Shields.

Newcastle Group: JD Gallery, Corbridge,
Northumberland.

1995 Middlesbrough Open 95: Middlesbrough Art Gallery.

Newcastle Group: Design Works, Gateshead.

Newcastle Group: The Barracks, Berwick Upon Tweed.

Towards a Place for Art: Surikov Institute, Moscow.

1994-1997 Sculpture at Goodwood: Hathill Foundation, Sussex.

Newcastle Group: Hatton Gallery, Newcastle.

1993 'Ha-Ha': Killerton Park, Devon.

Newcastle Group: Latvia Academy of Art, Reiga.

Doxford International, Sunderland.

1992 Newcastle Group: Central House of Artists, Moscow.

Newcastle Group: Tampera Art Museum, Finland.

Alfresco: Seaton Delaval Hall, Northumberland.

1991 Newcastle Group, Northern Lights: DLI Gallery, Durham;
JD Gallery, Corbridge, Northumberland;
Design Works, Gateshead.

National Garden Festival, Gateshead.

Festival Landmarks '90: Central Library, Gateshead.

1990 Newcastle Group: Bergens Kunstforening,
Bergen, Norway.

Small Works: Yorkshire Sculpture Park.

1989 Art London '89: Olympia, London and
RIBA, London.

1988 Steel Sculpture: Yorkshire Sculpture Park
and Wantijpark, Dordrecht, West Germany.

Landscape & Environment: Ward Jackson Park and
Grey Art Gallery, Hartlepool.

Summer Exhibition: Polytechnic Gallery, Newcastle.

Glass House Exhibition: Westgate Road, Newcastle.

Newcastle Group: Richard Demarco Gallery, Edinburgh.

Newcastle Group: Grunigen, Holland.

Sculpture in the Forest: Grizedale, Cumbria.

Steel Sculpture: Middleheim Statpark,
Antwerp, Belgium.

1987 International Sculpture Symposium: Krefeld,
West Germany.

The Newcastle Group: Laing Art Gallery, Newcastle.

1986 Friends of Hatton Exhibition: Hatton Gallery, Newcastle.

Holbeck Triangle Project: Bond Street, Leeds.

Impressions of Jarrow: Bede Gallery, Jarrow.

Art in Public Places: Shipley Art Gallery, Gateshead.

1985 A Sense of Place: Sunderland Arts Centre, and UK Tour.

1984 Attitudes 1: Yorkshire Sculpture Park.

1982 Small Works: Polytechnic Art Gallery, Newcastle.a
Anniversary Exhibition, Polytechnic Art Gallery,
Newcastle.

1979 Northern Young Contemporaries:
Whitworth Gallery, Manchester.

1978 Recent Work by Graduates: Newcastle Polytechnic.

The Northern Art Exhibition: Shipley Art Gallery,
Gateshead, and UK Tour.

1977 International Drawing Biennial: Cleveland Gallery,
Middlesbrough and World Tour.

1975 Northern Young Contemporaries: Whitworth Gallery,
Manchester.

Collections, awards and residencies

2001 Winner, National Design Competition,
Highways Agency, UK.

2001 Northern Arts Award.

1995 Artist Exchange, Lewers Gallery, Penrith NSW
and the University of Western Sydney, Australia.

1994-1996 Resident Artist, Great North Forest.

1992 Winner, Northern Electric Visual Arts Award.

1991-1992 Henry Moore Foundation Bursary at
Yorkshire Sculpture Park.

1990 Artist in Residence, Duchess's High School,
Alnwick, Northumberland.

1989 Artist in Residence, Arts in Schools Project,
Northumberland and North Tyneside.

1987 Northern Arts Travel Award.

Artist in Residence, Community Centre, Ashington.

1985-1986 Northern Arts Major Bursary.

1984 Mid-Nag Production Award.

1982 ACGB Purchase.

1979, 80 & 84 Northern Arts Purchase Awards.

1977 ACGB Award.

Works in Regional and National Collections

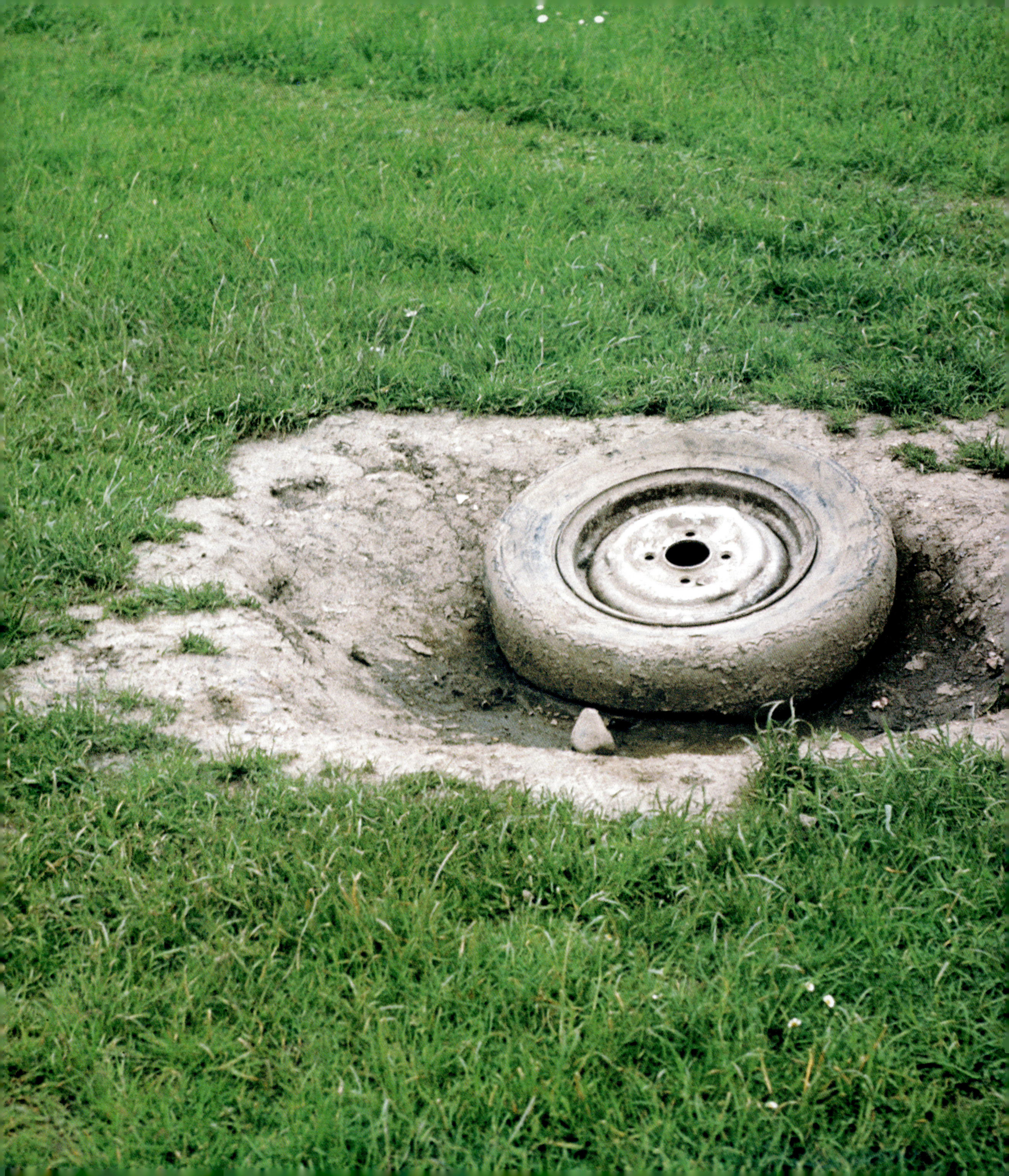

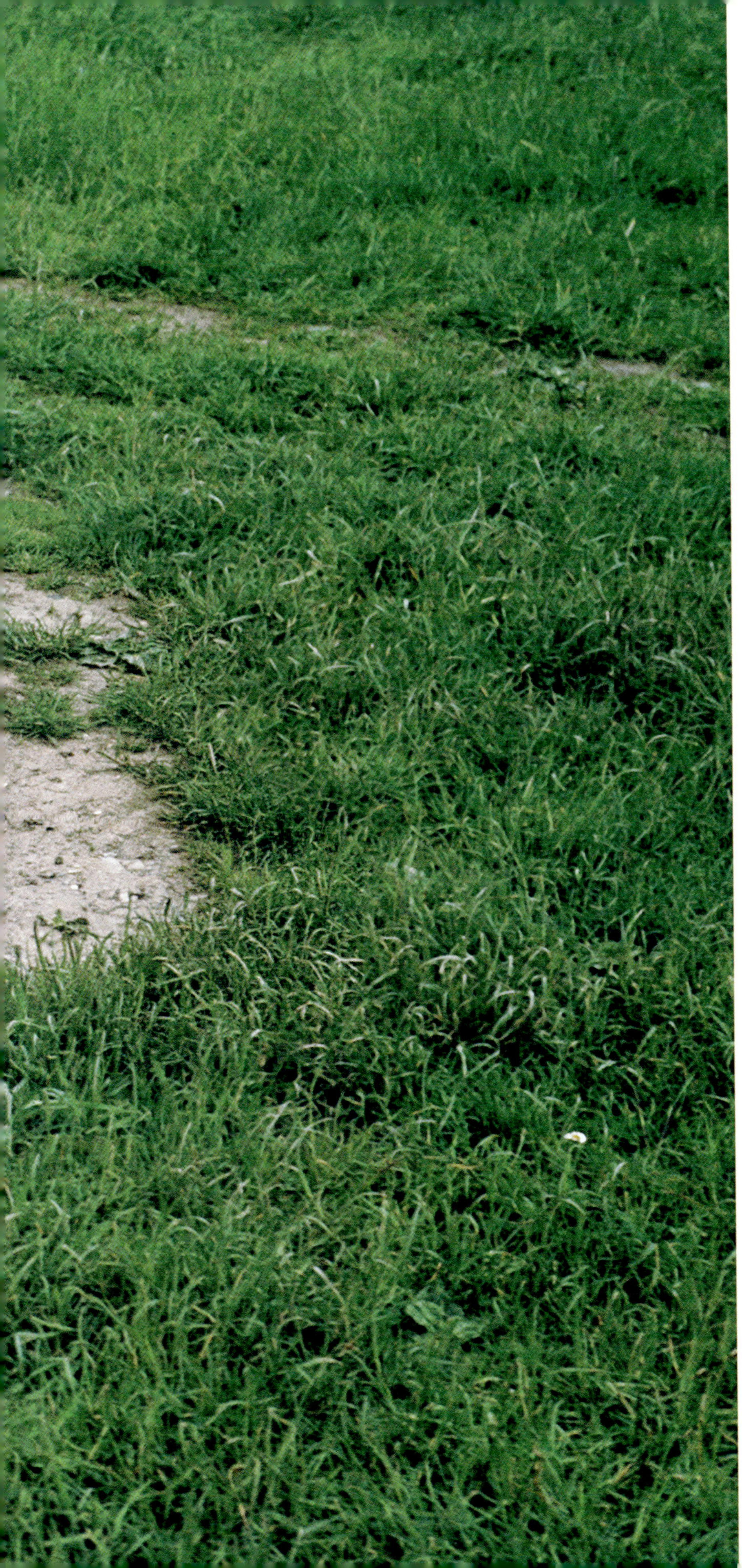

For all the generous support and belief people have shown me over the years. With special thanks to all those who have climbed trees, hung off cranes, balanced on rafts, dug holes and struggled in all weathers to help me work.

edge to edge

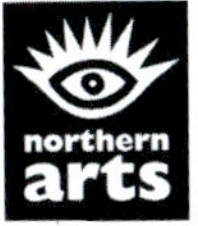

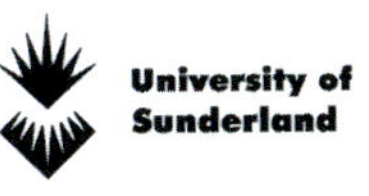

Yorkshire **Sculpture** Park

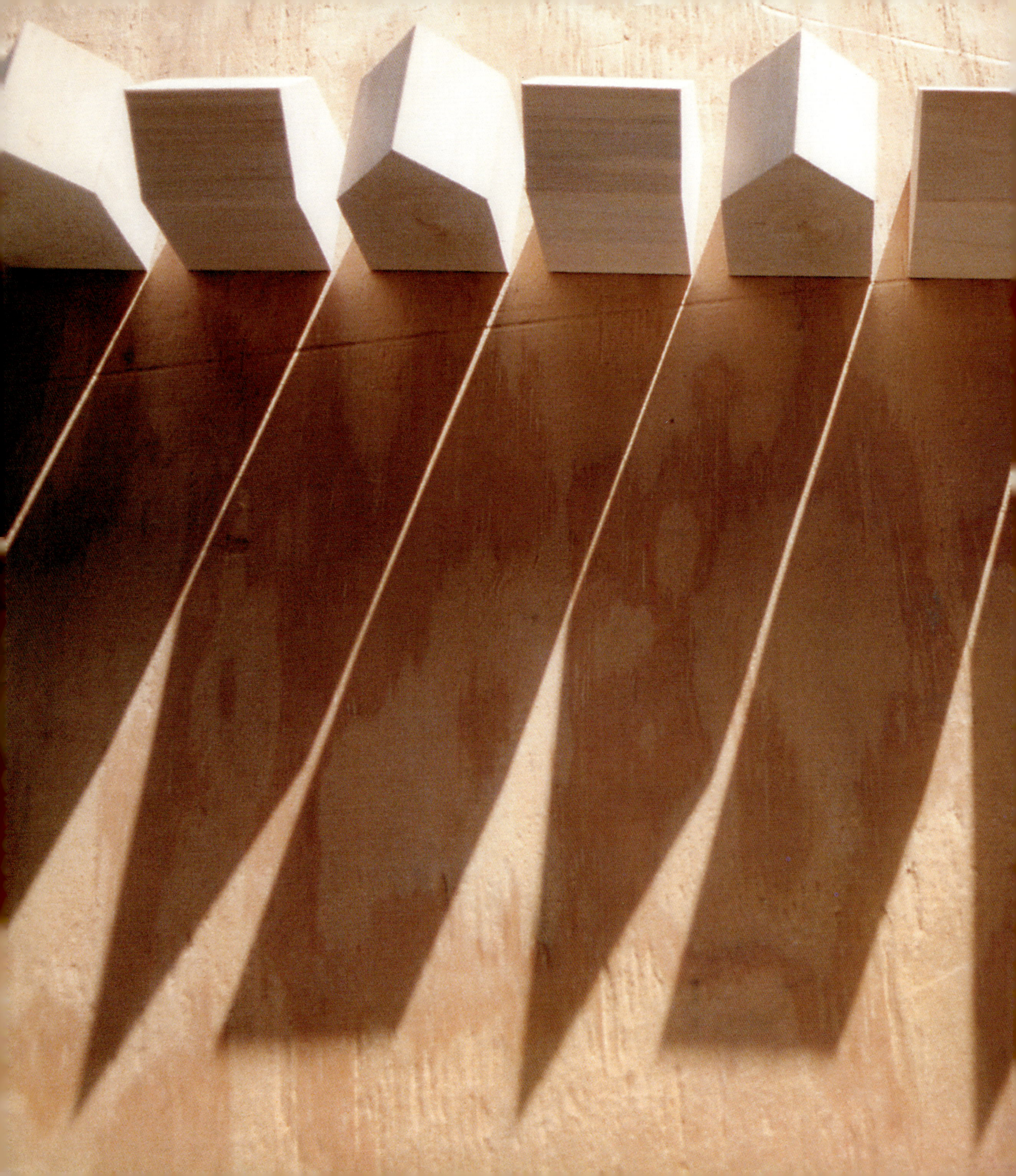

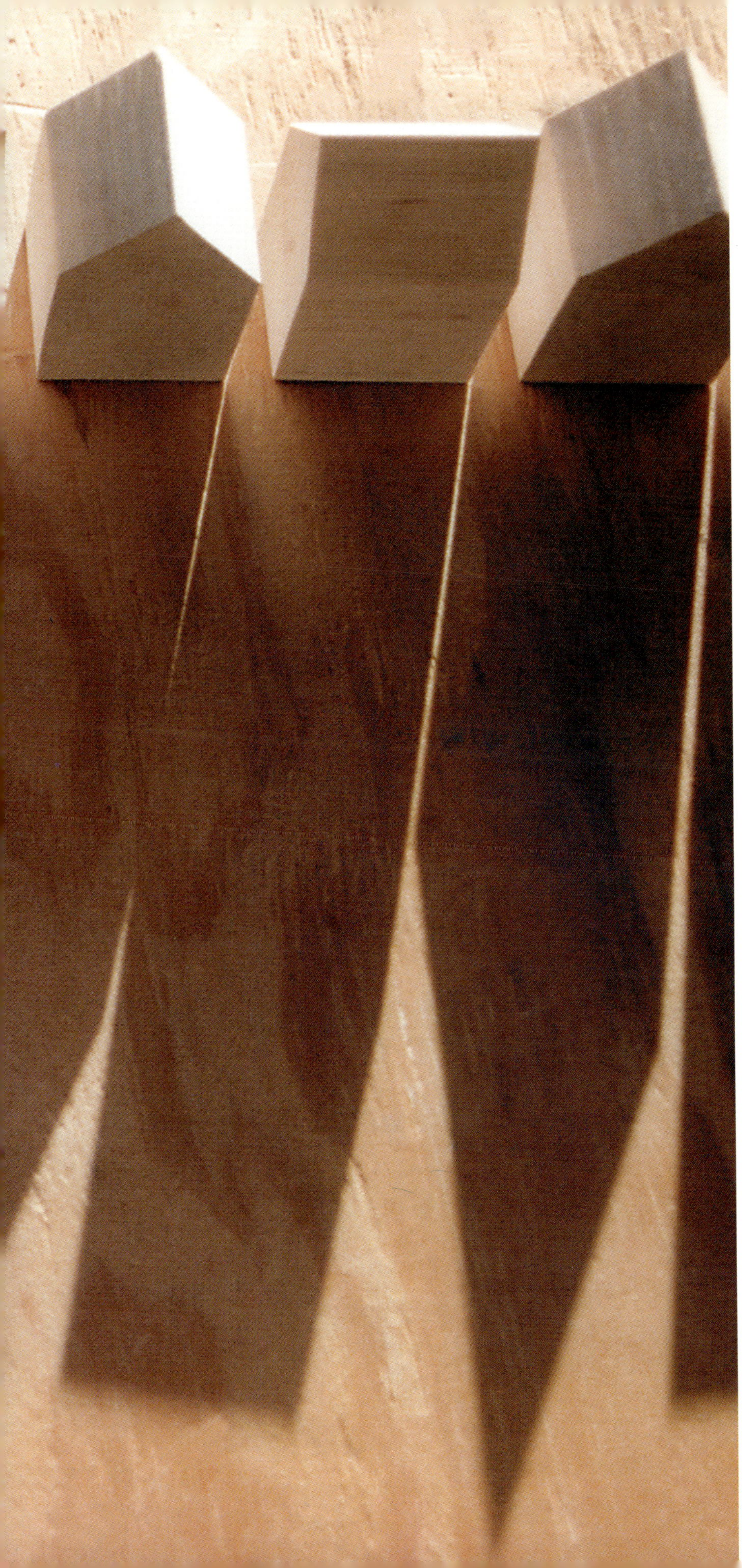

Edited by Catherine Grant and Duncan McCorquodale

Designed by Gavin Ambrose

Printed in Thailand by Imago

All photographs by Colin Rose except for:
Page 7 Ray Gray
Pages 13, 24, 25, 35, 53, 112 and 118 by Jerry Hardman Jones
Page 135 Linda Kent
Page 146 by Chris Growcott

**Architecture Art Design Fashion History
Photography Theory and Things**

Black Dog Publishing Limited

5 Ravenscroft Street
London
E2 7SH
UK

T 44 020 7613 1922
F 44 020 7613 1944
E info@bdp.demon.co.uk
www.bdpworld.com

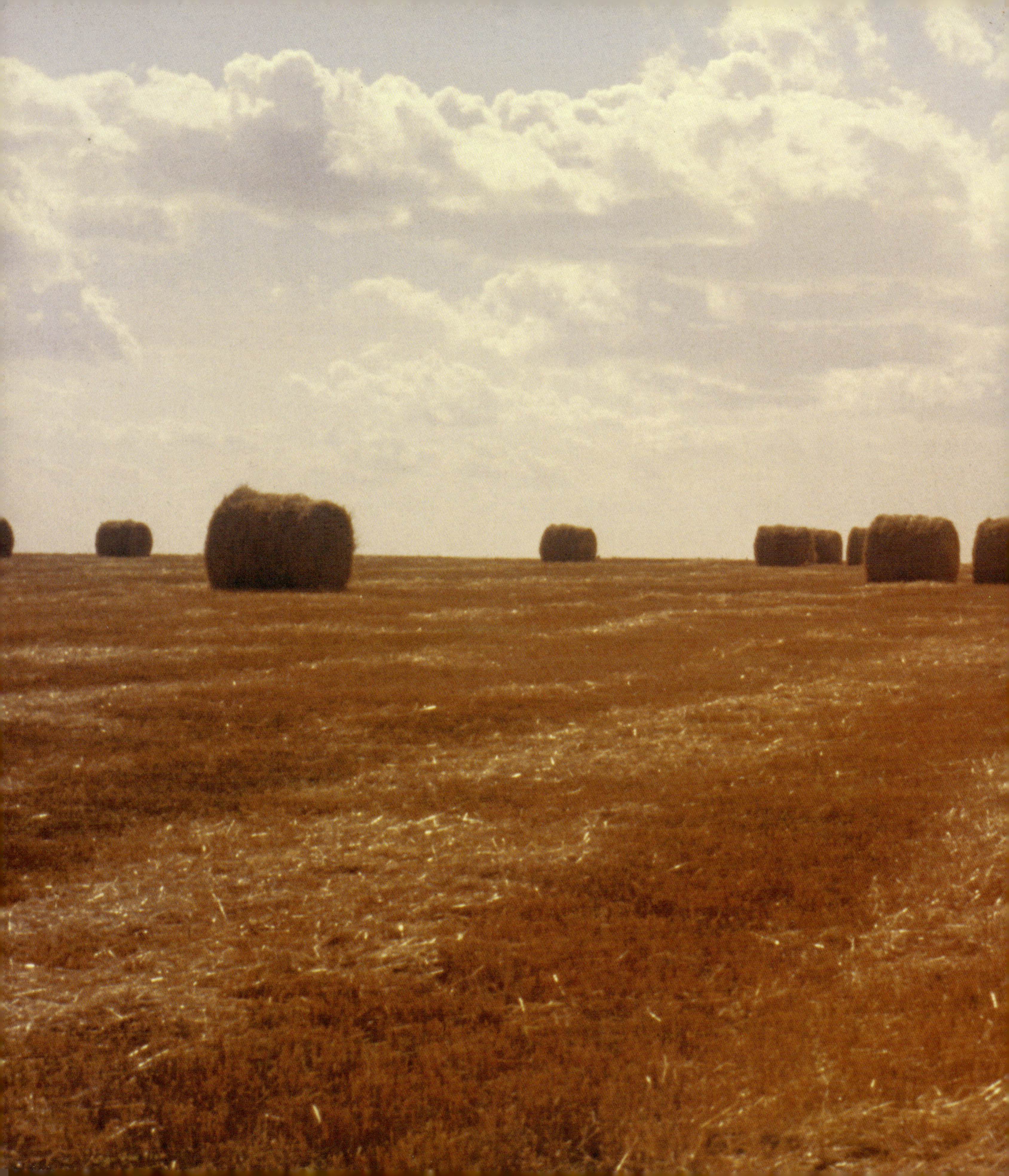

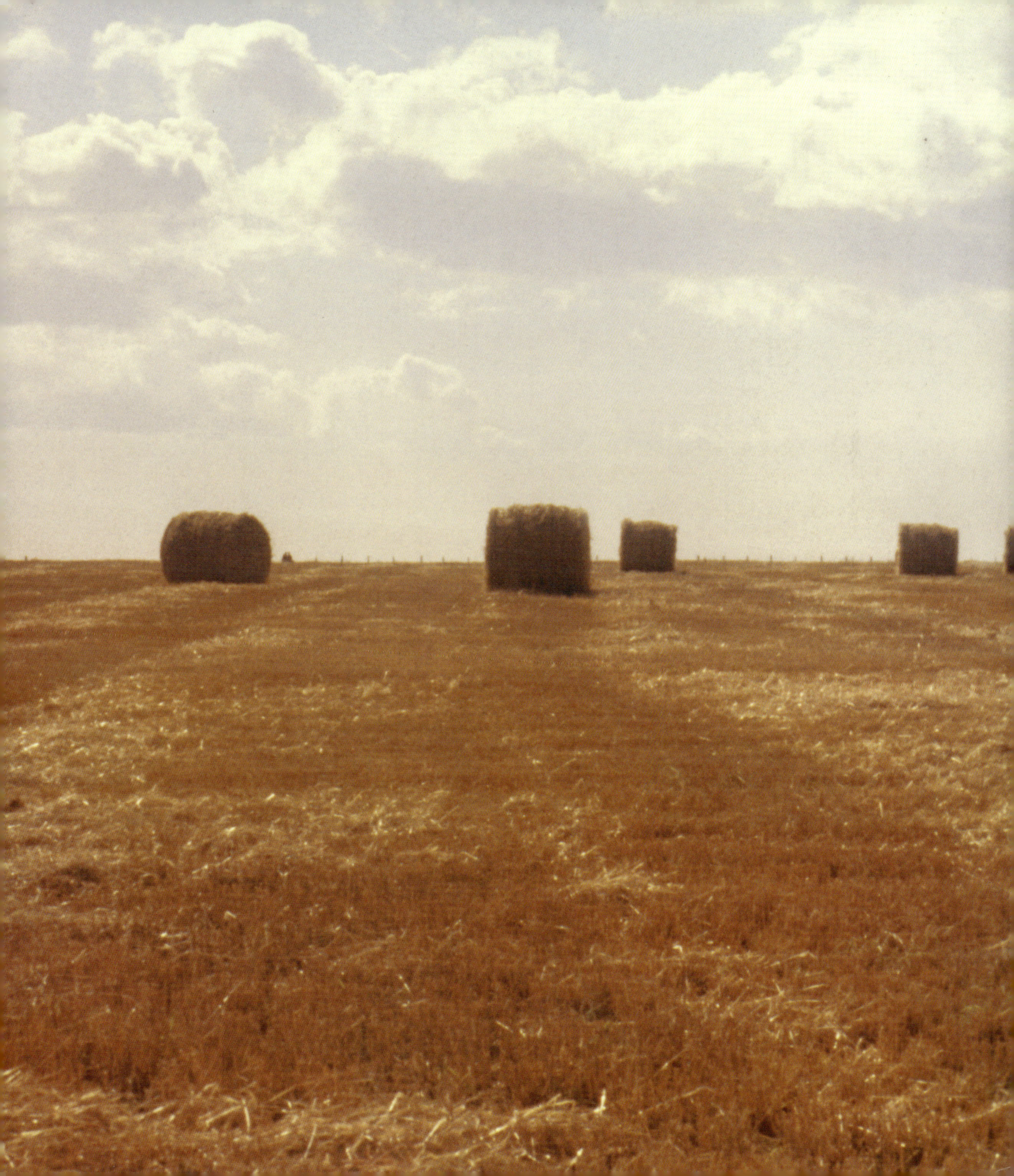